PART-TIME FARMING

PROBLEM OR RESOURCE IN RURAL DEVELOPMENT

PROCEEDINGS OF THE FIRST RURAL GEOGRAPHY SYMPOSIUM

DEPARTMENT OF GEOGRAPHY UNIVERSITY OF GUELPH

JUNE 18, 19 and 20th, 1975

Edited by

ANTHONY M. FULLER and JULIUS A. MAGE

25. 4. 78

Supported by

Ontario Ministry of Agriculture and Food
The Canada Council
Rural Development Branch, O.M.A.F.
Ontario Agricultural College
Ontario Rural Geography Group
Department of Geography, University of Guelph

ISBN

© Department of Geography, University of Guelph 1976

The cover was designed by Margo Adamson,
Cartographer, Department of Geography,
University of Guelph

Information about the Symposium may be obtained
from the "Rural Research Group", Department of Geography
University of Guelph, Guelph, Ontario, Canada N1G 2W1

Copies of the published proceedings of the Symposium are available from the sole distributors;

GEO ABSTRACTS LTD.,
University of East Anglia,
Norwich NR4 7TJ
England

TABLE OF CONTENTS

PREFACE

This book represents the proceedings of the First Guelph Symposium of Rural Geography; Part-Time Farming — A Problem or Resource in Rural Development. The symposium evolved from a long standing interest in part-time farming by A.M. Fuller and J.A. Mage, the symposium organizers. Specifically, Fuller, working in Italian agriculture, had developed a conceptual model identifying and relating various types of part-time situations while Mage, in an independent study, had isolated several types of part-time situations on the basis of an objective multi-variate procedure applied to the Southern Ontario context.

Canada is presently at the forefront in collecting and making available to researchers census information pertaining to farm operators who report jobs in addition to farming. Much of the macro level information, augmented by micro level surveys in Ontario, had been analyzed by geographers at the University of Guelph. This research was a direct outcome of a continuing grant by the Ontario Ministry of Agriculture and Food under Programme 33 of the University of Guelph. It was therefore appropriate to present some of the major findings of the phenomenon in portions of Canada at a symposium designed to give rise to an international exchange of information and to stimulate interdisciplinary cooperation. The University of Guelph and the Department of Geography, both with a major interest in rural studies, were particularly suited to host a conference on part-time farming.

The rise of part-time farming in Canada and other western societies initiated the need to bring together an interdisciplinary group of scholars, government officials and interested individuals to present and debate the several aspects of the phenomenon. Accordingly, a sequence of papers was arranged to:

a) Identify who are the part-time farmers.

b) Assess whether part-time farming represents a problem or resource.

c) Identify the relationship between newcomers to agriculture and part-time farming.

d) Identify some policy implications.

We wish to acknowledge the enthusiastic response by local and international researchers who contributed major papers and critiques to the various sessions. Particular thanks go to B.B. Perkins and R.C. Crown of Agriculture Canada, who collaborated on the format of the conference.

The conference itself was made possible by financial support from the Ontario Ministry of Agriculture and Food, the Rural Development Branch of O.M.A.F., the Canada Council, the Ontario Agricultural College and the Department of Geography, University of Guelph. The membership of the Ontario Rural Geography Group (O.R.G.G.) also offered its encouragement and support.

We wish to thank the Geography Department cartographers, Fred Adams, Margo Adamson and Pat McAllister for their patience and efforts in producing the final maps and drawings. Technical assistance was rendered by Lynne Myers, Jackie McLean and Dianne Love.

The invaluable assistance of Heather Fuller (Geographer at large) and students in the Geography Department, University of Guelph is also acknowledged.

Delphine Abrahamse
(Graduate Student)

Doug Begg
(Graduate Student)

Gail Finlay
(Student)

Mario Finoro
(Staff)

John Galloway
(Graduate Student)

Bill Hodgson
(Graduate Student)

Michael Holland
(Student)

Kenneth Kelly
(Chairman, Geography)

Rick Knutson
(Student)

Michelle Phillips
(Graduate Student)

Brian Reynolds
(Staff)

Peter Stoddart
(Graduate Student)

Symposium Organizers

A.M. Fuller

J.A. Mage

RECEPTION-WELCOME AND OPENING ADDRESS

Reception Welcome

The symposium officially convened with a banquet at the University Center. Participants were welcomed by the organizers and the guests of honour.

The head table comprised:

A.G. Ball, Associate Dean, Ontario Agricultural College

D. Christodoulou, Agrarian Reform Policy Officer, F.A.O.

H.C. Crown, Head, Rural Development Branch, Ontario Ministry of Agriculture and Food

A.M. Fuller, Symposium Organizer, Geography, Guelph

K. Kelly, Chairman, Geography Department, Guelph

J.A. Mage, Symposium Organizer, Geography, Guelph

B.B. Perkins, Policy Advisory Group, Agriculture Canada

C. Rennie, Executive Director, Education and Research Division, Ontario Ministry of Agriculture and Food

Opening Address to the Symposium

B.B. PERKINS, Policy Advisory Group, Economics Branch, Agriculture Canada, Ottawa

1

OPENING ADDRESS

THE FIRST GUELPH SYMPOSIUM ON RURAL GEOGRAPHY

PART-TIME FARMING: A PROBLEM OR RESOURCE IN RURAL DEVELOPMENT

Brian B. Perkins

It is a great pleasure to be back in Guelph after an absence of several years. Before such an auspicious and interdenominational a gathering, I feel a little like Daniel. I am not quite certain why Julius Mage and Tony Fuller, the organizers of this Symposium, invited me to address you. On inquiry, I gathered that their main excuse was that I was an old-timer — in the part-time farming field, that is. I had not realized how quickly the field had matured.

Twelve years ago, when I first became interested in part-time farming, geographers were unheard of, and no self-respecting production economist or farm management specialist seriously considered part-time farming or part-time farmers. The field was left to odd-balls, like rural sociologists or those interested in farm policy. As for politicians, part-time farming was in the "expletive deleted" category.

Now geographers dominate the field, farm management and production economists are actively trying to catch up, and politicians have decided that part-time farming may be, just may be, the answer to rural depopulation problems.

Tony Fuller was fairly explicit in his instructions. They ran to about a page. I was to explain the phenomenon, comment on its international dimensions, state the Federal policy position, project the prospects, generally stimulate the symposium to get off to a good start, and tell a number of jokes!

This Symposium is remarkable because it is taking place here, in Canada. In an under-developed country, part-time farming would attract no special attention because it is so common. In most European countries and many others, experience with, and policies for part-time farming go back over many years.

Historically, North American agriculture was labour scarce, land extensive. The concept of full-time family farms has long been firmly embedded in the thinking, institutions and policies of agriculture in Canada and the United States.

It is only during the rapid economic growth of the past 30 years that part-time farming has emerged as a major feature of our agriculture. This emergence has been associated with rapid increases in wage rates and incomes, especially in non-farm sectors, and fundamental structural changes in agriculture, including the impressive enlargement of farms in area and as businesses, the substitution of capital for labour (in response to the rising price of the latter factor relative to others), and the steady net out-migration of people from farming and rural areas.

What do we mean by part-time farming? I ask the question rhetorically, in a sense, since you will be addressing it in your discussions in the next few days. Evidently, there are many answers to the question. We may speak of part-time farming in terms of the proportion of employment or earnings derived from a combination of farming and other occupations; we may speak of part-time farmers or part-time farms, of seasonal or year-round part-time farming.

These kinds of considerations raise broader structural questions, to which too little attention has been paid in Canadian policy. But more of that later. (By structure I mean to refer to the distribution of farms and farmers, not only by incomes and employment, but by location, soils, enterprise combination, capital, operator's education, and the many other factors which characterize the physical, social and economic matrix of farming).

Traditionally, Canadian agricultural policy has been oriented to commercial farming, along commodity lines, with limited questioning of the basic structural changes attending the development of the sector, or indeed, stimulated by the policies toward it.

Efforts since the early 1960's through the Agricultural Rehabilitation and Development Act and the Fund for Rural Economic Development were intended to deal more with low-income problems and economically depressed rural areas than with part-time farming and structural issues generally.

The more recent Small Farm Development Program is clearly different in orientation, in that it is focussed on structural change, but its foundations also were based on the concept of the full-time family farm, and did not embody the notion of a major role for part-time farming in the longer-term structure of the sector. Our agricultural credit programs in Canada are predicated generally on similar structural ideas.

Apart from these implicit approaches with respect to part-time farming, the Federal government has not taken a clear articulated position toward the phenomenon. In the light of a number of on-going policy developments, I am emboldened to suggest that the Federal position is in the process of reassessment — not in a direct, explicit way, but through several reviews of related policy areas.

The bases of concern motivating this re-thinking include, first and foremost, rural depopulation itself, which is alleged to be among the few issues on which politicians at all three levels of government can unite, albeit for different reasons. Closely related are the prospects implied by present demographic trends and the concern to seek a different and better spatial distribution for our population in the future. The form of urban and rural development envisioned by such aspirations is very different from that of the past. With respect to land use, a major component of urban and rural development, the Federal government is in the process of developing a national policy in collaboration with the Provincial governments. Another related policy area is social security, in the context of which income distri-.

3

bution concerns, in the broad sense, have been under review for sometime. Farm labour shortages in peak periods and for certain skills have prompted new manpower programs and consideration of new approaches to agricultural employment, such as cooperative farming arrangements which might permit more farm operators to work five day weeks. The recent international food crisis has raised many questions about our food policy and the capacity of agriculture to meet the demands made of it in the future. In this respect also, the future of part-time farming and more generally the future structure of farming patently is important.

These kinds of issues are extremely broad and complex. For this very reason political leaders need the aid of sound analysis and advice on alternative policies to focus clearly on the issues.

Specifically, with regard to part-time farming, we need to seek answers to the following kinds of questions. Is part-time farming to be merely a means of mopping-up surplus agricultural labor generated in the process of structural change in agriculture? Or is it a means to provide a rural pursuit for city-workers who want to live in the country? Or, should it be considered as an integral part of the future structure of farming? What in terms of policy influence are the feasible alternatives for the future structure of farming? How do these alternatives rate in terms of the several and often competing objectives for agriculture, the rural economy, and regional development?

This Symposium should serve as a useful catalyst to generate thinking and research on these issues. I am glad that many social science disciplines are now engaged in work on part-time farming, as the composition of participants at this Symposium attests. The questions I have identified are ones which will require a broad spectrum of professional skills. I hope that those of you responsible for part-time farming research will orient those analyses to policy needs, and not confine yourselves to the interesting but narrow study of the phenomenon for its own sake.

The participation of professionals from several different countries should do much to stimulate useful exchanges in this Symposium. My fellow Canadians will forgive me if I say we stand to benefit most from this exchange. Not that we should copy the approach of any other country, but rather that we can and should learn from the experience of others, and adapt their ideas and knowledge to our own circumstances and needs.

It remains for me to wish you individually and collectively every success at this Symposium.

INTRODUCTORY SESSION

"WHO ARE THE PART-TIME FARMERS"

CHAIRMAN: J.L. GIRT (Geography, Guelph, Canada)

PAPER: J.A. MAGE (Geography, Guelph, Canada)
                 "A Typology of Part-Time Farming"

PAPER: A.M. FULLER (Geography, Guelph, Canada)
                 "The Problems of Part-Time Farming Conceptualised"

CRITIQUE: G.V. FUGUITT (Rural Sociology, Wisconsin, U.S.A.)

GUELPH REPORT 1

A TYPOLOLOGY OF PART-TIME FARMING

Julius A. Mage

Part-time farming has been growing in importance during the last few decades and has emerged as a complex and varied phenomenon in agriculture. The complexity of part-time farming situations necessitates a clear identification process based on objective methodology. There is a need to establish terminology which will aid in identifying who the part-time farmers are and which will serve as a basis for conceptualizing related problems. The purpose of this introductory paper is; 1) to present a methodological approach leading to the identification of general factors associated with the distribution of part-time farming on a regional scale and; 2) to present the results of an analysis contributing to terminology and a better understanding of who part-time farmers are.

PART-TIME FARMING — WHAT IS IT?

In this opening session before we attempt to answer the question "Who are the part-time farmers?" it is appropriate that we very briefly note what "part-time farming" has been considered to be by others in North America. The combination of farming and off-farm work by farm operators has undoubtedly existed since the art of farming came about.[1] However, contemporary researchers agree that the terms "part-time farming" and "part-time farmer" were first introduced in a Massachusetts study in 1930 by Rozman.[2] He defined a part-time farmer as a farm operator who spent 2 or more months per year in off-farm work.[3] Rozman was careful to make the distinction between the part-time farmer and the part-time farming enterprise. If cases were found where the head of the family, that is, the operator, was devoting only part of his working time to his farming activities and supplemented this through full-time hired or family labor, his enterprise was in reality a "regular" farm and was treated as a regular or full-time farming enterprise. Hence to Rozman, the term "part-time farming" meant a "part-time farmer" and a "part-time farming enterprise" whenever the equivalent of full-time male farm labor was not evident.

In 1930, the same year that Rozman's study appeared, the U.S. Bureau of the Census first took cognizance of the phenomenon of part-time farming. In this census, the principal off-farm occupation of the operator was recorded in days; these occupations were then classified as agricultural and non-agricultural. This procedure of identifying part-time farmers remained until 1950. From 1950 to 1959 the U.S. Census defined a part-time farm as a farm with gross sales of $250-$1199 with the operator working off the farm for 100 days or more and/or the family income from off-farm sources greater than sales from farm products. In 1960 the present definition was cast as follows: "Part-time farms have a value of products sold of $50 to $2499 and a farm operator under 65 years of age who works off the farm 100 days or more in the census year."[4] Thus the definition has been made more specific during the last 40 years as it now includes gross sales, age of operator and time worked off the farm (see Table 1).

In Canada, the Dominion Bureau of Statistics did not gather or publish data pertaining to part-time farming until the 1941 Census. For that year data were obtained with respect to: a) the number of farm operators who worked off the farm in order to supplement their farm income; b) the off-farm occupation of the operator; c) the gross returns received from off-farm work (by the operator and any family member) and d) the gross returns from other off-farm sources.[5] Apart from total numbers of operators reporting off-farm income and off-farm work, a specific definition of part-time farming was not established. However by 1951 the following definition was utilized by the Bureau: "Part-time farms include those with gross sales of farm products between $250 and $1199 and, 1) the operator reported that he worked 100 days or more off the farm in 1950, or 2) the farm operator reported the farm income less than his income from other sources. If the value of farm products sold was less than $250 the farm is classified as a small scale farm."[6] In 1961 this definition was modified slightly, so that part (2) of the above read, "the operator reported that income received by the operator and his family from all other sources, excluding investments, was greater than the income received from the sale of agricultural products."[7]

In the 1966 Census the definition was again changed. A part-time farmer was considered to be "a census-farm operator reporting income received from agricultural and non-agricultural work off the operator's farm of $750 or more or who worked 75 days or more off the farm during the past 12 months."[8] At the present (1971 Census) no specific definition is utilized but rather a variety of farm and farmer attributes are cross-tabulated by 10 categories of number of days devoted to off-farm work by the farm operator. Since it has been well documented (in the Ontario context) that part-time farming occurs in every gross farm sales class as well as every operator age class published in the census,[9] it appears logical initially to consider all farms whose operators report off-farm work as part of the part-time farming phenomenon. Table 1 presents a comparison of the changing definitions of part-time farming in the U.S. and Canada census reports.

Shortly after the U.S. Bureau of Statistics "officially" recognized the part-time farmer in 1930, a spate of literature appeared dealing specifically with the combination of farm and non-farm employment of farm operators and/or farm families. In an earlier study I examined nearly fifty North American part-time farming articles, reports and theses,[10] while Frauendorfer recently reviewed 460 part-time farming works pertaining to various parts of the world.[11] Included in this massive review were 128 U.S. references but only 4 Canadian papers. In spite of the quantity of literature available the concept of part-time farming is still the subject of some controversy and varies somewhat according to the whims of the researcher and possibly the data at hand. Reviewers of the subject matter have stated, "to date no completely acceptable definition has been offered and each writer on the subject tends to use a definition which suits his purpose."[12] Therefore there are problems of relating the various studies to each other and extracting general principles.

Table 1

Comparison of Canada and U.S. Census Definitions of Part-Time Farming [a]

	Canada	United States
1930-31	No data available	— No specific definition — Days of off-farm work recorded only for farm operator
1940-41	— No specific definition — Number of farm operators reporting off-farm work	— Same as 1930
1950-51	— Part-time farms include those with gross sales of farm products between $250 and $1199 and 1) the operator reported that he worked off-farm 100 or more days in 1950 and 2) the farm income was less than the operator's income from other sources	— Part-time farms are farms with gross sales of $250-$1199 with the operator working off-farm for 100 days or more and/or the family income from off the farm sources are greater than sales from farm products
1960-61	— Similar to 1951 except portion (2) of the 1951 definition was expanded to include off-farm income of operator **and his family**	— Farms with a value of farm products sold of $50-$2499 were classified as part-time if the operator was under 65 years of age and he worked off the farm 100 or more days per year
U.S. 1964 Canada 1966	— A part-time farmer is a census farm operator reporting income received from agricultural and non-agricultural work off the farm of $750 or more **or** who worked 75 days or more off the farm during the past 12 months	— Same as 1960
U.S. 1969 Canada 1971	— No specific definition. Number of operators reporting off-farm work	— Same as 1960

[a]Sources: U.S. Census of Agriculture, 1940, 1950, 1960, 1964 and 1969.

8

One can conclude that the majority of studies have defined part-time farming according to time devoted to off-farm work by the farm operator and have directly implied dual or multiple employment on the part of the head of the household.[13] Moreover it appears that time devoted to an off-farm occupation by the operator can be considered as a surrogate of the decision-making process culminating in a part-time situation. In this sense, although some would argue that a definition of part-time farming should be based on labour inputs and/or income accrued from farm and non-farm endeavours of the whole farm family,[14] a part-time situation as expressed by the terms part-time farm, part-time farmer and part-time farming is ultimately determined by the decision of a farm operator to farm part-time.[15] Therefore our approach in the Department of Geography at Guelph has been to apply initially a very liberal criterion to define the phenomenon which we consider to be a situation wherein the operator of a census farm engages in another job, for which he receives remuneration, in addition to running his own farm during the survey or census year period.[16]

A TYPOLOGICAL APPROACH TO IDENTIFYING WHO THE PART-TIME FARMERS ARE

In 1958 Metzler suggested that various types of part-time farmers could be identified and that these groups would theoretically reflect one of;

1) a transitional stage out of full-time farming
2) an advantageous economic position of stability, or
3) refuge from congested cities.[17]

Such groupings imply that it is possible to approach part-time farming types from the standpoint of the agricultural enterprise or from the non-farm point of view. That is, in the first instance outside income supplements the farming income, and in the second and third, farm income supplements non-farm sources. From the available literature it appears that researchers have not pursued types of part-time situations. The notable exception is the work of Fuguitt who, over a decade ago, proposed and briefly tested a typology of part-time farmers based on past, present and future farm and non-farm occupational commitment.[18] His system made a significant contribution to the notion that "the part-time farmer category is likely to be a very heterogeneous group, with varying backgrounds, goals and types of occupational commitments."[19]

In pursuing the question of what is part-time farming and, more specifically, who are the part-time farmers, and in attempting to establish some general principles related to the phenomenon one can advocate a two tier approach involving two levels of analysis.

THE MACRO LEVEL APPROACH

In an area such as Ontario the incidence of part-time farming is unequally distributed spatially (at the county level of aggregation, Figure 1). Such a distribution suggests that there are regions and/or areas of Ontario with attributes which are particularly conducive for part-time farming situations. One can also hypothesize that in

9

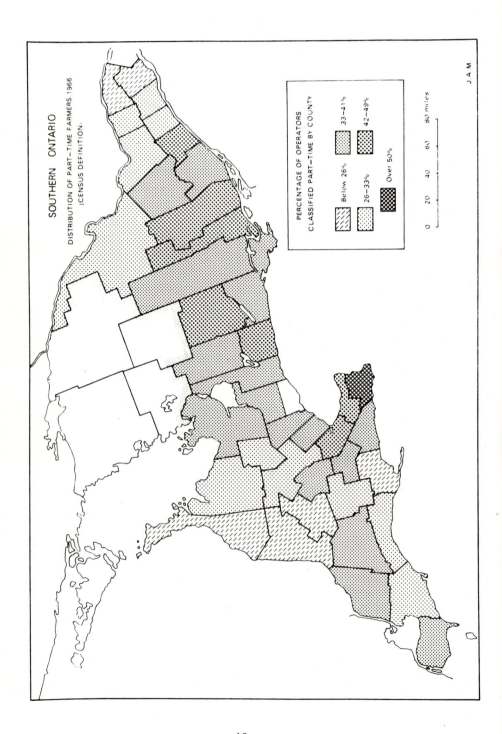

SOUTHERN ONTARIO

DISTRIBUTION OF PART-TIME FARMERS 1966
(CENSUS DEFINITION)

PERCENTAGE OF OPERATORS
CLASSIFIED PART-TIME BY COUNTY

Below 26%
33-41%
26-33%
42-49%
Over 50%

0   20   40   60   80 miles

J A M.

different areas of the Province part-time farming will be associated with different factors. The first task then, is to isolate and identify these broad areas using statistical units such as counties or townships for which relevant census data are available. An example, taken from my earlier study, illustrates this approach.[20]

The purpose of this exploratory study was to identify the nature of circumjacent environment types within which farmers operate.[21] Given the lack of well founded theoretical models to explain the phenomenon of part-time farming the researcher is faced initially with the necessity of working from the available data toward a descriptive model. A synthesis of the literature led to the conclusion that part-time farming is a multivariate construct characterized by numerous variables, therefore a series of "characterizing" measures was chosen from the census for each of the counties of southern Ontario.[22] These measures were transgenerated into proportions or ratio values to overcome scalar problems which may have arisen in the comparison of large and small counties. An intercorrelation matrix computed for the basic data set indicated which measures were correlated with the variable "proportion of farmers part-time". Table 2 lists these 44 measures.[23]

Because the number of measures is rather large and because an inspection of the intercorrelation matrix revealed moderate to high correlation coefficients between numerous pairs of variables, an analysis of the spatial association between "part-time" farming and each individual "predictor" variable would be redundant. Therefore an analytical technique was sought that would identify the underlying dimensions of the data without the assumptions of a closed hypothesis testing system. A principal components model was used to define significant interrelationships in unordered associations of variables and to identify the few underlying patterns called factors which are responsible for the variations among the census variables.[24]

The factor analysis yielded 5 factors which were interpretable and which together accounted for 75.5 per cent of the variation within the data matrix. Table 3 presents the factor loadings of the variables comprising the 5 factors used and the per cent variance accounted for by each factor. The factors were labelled as follows;

1) Small farm size and few acre enterprise type
2) Age of operator and scale of sales
3) Rural-urban differences
4) Dairy emphasis
5) Sheep emphasis

Using factor scores as input, the correlation coefficient was calculated between the distribution of each factor and part-time farming (as measured by the variable "proportion of farmers part-time").[25] Because factor constructs are statistically independent of each other one can state, from Table 4, that the degree of part-time farming in the counties of southern Ontario is positively associated firstly with socio-economic characteristics measuring the degree of small scale (low farm income) farming and the preponderance of aging operators

11

Table 2

Variables Correlating with the Part-time Farming Measure

Variable No.	Variable Name	R Value	Variable No.	Variable Name	R Value
1	Percent of farms less than 10 acres in size	0.34	22	Percent of farm operators 45-64 years of age	0.38
2	Percent of farms 10-69 acres in size	0.36	23	Percent of farm operators over 64 years of age	0.55
4	Percent of farms over 399 acres in size	0.40	24	Percent of farm operators under 45 years of age	-0.55
5	Percent of farms reporting less than 70 acres improved land	-0.66	31	Percent of farms reporting sales of $25,000 plus	-0.35
6	Percent of farms reporting 70-179 acres improved land	-0.63	32	Percent of farms reporting sales of $10,000-$24,999	-0.47
7	Percent of farms reporting 180-399 acres improved land	0.52	33	Percent of farms reporting sales of $5,000-$9,999	-0.56
9	Percent of farms reporting less than 33 acres of crops	-0.65	35	Percent of farms classified small scale (census classification)	0.75
11	Percent of farms reporting over 72 acres of crops	-0.68	37	Percent of farms reporting 2 automobiles	0.40
13	Percent of farms reporting 8-72 acres of improved pasture	-0.41	38	Percent of farms reporting more than 2 automobiles	0.34
20	Percent of farm operators under 25 years of age	-0.54	40	Percent of farms reporting 2 tractors	-0.54
21	Percent of farm operators 25-44 years of age	-0.52	46	Percent of farms reporting milking machines	-0.31

Table 2 (cont'd)

Variable No.	Variable Name	R Value	Variable No.	Variable Name	R Value
56	Average acreage of improved land/farm	-0.58	92	Percent of improved land in tree fruits	0.36
57	Average acreage in crops/farm	-0.65	93	Percent of improved land in small fruits	0.33
63	Percent of farm operators resident 1-4 months	-0.32	95	Percent of farms reporting milk sales	-0.35
67	Percent of improved land in summer fallow	0.36	96	Percent of population classified urban	0.35
70	Percent of improved land in mixed grains	-0.38	99	Percent of population classified rural farm	-0.55
72	Percent of improved land in buckwheat	0.32	104	Number of sheep per 100 improved acres	0.32
73	Percent of improved land in fieldbeans	-0.36	111	Percent of farms 70-129 acres	-0.51
76	Percent of improved land in other fodder crops	0.51	112	Percent of farms 130-137 acres	-0.62
			113	Percent of farms with less than 10 acres improved land	0.46
79	Percent of improved land in turnips	-0.33	114	Percent of farms with 10-69 acres improved land	0.68
87	Sheep (converted to animal units) as a percent of total animal units	0.36			
88	Poultry (converted to animal units) as a percent of total animal units	0.37			
89	Chickens (converted to animal units) as a percent of total animal units	0.41			

13

Table 3

Factor Loadings

Variable No.

	I 25.1%	II 24.6%	III 12.7%	IV 7.6%	V 5.5%	
1	-0.855					% farms 10 acres in size
2	-0.782					% farms 10-69 acres in size
5	-0.762					% farms with 70 acres improved
9	-0.877					% farms with 33 acres crops
88	-0.937					all poultry as % of animal units
89	-0.912					chickens as % of animal units
92	-0.948					% improved land in tree fruits
93	-0.913					% improved land in small fruits
113	-0.846					% farms with 10 acres improved
114	-0.587					% farms with 10-69 acres improved
6	0.721					% farms with 70-179 acres improved
7	0.599					% farms with 180-399 acres improved
11	0.656					% farms with 72 acres pf crops
56	0.778					average acreage improved/farm
57	0.670					average acreage crops/farm
112	0.643					% farms 130-179 acres in size
22		-0.667				% operators 45-64 years old
23		-0.889				% operators 64 years old
35		-0.911				% farms small scale
76		-0.668				% land in fodder crops
20		0.563				% operators 25 years old
21		0.958				% operators 25044 years old
24		0.594				% operators 45 years old
31		0.684				% farms with sales $25,000
32		0.877				% farms with sales $10,000-$25,000
40		0.865				% farms with 2 tractors
37			-0.500			% farms with 2 cars
38			-0.646			% farms with 2 cars
96			-0.919			% county population urban
99			0.912			% population rural — farm
13				-0.737		% farms with 8-72 acres imp. pasture
46				-0.713		% farms with milking machines
95				-0.721		% farms with milk sales
87					0.813	sheep as % of animal units
104					0.872	no. of sheep per 100 acres imp. land

Table 4

Correlation Coefficients Between the Five
Factors and the Part-time Farming Measure

Factors	R. Value	Percent Variation
1) Small farm size and few acre enterprise	+0.395	15.60
2) Age of Operator and Scale of Sales	+0.580	33.64
3) Rural-Urban Differences	+0.302	9.12
4) Dairy Emphasis	-0.102	1.04
5) Sheep Emphasis	+0.124	1.53
Multiple R value	0.780	60.93

(Factor 2), secondly with structural variates indicating the presence of small area farms and types of agricultural enterprises requiring few acres (Factor 1) and thirdly with the intensity of urbanization (Factor 3). Together, nearly 59 per cent of the variation in the distribution of part-time farming is reflected in the spatial distribution of these 3 dimensions. Figures 2, 3 and 4 indicate the actual distribution of each factor.

Although the 3 main underlying dimensions are orthogonal there may be similarity among several counties in the relative amounts of each factor contained. The problem is to combine the 3 main patterns into one composite map which will portray similar groups of counties. This was achieved in an objective manner by subjecting the factor score values to a hierarchical grouping technique. This technique has been widely used in classification or taxonomic procedures leading to types and regions[26] and in this study was employed as a summarizing technique to obtain types of areas whose component members are similar on the basis of the 3 main factors.

A 6 group optimal solution emerged. The component members of each group appear in Figure 5 which traces the successive grouping sequences from a ten to a one group solution. The results of such a synthesis can have merit for geographical research if the groups can be identified spatially and labelled from a conceptual point of view. That is, some meaning, on the basis of the input variables must be associated with the area occupied by each group. According to the factor score attributes the groups were interpreted to represent the following;

    1) Group 1   Intensive horticulture and poultry
    2) Group 2   Urbanizing area — small farm emphasis
    3) Group 3   Urbanizing area — viable farming[27]
    4) Group 4   Non-specific transitional
    5) Group 5   Low sales — aging farmer
    6) Group 6   Rural emphasis — viable farming

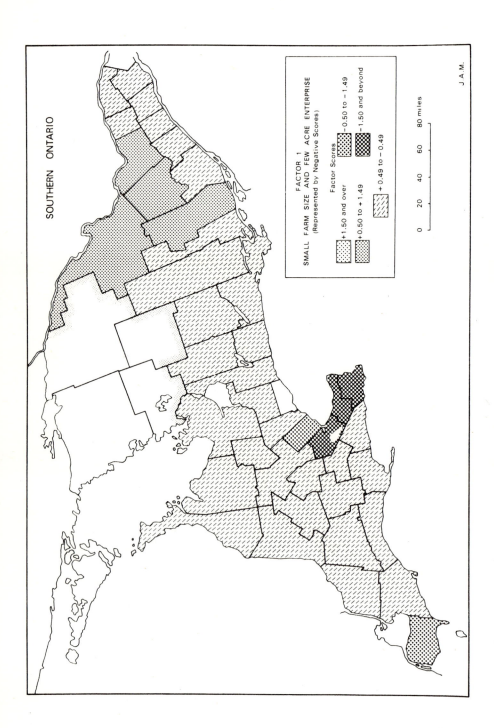

SOUTHERN ONTARIO

FACTOR 1
SMALL FARM SIZE AND FEW ACRE ENTERPRISE
(Represented by Negative Scores)

Factor Scores

+1.50 and over
+0.50 to +1.49
+0.49 to −0.49
−0.50 to −1.49
−1.50 and beyond

0   20   40   60   80 miles

J. A. M.

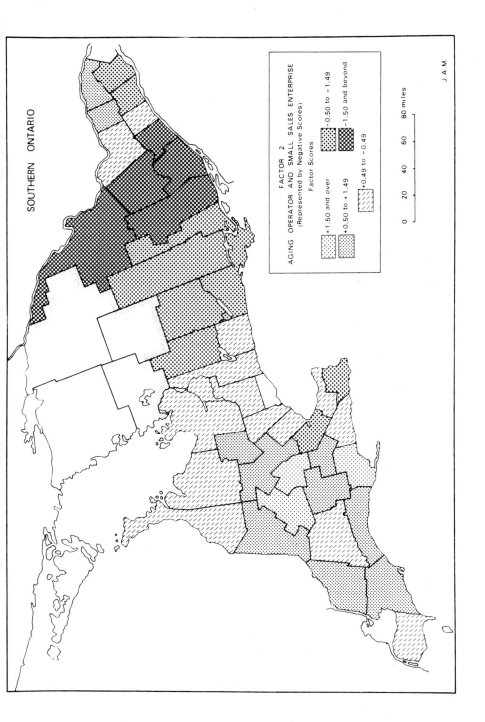

SOUTHERN ONTARIO

FACTOR 2
AGING OPERATOR AND SMALL SALES ENTERPRISE
(Represented by Negative Scores)

Factor Scores

+1.50 and over   −0.50 to −1.49

+0.50 to +1.49   −1.50 and beyond

+0.49 to −0.49

0   20   40   60   80 miles

J.A.M.

Figure 3

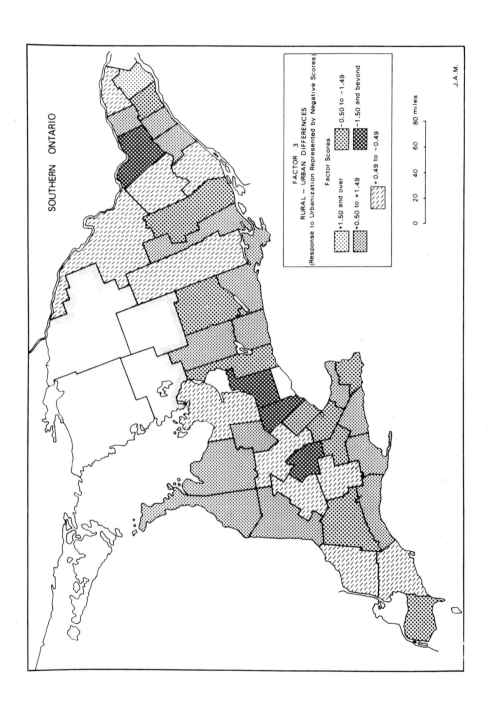

SOUTHERN ONTARIO

FACTOR 3
RURAL — URBAN DIFFERENCES
(Response to Urbanization Represented by Negative Scores)

Factor Scores

+1.50 and over

+0.50 to +1.49

+0.49 to −0.49

−0.50 to −1.49

−1.50 and beyond

0   20   40   60   80 miles

J.A.M.

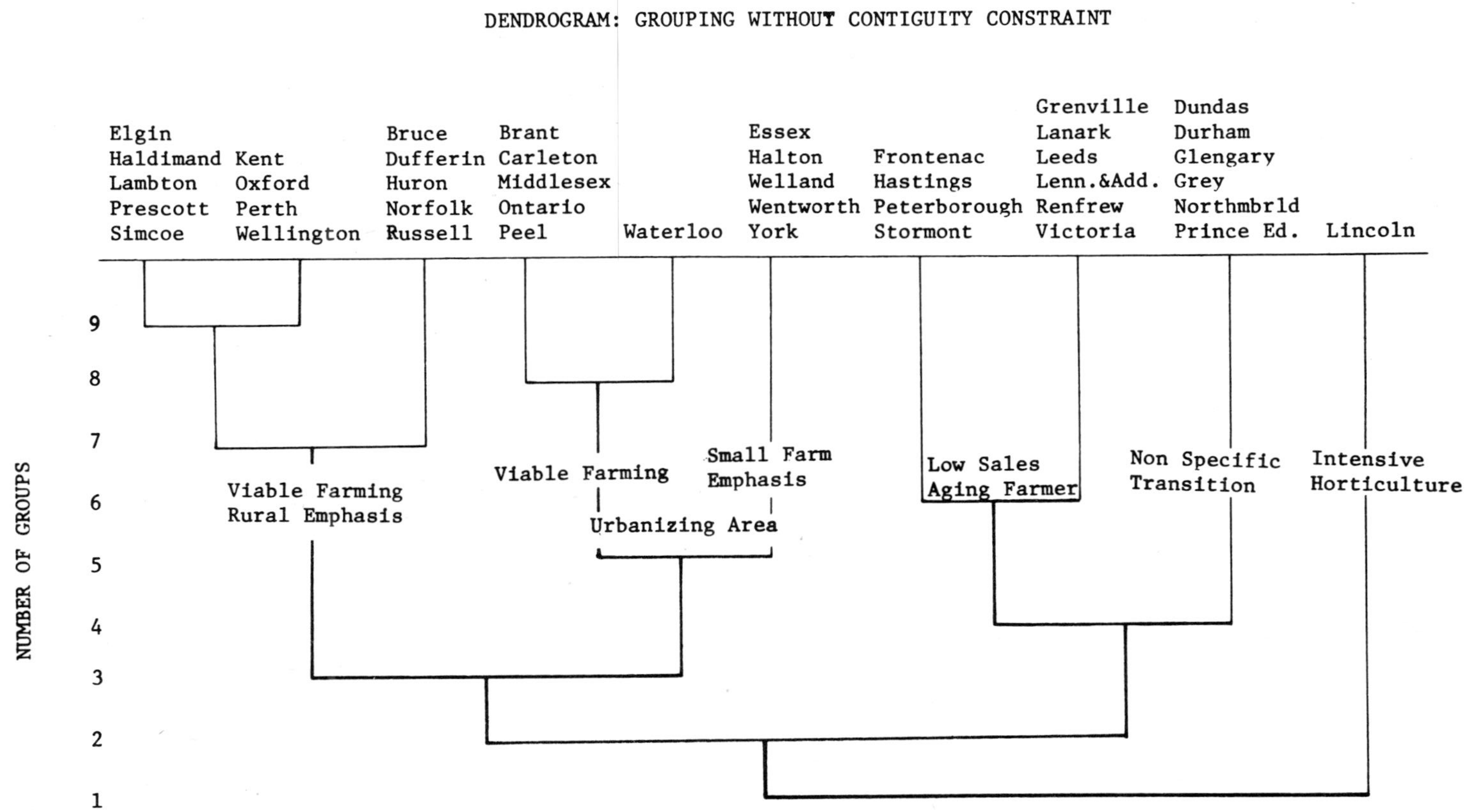
DENDROGRAM: GROUPING WITHOUT CONTIGUITY CONSTRAINT
Elgin
Haldimand
Lambton
Prescott
Simcoe
Kent
Oxford
Perth
Wellington
Bruce
Dufferin
Huron
Norfolk
Russell
Brant
Carleton
Middlesex
Ontario
Peel
Waterloo
Essex
Halton
Welland
Wentworth
York
Frontenac
Hastings
Peterborough
Stormont
Grenville
Lanark
Leeds
Lenn.&Add.
Renfrew
Victoria
Dundas
Durham
Glengary
Grey
Northmbrld
Prince Ed.
Lincoln
Viable Farming Rural Emphasis
Viable Farming
Small Farm Emphasis
Urbanizing Area
Low Sales Aging Farmer
Non Specific Transition
Intensive Horticulture
NUMBER OF GROUPS
9
8
7
6
5
4
3
2
1

Figure 5

Recall that the degree of part-time farming varied positively throughout the counties of southern Ontario with the following main factors (in order of importance):

a) socio-economic characteristics depicting low farm income and aging farmers

b) structural variates indicating small farms and few acre enterprise types

c) intensity of urbanization

The three independent concepts are concentrated either singly or in combination in groups 1, 2, 3 and 5. All of these groups contain average or above average proportions of farmers classed part-time. If one assumes that factors correlated with a measure of part-time farming could reflect the general nature of part-time farming in areas where concentrations of both phenomenon occur, then the results of the analysis suggest differing types of part-time situations portrayed by the several types of county groups. Figure 6 summarizes generally the main areas of concentration of part-time farming and aspects of the circumjacent environment (identified here on the basis of the group types) within which the farmers operate. Each group provides a conceptual and spatial setting within which microlevel (individual farm) investigations into the varying nature of part-time farming can take place.

A note of caution must be introduced. When one applies correlation and factor analysis to data ordered spatially by counties the problem of stating relationships between "ecological correlations" and the "behaviour of individuals" arises. That is, inferences concerning the behaviour of individuals cannot be made from ecological correlations resulting from data pertaining to an areal unit. The correlations presented in Tables 2 and 4 represent the areal association between the intensity of each variable and the intensity of the variable "proportion of farmers part-time". Therefore to assess the particular mix, of social, economic and farm structure variates, which has resulted in a decision to farm part-time or, which may itself be the result of a decision to farm part-time, one needs to research the phenomenon at the individual farm level.

THE MICRO LEVEL APPROACH — IDENTIFYING THE PART-TIME FARMERS AND A CONTRIBUTION TO TERMINOLOGY

The Rural Research Group at Guelph has conducted a number of microlevel surveys in various areas of Ontario using the circumjacent environment types identified in the previous section.[28] The example here is based on my work in Waterloo County,[29] an area within the "urbanizing area — viable farming" circumjacent environment type. (See Figure 7 for the location of Waterloo County.) It was hypothesized that in this area part-time farming would represent a response to urban pressures and opportunities. The major purpose at hand is to identify, in an objective manner, sub-groups representing types of part-time situations and to emphasize the distinctiveness of these several part-time farming types.

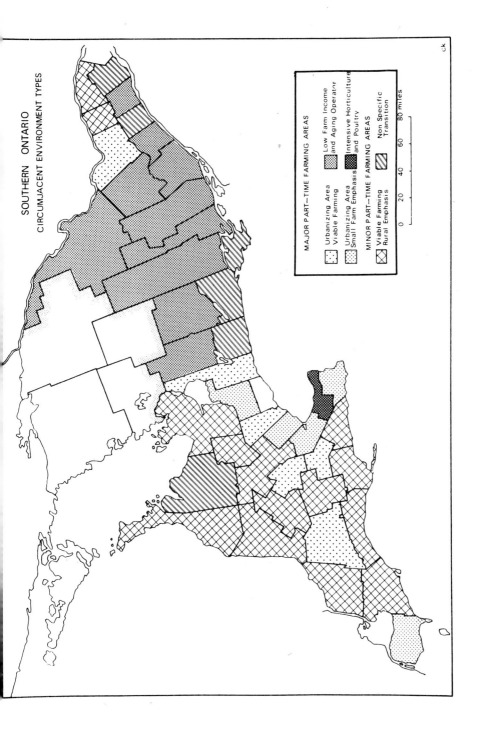

SOUTHERN ONTARIO
CIRCUMJACENT ENVIRONMENT TYPES

MAJOR PART-TIME FARMING AREAS

Urbanizing Area
Viable Farming

Low Farm Income
and Aging Operator

Urbanizing Area
Small Farm Emphasis

Intensive Horticulture
and Poultry

MINOR PART-TIME FARMING AREAS

Viable Farming
Rural Emphasis

Non Specific
Transition

0   20   40   60   80 miles

Figure 6

21

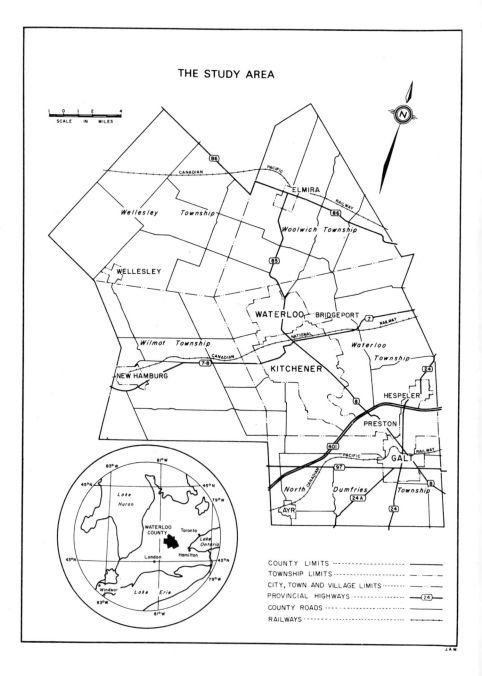

THE STUDY AREA

Figure 7

22

The typology was formulated on the basis of the interrelationships of the social, ownership, organizational and technical variates that have been suggested by the Typology Commission of the International Geographical Union.[30] Twenty measures, encompassing characteristics of the farm and the farmer were selected for a sample of part-time farm operators (Table 5).[31] Thus the resultant typology goes beyond the simple grouping of farmers.

In any objective grouping procedure it is desirable to use input measures which are independent of each other. Orthogonal variates, usually fewer in number, also expedite the problem of cluster identification which may prevail in the case of groupings emerging from many variables (some of which may be highly intercorrelated and hence "forcing" a solution in a particular way.) Therefore, the factor analytic method was again utilized to remove possible redundance and to produce a set of independent input measures. The factor scores, representing the new input data, were entered into a hierarchical grouping analysis.

The factoring procedure provided 5 interpretable underlying dimensions[32] labelled as follows;

Factor 1, Economic attachment to farming

Factor 2, Economic success syndrome

Factor 3, Part-time farming persistence

Factor 4, Social and ownership attachment to farming

Factor 5, Operator age and future status

The specific variable loadings for the 5 factors are presented in Table 6.[33]

The 5 factors extracted represent independent economic and social measures from which types of part-time situations can be developed. A hierarchical grouping procedure, using the factor scores of the 47 part-time situations as input, was next utilized. The resultant groups would therefore be formed both on the basis of farm and farm operator characteristics.

The grouping analysis yielded a mathematically "optimal" solution of 6 groups. The number of component members within each of the 6 groups ranged from one to 15. Interpretation of the meaning of each cluster must initially proceed solely from the relative common association that group members display with the input factors. This association, summarized in Table 7, led to the labelling of the type of situation represented by each group. In order of decreasing numbers of component members the groups have been subjectively identified as follows:

Group 1 — Small scale hobby and miscellaneous situation. This largest cluster contains 15 component members, or nearly one-third of the total sample. High positive scores for factor 4 indicate a low social and ownership attachment to farming while high positive scores for factor 3 reflect a low level of part-time farming persistence. The majority of cases (11) were characterized by very small farms with less than 32 acres being operated.[34] All operators reported full-time off-farm employment and had no intention of becoming full-time

Table 5

Data List 20 Selected Measures

Social and Ownership

Variable Number and Name
1) Acres rented to others

2) Total area operated

3) Years as a part-time farmer (present situation)

4) Operator born and rased on a farm*

5) Age of operator

6) Son plans to farm here*

7) House amenity index

8) Number of pleasure horses

9) Future plans to be a full-time farmer*

10) Operator days off-farm work

11) **Operator distance in miles to off-farm work**

12) Operator number of years in present or similar off-farm work

Organizational and Technical

13) Total animal units

14) Present $ value of farm equipment

15) Total man hours per year farm labour input

16) Gross value of products sold

17) Net farm income

18) Desired net return from farming

19) Total of net farm sales plus all other income

20) Net hourly farm wage to operator and family labour

*nominal scale variables

Table 6

Factor Loadings — Part-Time Typology Phase

Variable	Factor Loadings and Proportion of Variance				
	I 20.7%	II 12.5%	III 8.9%	IV 12.3%	V 7.7%
2) Total area operated				-0.687	
3) Years in this part-time situation			-0.724		
5) Age of operator					-0.733
6) Son plans to farm here				-0.752	
7) House amenity index		0.534			
9) Future plan to be full-time farmer					0.757
10) Operator, days of off-farm work				0.587	
12) Years of off-farm work experience			-0.813		
13) Total animal units	0.717				
14) Present $ value of farm equipment	0.743				
15) Total man hours/years farm labour				-0.653	
16) Gross $ value of products sold	0.879				
17) Net farm income	0.903				
18) Desired net farm income		0.897			
19) Total, net farm plus all other income	0.723				
20) Net hourly farm wage to operator and unpaid family labor	0.858				

Table 7

Dominant Factor Characteristics of Each
Type of Part-Time Situation

Group 1 — Small scale hobby and miscellaneous situation (31.9% of sample)

— Low social and ownership attachment to farming
— Low part-time farming persistence

Group 2 — Aspiring element situation (25.5% of sample)

— Younger operator
— Fairly high social and ownership attachment to farming
— Fairly low economic attachment to farming

Group 3 — Part-time farming persistence situation (21.3% of sample)

— High part-time farming persistence
— Fairly low social and ownership attachment to farming

Group 4 — Sporadic part-time situation (12.8% of sample)

— Low economic success syndrome
— High social and ownership attachment to farming
— Aging farm operator

Group 5 — Large scale hobby situation (6.4% of sample)

— High economic success syndrome
— Fairly high social and ownership attachment to farming
— Fairly low economic attachment to farming
— Fairly low part-time farming persistence

Group 6 — The "unique" situation (2.1% of sample)

— High economic attachment to farming
— High economic success syndrome
— Low part-time farming persistence

farmers. Farm labour inputs were the lowest of any of the emergent groups and ranged from 160 total man hours per year to 1500 man hours. Corresponding sales were also low with 11 of the 15 cases obtaining negative farm returns.

The core operators within this group stressed that their situation was strictly "hobby farming" and that their interests were in rural living with farm produce sales being a result of farming in spare time. In certain instances the "farming" activity was initiated by the wife and children with the male of the household being a reluctant participant.[35] Most of the individuals involved realize they are not, nor will they ever be, in the business of farming and do not think of themselves as farmers. For some the selling of agricultural products arose by chance. Hence, although all but 2 operators in this whole group were born and raised on a farm and had some farming experience the attempt to "farm" is characterized by inefficiency and the results, or outputs, by uncertainty.

The high factor scores for factor 3 (meaning a low level of part-time persistence) appear to be a result not only of relatively recent "entries" into the farming community, but also of a certain amount of "dabbling" in agriculture. Most of the cases entered "farming" in the part-time situation with the farm families involved moving out of an urban centre. None of this group was dependent on the sale of agricultural products and some respondents admitted that the selling of produce did not necessarily occur every year. Hence a low value for the variable "years in the present situation" could have resulted from the simple fact that the operators "jumped" in and out of agriculture in the past.[36] Clearly, this group represents mainly a rural residence situation. The operations involved have been classified as farms on the basis of the present census definition (1 acre or more of land and $50 or more of produce sold the previous year) but appear to belong more logically to the rural non-farm category.

Group 2 — The aspiring element situation. Nearly 26 per cent of the total sample clustered within Group 2. A high positive index for factor 5 (operator age and future status) indicates relatively young farmers intending to achieve a full-time farming status in the future. Secondary characteristics show a fairly high social and ownership attachment to farming (factor 4) and a trend to a low economic attachment to farming (factor 1). In combination these factors suggest a young farmer element possessing a substantial land resource base but yet perhaps suffering from low farm incomes.

Most of the respondents owned relatively large farms varying from 63 to 200 acres. All group members indicated they were in a part-time situation solely for economic reasons. Half were previously full-time farmers who took on extra work to supplement low farm incomes while the other half were entering farming via the part-time route. Born and raised on farms, these operators required additional income either to expand their land holdings, or for livestock or machinery purchases. All expressed a strong desire to become full-time operators within the next 5 years, but most were presently devoting the equivalent of a full year (250 days) to the off-farm job.

Group 3 — Part-time farming persistence situation. Ten cases (21.3 per cent of the sample) were grouped in the third cluster. The high negative scores on factor 3 reflect many years of off-farm work experience and an extended period of part-time farming. The actual number of years as part-time farmers ranged from 8 to 20 years with the majority of operators reporting 12 or more years on this farm and in the present part-time situation. All operators had entered farming on a part-time basis and have full-time off-farm jobs. This group thus represents a "persistent" part-time type.[37]

The off-farm income level is fairly substantial and over a period of time a satisfactory balance of primary dependency on non-farm income and secondary dependency on farm generated income has emerged. Some individuals had originally anticipated full-time farming situations but have remained part-time farmers. All members had lived in urban areas prior to their present status, and now stressed the virtues of rural living and personal satisfaction derived from working the land and with animals. One could argue that these operations go beyond an apparent "hobby situation" because most units are operated at a profit with the output level having been carefully chosen on the basis of years of experience. In certain instances the adjustment process led to substantial portions of land owned being rented out. The resulting combinations of effort put into farming and non-farming is satisfactory to the operator and likely to be continued in the future.

Group 4 — Sporadic part-time situation. The 6 members of this cluster (12.7 per cent of the sample) obtained high negative scores for factors 2, 4 and 5 reflecting limited economic success, small amounts of off-farm work, and aging operators. All displayed a very low relative dependency on off-farm income which undoubtedly reflects the short off-farm work periods (range 40-90 days). Furthermore each operator's job was of the occasional "sporadic opportunity" type which supplied a semi-skilled or unskilled service sought by others in the immediate area.[38] Operators cited this chance opportunity reason for obtaining extra work rather than economic incentive or gain reasons and pointed out that they were in a previous full-time situation. Some simply derived personal satisfaction from the variety of an occasional off-farm job. It appears that farm, farmer and farming characteristics associated with sporadic off-farm work are really "full-time" in nature even when the accumulated number of days approaches the 100 level in this area.[39]

Group 5 — Prosperous large scale hobby situation. The fifth group consisting of 3 members (about 6.3 per cent of all cases) can be considered as a residual element whose characteristics form a specific combination of factors resulting in an unusual part-time situation. The factor score values reveal a strong positive association with factor 2 (economic success syndrome), a high degree of social and ownership attachment (factor 4) and a fairly low economic attachment to farming (factor 1). Furthermore, moderate positive trends on factor 3 (part-time farming persistence) suggested relatively recent entry into the part-time situation. A situation of relative prosperity based mainly on high off-farm incomes and lack of a relative dependency on farm income is implied. The area operated and total labour input were rather high, suggesting a prosperous large scale hobby farming situation.

The rationale for the "labelling" of this group is supported by an examination of each operation. All three operators were professional men with substantial off-farm incomes.[40] Although the areas operated varied from 100 to 260 acres, all units operated at a net loss varying from -$2250 to -$7600 for the study year. All operators entered farming recently (range 2 to 7 years) as part-time operators and each cited a preference for country living and the desire to "escape" from the city as the main reason for combining farming with some other job. In 2 cases additional hired labour was present. All individuals expressed the desire to expand the farming operation into a viable state in the future but no one planned to discontinue the full-time off-farm job. For this small group with relatively high off-farm incomes the current losses from the farming operation were offset by income from off-farm sources. In this sense the term "hobby" may be applied to the situation. However, in view of the scale of each operation (i.e. the size of area operated and sales exceeding $10,000) the term "large scale" must be an added qualification.

Group 6 — The unique situation. One can argue that a group can consist of only one entity representing a unique situation whose factor score profiles are unlike that of any other member of the sample. In reality this unique case embraced a small (3 acre) poultry unit specializing in egg production (from some 10,000 hens) yielding gross sales of about $70,000. The operator devoted about 90 days per year to bus driving and driver training instruction at a local high school. He cited a combination of farm work boredom and an automated procedure of egg collecting as the chief reasons for being in a part-time situation. This operation is characterized by viable farming, relative prosperity and low part-time farming persistence.

SOME GENERAL PRINCIPLES SUGGESTED BY THE TYPES OF PART-TIME SITUATIONS

The Continuum of Part-Time Farming Types

In addition to establishing the 6 types of situations on the basis of the "optimal" grouping level, one can also determine which groups are most similar (and conversely which are most dissimilar) by tracing the hierarchy of types through the grouping procedure. The dendrogram (Figure 8) presents the ever increasing generalization of types which emerged from 6 to 2 groups. Notice that 2 main streams appear. One stream comprises the large and small scale hobby elements which cluster first into a "general hobby" situation (grouping level 5). This is joined at the next step by the persistent type to form a potential "continuing" part-time situation (grouping level 4). Another stream forms at grouping level 3 when the aspiring and sporadic types merge to create a potential full-time farming situation. The unique case associates itself with the potential continuing part-time types when only 2 groups are evident.

The 2 most dissimilar situations (potential full-time and potential continuing part-time) appear to be a function of the "intent" of the operator.[41] Fourteen of the 18 members of the potential full-time group (or about 78 per cent) indicated a desire to be full-time farmers within the next 5 years,[42] whereas 27 of the 29 members

GROUPING PROCEDURE TYPES OF PART-TIME SITUATIONS

47 Part-Time Operations

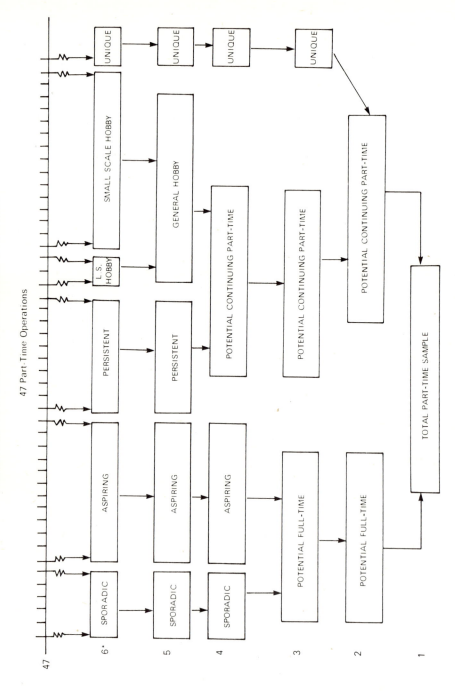

Number of Groups
* Optimal Group

of the potential continuing part-time element (about 93 per cent) maintained they will continue part-time farming. This suggests that in Waterloo County two fundamental types of part-time situations exist based on the "intent" and activity focus of the operator. As a general principle then, either the potential full-time or the potential continuing part-time situation underlies nearly all part-time operations in this area. There appears to be no significant "exist" element whereby farmers effectively withdraw from farming using the part-time route as a temporary bridge.

Since reality seldom follows the simple dichotomy suggested above the original 5 types of situations (omitting the unique) were placed on a continuum ranging from full-time farming to non-farming. Figure 9 incorporates the activity focus, intensity of off-farm work and reason for the part-time situation displayed by the emergent types. Note that the small scale hobby type and the sporadic type have been placed in the extreme positions with the former being basically a rural residence and limited farming situation and the latter displaying characteristics very similar to the full-time farming element. Furthermore, as one progresses through the other types of situations (left to right on Figure 9) there is an increasing amount of "dependency" on farming and an increasing tendency for the source of the off-farm employment to be non-urban.

Initially it appears that two-thirds of the total sample is "responding" to urban job opportunities. However, former full-time farmers did not gravitate to the city for extra work. Table 8 indicates that over half of all part-time situations involved a move by the operator from the city to the farm. In most instances, the actual job

Table 8

Present Off-Farm Work Source and Former Residency and Farming Status (absolute number and proportion of sample)

	No. moving from urban centre	No. former full-time	No. starting farmers[1]	Totals
No. of respondents with urban jobs	24[2] (51.1%)	1 (2.1%)	7[3] (14.9%)	32 (68.1%)
No. with farm based or local job	2 (4.3%)	13[4] (27.6%)	0	15 (31.9%)
Totals	26 (55.4%)	14 (29.7%)	7 (14.9%)	47 (100.0%)

1. No previous city residency.
2. Includes 13 of the 15 small scale hobby, all 3 large scale hobby and 8 of the 10 persisting type.
3. All 7 are of the aspiring type.
4. Includes 2 small scale (exit) type, 5 of the 12 aspiring type and all 6 sporadic type.

31

GENERALIZED ACTIVITY FOCUS OF THE TYPES OF PART-TIME SITUATIONS

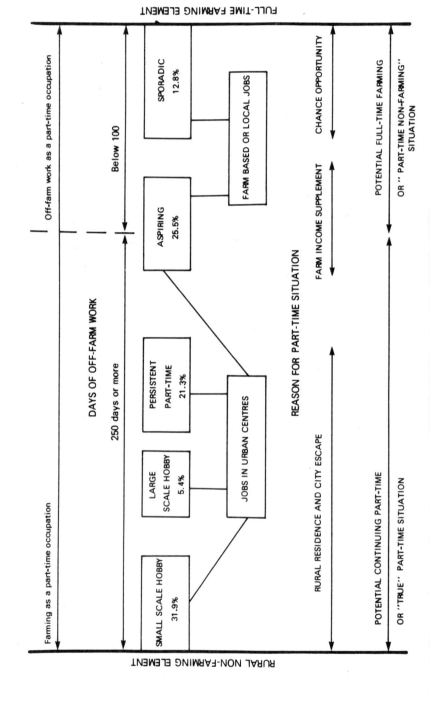

source remained unchanged. Note also that a further 15 per cent of the sample (all aspirants) were taking advantage of employment opportunities in the city to build up capital for full-time farming. No operator replied that he had de-emphasized farming because of urban work availability.[43]

CONCLUSIONS — A PHILOSOPHICAL NOTE

Part-time farming is a very complex phenomenon. A holistic typological approach can further the understanding of part-time farming generally. Pressures and opportunities resulting in the decision to farm on a part-time basis appear to vary spatially (as indicated by the several circumjacent-environment types). The numerous basic ramifications of part-time farming (expressed in this paper by the types of situations) preclude interpretation of the phenomenon as simply "opposite" to full-time farming. Moreover, we must consider part-time farming positively. Popular quotes, such as the following, appear to apply to only a segment of the part-time farming population and should be challenged;

> To be a part-time farmer! To come home from
> a day in the office or shop and spend a few
> minutes feeding the chickens and patting Bossie
> affectionately on the rump; then to sit on the
> front porch and watch the sun sink slowly behind
> the distant hills as the crickets sing and the
> breeze wafts gently across the green pastures
> and fields of corn. To be a part-time farmer. . . .
> paradise on earth![44]

Indeed, Perkins has argued that "it is no longer appropriate to regard multiple jobholding as a temporary phenomenon, as an aberration in the structure of farming to be corrected by public policies. Programs to facilitate off-farm employment by farm operators and their families merit serious consideration as a complement to other forms of adjustment assistance".[45] In this sense the part-time route could lead, in certain instances, to a greater measure of stability in the rural environment. We need, however, to identify who the part-time farmers are (both on a regional and local scale) and establish terminology which will reflect more accurately the variety of situations which the term "part-time farming" presently encompasses.

The soundness of the part-time farming types offered here should be tested in other portions of the urbanizing area-viable farming circumjacent environment type. One can hypothesize that in these portions of southern Ontario part-time farming would represent a response by; a) urban folk leaving the city to become part-time farmers; b) young starting farmers using city jobs to acquire additional income and c) farm operators wishing to maintain long term positions of economic stability based on farm and non-farm income. If part-time farming types similar to those identified in this study emerge some progress will have been made in the search for general principles of part-time situations in an urbanizing area.[46]

33

Whether our typologies are theoretically, or empirically founded, the types must be derived via objective means based on measurable data incorporating a variety of social and economic characteristics of the farmer and farm family and structural attributes of the farm itself. It is the functional interrelationship of these variates that culminates in types of situations. But this analytical approach must also be based on the premise that we are dealing with believable people and not just numerical combinations of events. Hence in interpreting and identifying the emergent types of situations one needs to incorporate more subjective elements such as motives, aspirations and needs among the facts.

Finally, very little has been stated here about cause and effect relationships or about dynamic aspects involving the movement of idividuals by some adjustment process through the continuum of types (which themselves are not mutually exclusive). Some theoretical notions have been formulated.[47] These theories however, require more empirical validation via specific hypotheses testing. At the moment, insufficient time has passed to have conducted longitudinal studies under proper control conditions. The Rural Research Group at Guelph expects to do this in the future. To date we have concentrated on attempting to understand some of the complexities of our subjects (part-time farmers) and of our subject matter (part-time farming).

NOTES AND REFERENCES

1 It had been noted by St. Thomas Aquinas that various craftsmen-farmers cultivated small plots of land in the immediate suburban districts of the Italian town of Sambuca in the 13th Century, see G.H. Speltz, **The Importance of Rural Life According to the Philosophy of St. Thomas Aquinas,** Washington, D.C: Catholic University of America Press, 1945.

2 D. Rozman, **Part-Time Farming in Massachusetts,** Massachusetts Agricultural Experiment Station, Bulletin No. 266, October, 1930.

3 Rozman, p. 105. Previous authors had alluded to the practice of agriculture on a part-time basis with terms such as "farming in the twilight zone", "one-cow farmer", "back-yard farmer", "amphibian", and so on.

4 See **U.S. Census of Agriculture,** Volume 1, Part 8, 1964 and **1969 Census of Agriculture,** U.S. Department of Commerce, Part 38 (Montana), Section One, Volume One, p. A-4.

5 **Canada Census, 1941, Agriculture,** Volume VIII, p. xxiii.

6 **Canada Census, 1951, Agriculture,** Volume VI, Part 1, Table 26.

7 **1961 Census of Canada — Agriculture — Ontario,** Bulletin 5.2-2, Table 36.

8 **1966 Census of Agriculture — Agriculture — Ontario,** Volume IV(4-2), p. ix.

9 See for example J.A. Mage, "Part-Time Farming" in A.R.D.A. Report No. 7, **Planning for Agriculture in Southern Ontario.** Centre for Resources Development, University of Guelph, 1972. pp. 152-168.

10 J.A. Mage, "Part-Time Farming in Southern Ontario With Specific Reference to Waterloo County", Unpublished Ph.D. Thesis, University of Waterloo, 1974.

11 S.V. Frauendorfer, "Part-Time Farming — A Review of World Literature", **World Agricultural Economics and Rural Sociology Abstracts,** Vol. 8, No. 1, March 1966.

12 A.L. Bertrand, "Research on Part-Time Farming in the United States", **Sociologica Ruralis,** Volume 7, No. 3, 1967, p. 296.

13 The term "multiple jobholding" by farmers has been utilized by numerous researchers to define part-time farming in general. See for example B.B. Perkins, **Multiple Jobholding Among Farm Operators — A Study of Agricultural Adjustment in Ontario,** O.A.C. Publication AE/72/5, University of Guelph, May 1972.

14 P. Roy and W.L. Slocum, "Demographic Factors and Definition of Part-Time Farming", **Clinical Session on Part-Time Farming,** Washington, 1958.

15 A.M. Fuller, "The Part-Time Farm Problem — A Scheme for Geographers", Proceedings of the C.A.G. National Meeting, Winnipeg, May 1970. pp. 121-128.

16 The terms part-time farm, part-time farmer and part-time farming are used interchangeably here.

17 W.H. Metzler, "Discussions: Proposed Investigation of the Role of the Part-Time Farmer in Agriculture", **Clinical Session on Part-Time Farming,** Pullman, Washington, 1958.

18 G.V. Fuguitt, "A Typology of the Part-Time Farmer", **Rural Sociology,** Volume 26, No. 1, 1961, pp. 39-48.

19 Fuguitt, 1961, p. 48.

20 Mage, 1974. Only the 42 mainland counties of southern Ontario were used. The example is based on 1966 census data and uses the census definition of part-time farming.

21 This term was coined by Olmstead. See C.W. Olmstead, "The Phenomena, Functioning Units and Systems of Agriculture", **Geographica Polonica,** Volume 19, 1970, pp. 31-41.

22 Previously, Sterrett had indicated over 100 census variables which could be used to describe holistically the types of agriculture in southern Ontario. See D.J. Sterrett, "A Factorial Typology of Ontario Agriculture", (Unpublished M.A. Thesis, University of Waterloo, 1969).

23 Acceptance of individual variables occured at simple R values of ± 0.31 or greater (the 0.5 level of significance).

24 The terms factor, component and dimension are used interchangeably as are the terms factor analysis and principal components analysis. The varimax rotation solution was used.

25 A factor score represents an index of the relative strength of a factor on an entity (in this case a county).

26 For example see B.J.L. Berry, "A Method for Deriving Multifactor Uniform Regions", **Przeglad Geograficzny,** Volume 33, 1961, pp. 203-282.

27 The term "viable" is used here to reinforce the particular concentration of the combination of young farmers and generally high gross sales in these areas relative to other portions of southern Ontario.

28 Some of the findings are reported in papers by A.M. Fuller "The Problems of Part-Time Farming Conceptualized" and by R.C. Benson "Part-Time Farming in a Physically Marginal Area of Northern Ontario".

29 Mage, 1974. For more details pertaining to the agricultural economy of Waterloo County see J.A. Mage "Selected Aspects of the Agricultural Economy of Waterloo County", **The Waterloo County Area — Selected Geographical Essays,** ed. A.G. McLellan, University of Waterloo, Department of Geography, 1971, Chapter 8.

30 J. Kostrowicki "The Typology of World Agriculture — A Preliminary Scheme",. **Agricultural Typology and Land Use,** ed. L.G. Reeds, Proceedings of the Agricultural Typology Commission Meeting, McMaster University, Hamilton, July 1973. pp. 3-52.

31 All but the 3 nominal scale variables also represented key differentiating measures between the part-time and full-time farming group. Hence these variables portray the "essence" of the part-time farming group. The master sample included 61 full-time and 47 part-time cases. See Mage, 1974.

32 The rotated varimax solution was used. The 5 factors interpreted accounted for nearly 63 per cent of the variance within the original data.

33 The logic of factor labelling is apparent by interpreting the loadings in Table 6.

34 Seven situations embraced farms of 2 to 19 acres.

35 Activities ranged from the selling of sweet corn and small fruit from roadside stands to the keeping of small pig and/or beef herds.

36 Unfortunately the number of past incidences of selling or non-selling of agricultural produce was not pursued in detail for this study.

37 The "persistent" situation as a type is covered more fully in other symposium papers by Benson, 1975 and Fuller, 1975. Refer also to J. Galloway, "The 'Persistent' Part-Time Farmer", C.A.G. Regional Conference, Ottawa, March, 1975.

38 "Occasional job" types included carpentry, saw milling, chicken catching, grain bin making, stock yard work and night watchman work.

39 The results of a discriminant analysis (part-time vs. full-time) indicated that members of this group logically "belonged" in the full-time farming category.

40 Included in this group were a sales manager, a high school teacher and a physician. The income range was $10,500 - $37,300 and all jobs were full-time off the farm.

41 This finding coincides with Fuguitt's idea that a typology of part-time farmers be based on the past, present and future commitment by the farmer to farm and non-farm occupation. (Fuguitt, 1961).

42 The remaining 4 were aging farmers and wished to retire.

43 It must be emphasized, however, that in about 6 per cent of the cases the part-time situation was the result of former full-time farmers selling land for urban development purposes but retaining the house and a few surrounding acres.

44 Editorial comment in **Canadian Swine,** Canadian Swine Breeders Association, Fall 1974.

45 Perkins, 1972, p. 37.

46 Inherent in this suggestion is that types of situations be also identified under the umbrella of the various circumjacent environments themselves.

47 Fuller, 1975.

GUELPH REPORT II

THE PROBLEMS OF
PART-TIME FARMING CONCEPTUALISED

Anthony M. Fuller

The Guelph Report I[1] has established that part-time farming in Ontario is a varied and complex phenomenon. A number of questions and problems derive from the conclusion that there are five basic types of part-time farming,[2] and it is the intention of this paper to examine some of these problems in order to more fully understand their implications, particularly in relation to agricultural adjustment and rural development. In searching for underlying conceptual principles regarding the different types of part-time farming, examples will be drawn from a series of micro-level surveys conducted in various counties and districts of rural Ontario.[3]

The fact that part-time farming can be classified into a number of types may be very satisfying academically, but should cause some concern among planners and administrators who, in dealing with rural development, will always be faced with the problem of identifying the mix of part-time farming types which contribute to the make-up of their target population. If one of the basic tenets of rural development is to understand and to cater for all human elements in a community (however defined), in order to maintain or alter the integrity of that community, then an holistic approach to part-time farming is required, at least at the outset. Geographers, concerned with systems theory, can contribute to the essential task of developing frameworks by which the different types of part-time farming can be seen interacting as a whole.[4] Only in this manner can the separate drives, problems and needs expressed by each type be understood in relation to the general rural system.

As occupiers of rural space producing goods, as farmers and also as members of the non-farm sector, part-time operators are a little known and multifaceted element in any rural community. Bunce[5] has begun to explore the activity patterns of part-time farmers, but as yet this aspect is little understood. Their behaviour as a group or as sub-group types will influence the regional economy in terms of both the supply and demand for goods and services which, in turn, depends upon the structure of the group and upon the stability or permanence of that structure. Since sub-group types of part-time farming are defined by motive and as one major motive is to use part-time farming as a means to an end (to enter or leave farming), then one can expect a high level of turnover within the structure, which may cause a shift in the equilibrium of the part-time farming mix. Mobility and change are thus features of most part-time farming groups and the subject becomes a question of **adjustment behaviour;** implying process and dynamism between farming and the rural sector at large.

Part-time farming is a mechanism by which rural residents attempt to satisfy their perceived needs and ambitions: to adjust to changing personal circumstances or external pressures. This mechanism of change is a major source of the problems associated with part-time farming. Problems are created at the local and regional level; for example, there may be a conflict between the appropriate use of land and the achievement of individual life goals. The motives for part-time farming are thus the key to understanding both the nature and origin of the resultant problems, be they associated with the adjustment of physical and human resources, economic costs or psychological stresses that emanate from a changing rural system.

Whatever the motive, the majority of part-time farming situations involve two fundamental processes:

1) DECISION MAKING: Part-time farming is a status of both economic and social significance and consequently is the result of a distinct decision making process and is not a natural, inherent or evolved status. Operators must choose, and most do so consciously, to be a farm operator and to hold an off-farm job.

2) DYNAMISM: The conscious attempt to reach a self-defined "new" status means that part-time farmers are associated with **change** (farm enterprise, rural life style) and **mobility** (personal, occupational).

By focussing attention on the decision-making process of part-time farmers and by considering the nature and outcome of their adjustment behaviour, some of the motivational causes and implications of part-time farming can be more fully understood.

Inherent in the concept of part-time farming is the question of time. The word appears in the actual term, but instead of having an explicit connotation has come to have a very confused meaning, probably because of the complex nature of the phenomenon itself. Time and income have been the classic definitional measures of part-time farming in the past and the Guelph surveys have taken into consideration the importance of both parameters.[6] However, at the micro-level study of part-time farming the time factor has been selected as the central element of hypothetical importance. In addition, it provides a medium for identifying the problems which result from part-time farming.

Time has two important dimensions in considering part-time farming as an adjustment process in rural development. There is the concept of time operating as the allocation of **work** or **labour time** between farm and off-farm employment during the cycle of a farming year. This is the more traditional view of time in part-time farming research and calls into play all the factors which potentially affect and result from dual employment in relation to labour time as a resource. Decisions concerning the allocation of labour time are governed by the perception of opportunities and constrained by the conformity of tradition. A study of labour-time allocation can illuminate the conditions which generate multiple job-holding and can also measure the outcome in terms of productivity, benefit or cost. The second measure of time, and one of more radical importance at this stage, is that of **adjustment time,** the notion of part-time farmers modifying their behaviour over a period of years, such adjustments collectively forming identifiable patterns of change. If part-time farming is a means to an end, as most people who enter the dual role perceive it, then it is important to determine how long it takes for different groups to achieve their goal — that is, the time required for the transition into or out of agriculture via the part-time farming route. A notion of transition time will enable the problem of assessing the social and economic costs of adjustment to be approached. These are fundamental questions and although they have been pursued before, the recent micro-level surveys permit a reconsideration in detail.

WORK-TIME ALLOCATION

In order to effectively measure the labour-time allocation of farmers with two occupations attention will be focussed on the home operation, this being the residence and thus the common core of the dual arrangement. In addition, as one of the main criticisms of part-time farming is that it underutilizes land and farm resources, it is useful to establish a procedural framework based on labour time such that this problem can be examined for the different types of part-time farming.

There is an important difference between the farm, the farm operator and the farm enterprise, these being theoretically separate elements in the concept of part-time farming. A **part-time farm** is a land holding unit that provides less than a full year's work, a **part-time farmer** is one who holds an additional job to that of farming, and **part-time farming,** in the pure sense, occurs when a part-time farm is operated by a part-time farmer.

If a part-time farm is one that provides less than a full year of work under normal circumstances, and 250 days of work is considered to be a standard working year,[7] then all units with less than 250 days of work may be considered part-time farms. One method of empirically testing this concept is to calculate the work requirement of any one operation by assessing its crop and livestock combination and expressing this in terms of the number of standard man-days (eight hours) required to run the total enterprise. This procedure was conducted for 187 part-time farmers in Hastings County, based on their farm performance statistics for the 1973 tax year.

As can be seen from Figure 1(a), 113 farms or 61 per cent of the sample had less than a full year of work in 1973; a high figure which suggests one of two causal possibilities. On the one hand, the large number of operators reporting off-farm work in Hastings County (47 per cent of all farmers, 1971) might be explained by low work-requirement units reflecting such structural attributes as poor physical quality of land or small size of production unit: in effect, a **marginal opportunity** to farm full time. On the other hand, it could imply that an adjustment or reduction in the scale of operation has already taken place. In the former case operators can be assumed to have taken an off-farm job because of low income returns from a part-time unit, while in the latter the holding of an off-farm job may have

WORK TIME ALLOCATION OF SAMPLE FARMS REPORTING OFF -FARM WORK

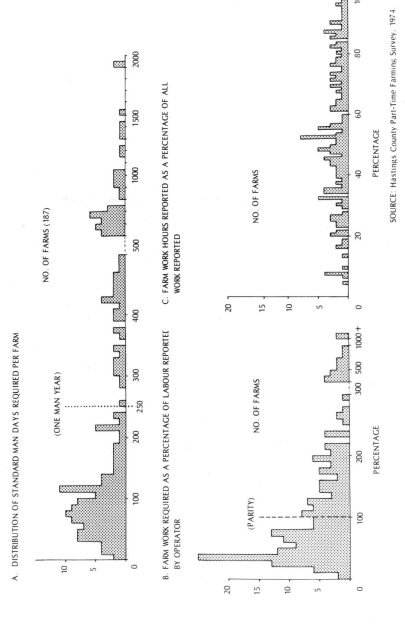

A. DISTRIBUTION OF STANDARD MAN DAYS REQUIRED PER FARM

C. FARM WORK HOURS REPORTED AS A PERCENTAGE OF ALL WORK REPORTED

B. FARM WORK REQUIRED AS A PERCENTAGE OF LABOUR REPORTED BY OPERATOR

SOURCE: Hastings County Part-Time Farming Survey, 1974.

Figure 1

41

led to a de-escalation of the farm operation to accommodate the time commitment of working off farm. Both situations were evident in Hastings County[8] and emphasize the problem, especially in rural planning, of distinguishing between the two.

A number of other observations can be made from the distribution of Hastings farms by labour-time allocation. Figure 1(b) depicts the relationship between work required and farm work actually reported by the operator for all sample farms. Those operations which lie near the 100 per cent line reflect a parity situation between work required and work reported, implying that the farm operation is largely run by the operator. It is clear from Figure 1(b) therefore that many operators supply only a little of the farm work required, the residual being made up by the farm wife, members of the farm family and hired help. Some operators also report far more personal labour expended than is statistically required by the nature and scale of the enterprise, suggesting a labour intensive operation in most cases.

When considering the ratio of farm work time as a percentage of off-farm work time the allocation decision of Hastings farmers also shows high variation (Figure 1(c)). Thirty-three operators spent 85 per cent of their total time doing farm work, while the majority (58 per cent) spend at least 40 per cent of their time in the off-farm job: six operators allocated over 90 per cent. Such trends reflect the wide range of work-time commitments illustrated in **An Atlas of Part-Time Farming for Ontario, 1971.**[9]

The division of the part-time farming concept into three major elements (part-time farm, part-time farmer, part-time farming) and the measurement of the part-time farm unit by labour requirements facilitates a more precise view of the problems resulting from the decision to farm part time. There is immediately the question of the efficiency of those operations which have less than a full year of work requirement — a problem which is heightened in Hastings County by the fact that 37 per cent of the part-time farmers have less than 100 days of farm work (Figure 1), implying an extremely low commitment to agriculture and obviating the possibility of commercial livestock operations (unless large-scale labour substitution is involved).[10] In fifty-six cases out of 187, Hastings operators did not cultivate a crop other than hay in 1973. The question of whether such a low commitment is the result of marginal opportunity or simply an adjustment choice becomes critical at this point, as low work requirement in marginal areas is probably a good resource allocation, while adjusted farm work to accommodate an off-farm job in a good agricultural region is less desirable.

Another aspect of the problem revealed by work-time allocation decisions of part-time farmers concerns holdings which provide **more** than 250 days of work. There are seventy-four part-time farmers (39 per cent of the total) who have more than a full year of work for one man on the farm. Of these, thirty-two have over two years of work, which implies that in Ontario approximately one-fifth of all part-time farmers will have enough work on their holdings to keep at least two adults fully employed. One may question therefore why such operators take an off-farm job when there is ample work on the farm. Does it imply a low income despite high farm labour demand, which would suggest a very inefficient use of resources, or does it mean that operators take an off-farm job to maximize their income opportunities, to exercise a skill or because there are abundant labour resources within the farm family? This situation also raises the possibility of labour substitution; the employment of non-family members to assist in the operation of a farm while the operator himself is absent. Recently this has shown up particularly in the form of custom work.[11] In many cases the off-farm time commitment will be very low and, if this coincides with the winter season, then little impact will be felt by the operator's absence, especially on a cash crop operation. A final statistic concerning work-time allocation reflects the problem potential of part-time farming as an adjustment process. It was found that the average number of total eight hour days worked, both on and off-farm, by Hastings part-time farmers, was 432, an indication of a very high labour commitment. The geographical and social mobility required to facilitate this level of activity points to the potential problems of stress embodied in such behaviour.

Whatever the micro patterns of individual behaviour, there appear to be two basic poles of decision-making stimuli. On the one hand decisions to farm part-time are associated with a basic need to supplement family income and may be described as **necessity** orientated (marginal opportunity) while on the other, the term **choice** (opportunity maximization) would seem to be an appropriate description of that behaviour which is clearly the result of more than subsistence income considerations. Although neither term explains precisely the causal nature of part-time farming decision-making, they do provide a conceptual polarization around which most decisions can be placed, as on a continuum, and viewed as a collective pattern. It is also relevant at this point to note that a large number of farms which are run full time (where the operator has no second job) also have less than 250 days of work under their present organization. These are part-time units but are operated full-time and, if society is concerned about the underutilization of land resources by part-time farmers, a similar concern might also be expressed about these situations. In terms of decision-making the two unusual situations, where operators of part-time units choose to farm full-time and where operators of full-time units decide to farm part-time, are clearly somewhat deviant from the pattern of activity that one might expect and their behaviour may be said to be based on choice. These groups need to be examined more carefully to understand the motivations and consequences of such behaviour.[12]

In reviewing some of the main points derived from a consideration of work-time allocation a simple basis for identifying the problems associated with the major types of part-time farming can be established. The decision to farm part-time, that is, to hold another job in addition to farming, is not always governed (as the bulk of the literature suggests) by the need to supplement income, but can also be the result of opportunity maximization. It is also apparent that farm work requirement does not necessarily dictate the decision of the operator to allocate his work time accordingly. Nevertheless, the majority of part-time farmers interviewed in the Guelph rural geography surveys to date have less than a full year of work requirement on their operation. The question still remains therefore as to whether the low work requirement on many Ontario holdings is the result of poor structural features or whether a conscious de-escalation of the farm operation has taken place subsequent to the operator becoming a part-time farmer. In order to consider this question the second dimension of time, adjustment time, can be usefully employed.

ADJUSTMENT TIME

The concept of adjustment time is primarily a consideration of accumulated annual behaviour in relation to the decision to operate a farm part-time. It incorporates a notion of motive in that the objective of holding two jobs is accounted for. Fortunately, such behaviour can be measured, albeit generally, over a medium period of time. In addition, the concept takes into consideration the origin of the part-time farmer, whether from a farm or a non-farm background, such that a measure of spatial as well as occupational mobility is incorporated into the scheme.

Classic literature on part-time farming, especially the work of Fuguitt,[13] has consistently pointed to the function of part-time farming as a transition stage for people moving into or out of agriculture. Although farmer mobility is still highly associated with this stepwise process, a shift in the balance of mobility patterns appears to be taking place. Currently part-time farming functions less as an intermediate stage in the process of out migration than as a means of assisting newcomers to enter agriculture, many with the intention of eventually farming full time. In the four micro-level surveys in Ontario over 60 per cent of the 414 part-time farmers interviewed had entered from the non-farm sector and it is clear that of the two standard transition flows the "entrant" is by far the most prominent. However, a third and hitherto largely unidentifiable status of part-time farming has become important, both numerically and functionally, in the contemporary structure of part-time farming. This group may be referred to as the "persistent" part-time farmer group and it is made up of people who maintain their status as dual job-holders over long periods of time. It appears that formerly many of the "persistent" group remained as part-time farmers because they were unable to achieve the full transition into or out of agriculture. A more contemporary, reason is that "persistent" part-time farmers perceive the advantages of holding a dual occupational status and fully intend from the outset to remain part-time farmers. Many of these are hobby farmers. Whatever the reasoning behind the decision to farm part-time on a permanent basis, the number in this group is expanding rapidly. When defined in terms of being continuous dual job-holders for more than six years, "persistent" part-time farmers form the major group in all the Guelph regional studies.

The concept of adjustment time therefore concerns three basic groups:

Group A   — operators who have entered part-time farming **from**
(LEAVERS)   **full-time farming** within the last six years;

Group B   — operators who have been part-time farmers for a
(PERSISTENT)   for a continuous period of not less than six years;

Group C   — operators who have entered part-time farming **from**
(ENTRANTS)   **the non-farm sector** within the last six years.

By combining the two concepts of time (work time and adjustment time), some initial observations concerning the adjustment behaviour of the three groups of part-time farmers can be made.

Of the 187 part-time farmers in the Hastings County survey, forty-five were classified as Leavers (Group A), eighty-three as Persistent (Group B), and fifty-nine were Entrants (Group C). When distributed according to the labour requirements of their 1973 farm operation, measured in standard man-days (Figure 2), the polarization of Groups A and C is apparent. Together, Groups B and C account for 87 per cent of the part-time units (below 250 days of work requirement), while Group A has only 33 per cent in this category (Table 1), implying that a separation of Groups A and C (Leavers and Entrants) can be based on their differential commitment to farming.

Table 1

HASTINGS COUNTY SURVEY, 1975

	No. of Part-Time	% Part-Time Units (< 250 days work requirement)	% Full-Time Units (>250 days work requirement)
GROUP A (LEAVERS)	45	33	66
GROUP B (PERSISTENT)	83	61	29
GROUP C (ENTRANTS)	59	81	19

SOURCE: Hastings County Part-Time Farming Survey, 1974

The differences between Groups A and C are emphasized when the general attributes of small scale farm operations (< 250 days of work requirement) are considered (Table 2). Group A part-time farmers are, on many counts, more committed to the farm than to the non-farm sector; a characteristic which is diametrically opposed to the average Entrant (Group C), whose main commitment is towards

WORK TIME ALLOCATION OF SAMPLE FARMS BY GROUP (A,B,C)

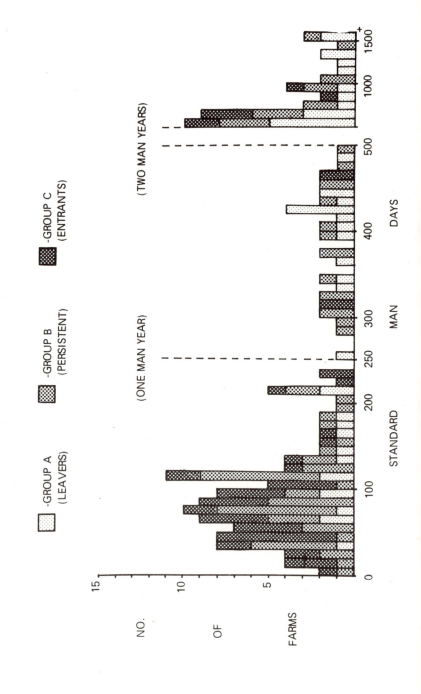

TABLE 2

SELECTED CHARACTERISTICS OF FARMS
WITH LESS THAN ONE YEAR'S WORK REQUIREMENT
(below 250 standard-man days)

	A — (LEAVERS)		B — (PERSISTENT)		C — (ENTRANTS)	
A. Distribution of Farms by Group and Work Time						
Total Farms	**No.**	**%**	**No.**	**%**	**No.**	**%**
With < 250 Man Days	15	33	51	61	48	81
Work Time < 100 Days	6	40	30	59	34	71
Work Time 100-250 Days	9	60	21	41	14	29

B. Characteristics of Farms and Farmers (Averages)

Structural Features

Land Owned (Acres)	238		204		143	
Improved Land (Acres)	66		59		53	
Agricultural Sales ($)	3,575		2,145		2,015	

Non-Farm Commitment

Off-Farm Income ($)	4,109		7,188		9,797	
Off-Farm Work (Days)	145		187		221	
Age (Years)	51		48		39	

Source: Hastings County Part-Time Farming Survey; Agridata, Rural Research Group, Department of Geography, Guelph, 1974.

the non-farm sector. Whether measured in terms of land resources (Leavers have more and better farm structures than
Entrants) or in terms of the non-farm job (Entrants spend more time
and earn far more income in the non-farm sector than Leavers), the
strength of the occupational commitment is clearly associated with the
origin and recency of the operator's former status, that is, his
position before entering the part-time farming situation. Judging from
the wide separation of the two poles of orientation (Table 2), it is not
difficult to understand why, over the last decade of rapid agricultural
capitalization, only a few aspirants actually achieve their original
transition goal and why so many embrace part-time farming as a
permanent compromise, giving a flexible but secure status.

Such findings only corroborate what one would tend to expect,
although there is evidence to suggest that motivational sub-groups
exist within the two transitional classifications (Groups A and C). The
age differential between Leavers and Entrants (average fifty-one and
thirty-nine years respectively) indicates that a majority of Group A
are elderly operators and that those with below 250 days of
work have probably de-escalated their operation in association with
retirement. In addition, a number have sought off-farm employment
as they are not making a living at farming.[14] Although the causes of
such inadequacy can only be speculated upon, the conceptual framework
of time enables this problem group to be identified.

Group C farmers, on the other hand, are much younger as a
whole and appear to fall into two categories. There are the Entrants
who aspire to be full-time farmers but who are handicapped by their
poor resources for agriculture and low farm work commitment
(71 per cent have less than 100 days of farm work requirement,
Table 2). These aspirants tend to have regular off-farm work of an
unskilled nature. The other category comprises hobby farmers who,
by definition, do not intend to become full-time farmers, except
perhaps on retirement. Hobby farmers also have regular off-farm
work, but can be divided into small and large scale by the status of
job held and by the amount of their non-farm income. In Hastings,
one-third of the Entrants held skilled jobs and a further 25 per cent
were classified as professionals.

If the six year time interval is accepted as being the normal
period required for a Leaver and Entrant to complete his transition,
then clearly the B group (Persistent) will consist mainly of non-
achievers from both A and C, including a number of hobby farmers,
the mix depending on geographical location. It can be assumed therefore that Group B will basically comprise an amalgam of all
the other part-time farming situations.

The validity of hypothesizing a significant difference between
Groups A, B and C has been tested by means of a discriminant
analysis.[15] Factors derived from a principal components analysis
on sixty-six variables collected and transgenerated from the Hastings
County survey were analyzed by the discriminant method to
produce two factor roots which respectively contributed 68 per cent

and 31 per cent to the discriminant model. According to the two roots, seven factors support and explain the separation of the three groups. The seven factors, in decreasing order of contribution to the discriminant model, are:

Factor	% Contribution to Discriminant Model
1. Aging	64.8
2. Low off-farm job commitment	24.4
3. Non-farm origin	9.6
4. Efficient dairy operation	9.5
5. High off-farm work commitment	3.7
6. High farm work requirement	3.7
7. Productivity	0.6

These are shown in diagramatic form in Figure 3 and demonstrate the consistent polarization of Groups A and C. The factors of age, time commitment to off-farm job (both negative and positive) and operator's background are ranked as the main discriminators and are noticeably social in origin, while economic factors (efficient dairy operation, high work requirement and productivity) although insignificant, are less powerful discriminators.[16] As well as confirming the separation of Groups A and C, the analysis also provides evidence of the orientation of Group B (whether towards A or C) and the degree of this orientation (Figure 3). Of the two poles, the farm and the non-farm sector, Group B tends to gravitate towards the former (Group A characteristics) although not with absolute consistency. Generally it can be concluded that Persistent part-time farmers and their operations have a socio-economic behavioural pattern that is separate from either the Leavers or Entrants.

This is an important finding for it demonstrates that in the time interval when future Persistent part-time farmers are in the A or C category they are, by definition, undergoing change. This period is one of adjustment such that by the time the individual has become a member of the B group, changes will have taken place not only in the aspiration of the operator and his family, but also in the structure of his operation.[17] As such, after six years the Group B operation is less likely to approximate the A or C norms. Group B therefore is not only an amalgam of characteristics of Groups A and C (as the statistics first imply, Table 2), but, as has been shown by discriminant analysis, is also a separate group with some distinct features of its own.

In terms of rural development this is a highly significant conclusion as, out of the three groups, it is with the Persistent part-time farmer that planning for rural development should begin. The Persistent group members are most numerous, are the most stable in that other types are adjusting in various ways, and, in addition, they have relatively fixed or resigned ambitions. Although Groups A and C should not be ignored, especially in regions where they form the dominant group, with the knowledge that Group B incorporates

THE DIFFERENTIATION OF PART - TIME FARMING GROUPS (A,B,C) BY DISCRIMINATING FACTORS

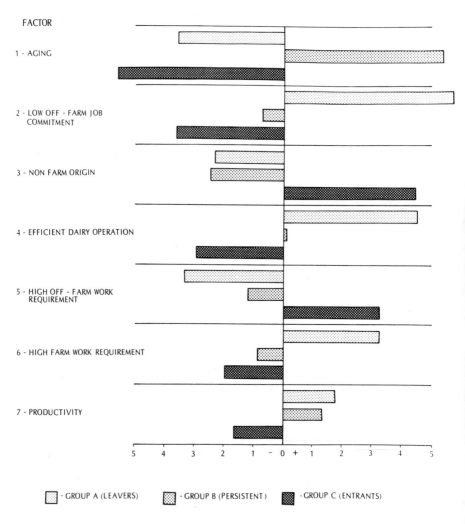

SOURCE: G MEANS, Group Discriminant Analysis.
Preliminary Report on Part-Time Farming
in Hastings County, 1975.

Figure 3

their main attributes, and that they are undergoing change, it is still advantageous to base planning perspectives on the general needs of the Persistent group. Having drawn this conclusion it is disappointing to note that very little is known about Persistent part-time farmers, although from the ongoing research at Guelph one or two summary points can be made.

Galloway[18] has observed, for example, that in a number of ways Persistent part-time farmers in Ontario are not substantially below the norms of full-time farmers and that in terms of their farm operation they reflect the general characteristics of the regional agricultural economy. These characteristics are shown in Table 3. It must be noted, however, that a large proportion (61 per cent) of Persistent part-time farmers occupy holdings with less than 250 days of work requirement, of which thirty out of eighty-three are below 100 days (Table 2.) This suggests the severe underutilization of land resources by multiple job-holders, especially in the light of some of the financial losses recorded by Hastings part-time farmers. For example, of the thirty operations with less than 100 days of work requirement, 73 per cent recorded a deficit at the end of the 1973 farm year, 40 per cent of which made net losses of over 200 per cent. This figure, even given a liberal margin of error, a single year sample, and the inadequacy of tax records as a measure of true earnings, implies either high inefficiency on behalf of the farmer aspirant or tax manipulations by hobby farmers.

From the preceding remarks it is evident that the dual concept of time has an important research function in the identification of problems associated with part-time farming. It is essential in any study of *de facto* adjustment behaviour to incorporate the idea of motive. By utilizing time frameworks, adjustment motives can best be understood in the context of the decision-making processes of part-time farmers. The value of the concept of work-time allocation lies in the clear demonstration of differential time commitments between work demands at several levels. From such allocations the problems that are assumed to characterize part-time farming can be verified and their real impact more effectively tested.

CONCLUSIONS

The most significant conclusion to be drawn from this paper is that part-time farming has become an end in itself as well as a means to an end. Its development has been a natural process as, until recently, it was neither supported nor encouraged by any agency, group of institution. Despite this, it has grown in almost every sector of the farming economy and is as pervasive spatially as farming itself. As part-time farming is a regular feature of almost all farming societies it must be recognized as a component part of any rural system.

If it is an objective to determine the contribution and needs of part-time farming in the rural system, then it must be comprehended not only in static but also in dynamic terms. As such, part-time farming is an ideal medium for understanding the needs of contemporary rural society. As a measure of rural adjustment it has

TABLE 3

SELECTED ATTRIBUTES OF 'PERSISTENT' PART-TIME FARMERS

	LAMBTON	DUFFERIN	HASTINGS	RAINY RIVER
A. Part-Time and 'Persistent' Part-Time Farmers[1]				
	%	%	%	%
All Operators Reporting Off-Farm Work	49.9	46.6	47.2	65.5
Part-Time Farmers Classified as Persistent	49.0	39.0	46.0	75.0
B. Basic Characteristics of 'Persistent' Part-Time Farmers[2]				
Average Per Farm	No.	No.	No.	No.
Land Owned (Acres)	148	131	220	395
Land Operated (Acres)	155	154	244	443
No. of Years as Operator	22	19	23	20
Age of Operator (Years)	46	47	49	48
Value of Machinery and Equipment ($)	12,500	22,055	10,313	10,762
Value of Agricultural Sales ($)	5,000	16,012	6,442	5,723
Off-Farm Income ($)	8,000	6,919	6,362	5,962
Total Sample	17	43	8.6	61

Source: 1) Statistics Canada, Census of Agriculture, vol. IV, pt. 2, 1971.
2) Survey data on 414 part-time farmers, Agridata, Rural Research Group, Department of Geography, 1973-74.

important predictive potential since it will always be at the interface of the farm and the non-farm sector. Perhaps in terms of mobility it still has its greatest significance for it permits adjustment via "trial and error" at the point of entry into or out of farming. These observations on the "function" of part-time farming testify to the importance of the subject, not only to academics in their quest to understand rural change, but also to applied scientists and policy makers who, in planning rural development, need to be aware of this phenomenon and its role in the rural system.

The list of general observations below summarizes the conclusions drawn from Guelph Report II on part-time farming research:

1) Part-time farming depends upon a conscious **decision** and under the present definitional concepts of farming almost anyone can be a part-time farmer. As such, part-time farming can be found in almost all rural systems.

2) Because to enter part-time farming a definite decision is required, the most valuable method of classifying the many part-time farming situations is by **motive.**

3) To understand the nature of decision-making it is necessary to distinguish between the **part-time farm** as a resource unit and the **part-time farmer** whose actions in operating his holding are not necessarily governed by the actual or potential labour opportunity of that unit.

4) The majority of decisions to farm part-time tend to be determined either by **marginal opportunity** (work and/or income) or **opportunity maximization.**

5) Part-time farming is a **dynamic** process in that it functions as a transitional status, at least at the outset, between the more traditional roles in the rural system.

6) Part-time farmers are at the **interface** between the farm and the non-farm sector and as such provide an excellent opportunity for studying the relationship between the two sectors.

THE PROBLEMS CONCEPTUALISED — SUMMARY

Part-time farming is a multifaceted form of labour organization. However, whether the features which characterize this phenomenon are seen as problems or as resources depends primarily upon location, that is, upon the nature of the specific rural system in which part-time farming is found. To generalize, there are three spatial contexts in which part-time farming, seen as an adjustment process of physical and human resources, can be hypothetically viewed:

1) the **marginal** rural area with poor physical resources for agriculture, low market opportunity, aging population;

2) the **ongoing** agricultural area in which conditions for a viable agriculture are generally favourable;

3) areas in the **urban shadow** which may exhibit either or both of the above characteristics.

Physical Resources Adjustment — The land question illustrates the dichotomy between part-time farming as a problem or as a resource. In the marginal area land which otherwise might have been abandoned may be retained in agriculture and, on occasion, part-time farming can act as a stimulus to a faltering local economy. In the context of withdrawal of land from agriculture, part-time farming may function as a selective process.

In a good agricultural area land resources may be slightly underutilized by part-time farmers and the growth of part-time farming may diversify an economy which might otherwise have been fairly independent. This is especially true when good land resources are adjacent to growing urban centers.

Human Resources Adjustment — In terms of human resources the dilemmas increase. In the marginal area the growing presence of part-time farmers may contribute to the survival of a community, yet the economic cost of providing services for dispersed rural dwellers is a serious problem. In the good agricultural zones part-time farming may function as a reservoir of labour for both agriculture and rural based industries. Stabilization of out-migration is an important goal in rural planning and if human resources adjustment can be satisfied by this means then the general balance of advantages and disadvantages must lie on the positive side. It may mean for example that with part-time farming there will be a slight under-utilization of agricultural resources but an overall gain in the general socio-economic well-being of the community.

Finally, there is the process of personal goal satisfaction and the opportunity part-time farming provides for individuals to adjust their roles to what they perceive as more desirable situations. The "trial and error" function of part-time farming is limitless and, as it has now been perceived as a satisfactory permanent way of life, its role is even more important in the rural system. The social and economic benefits of retaining people in marginal areas is a favourable outcome, just as the infusion of capital and ideas into ongoing farming regions may have stimulating effects on the economy. Against this however are the costs of adjustment — very high individual mobility and enormous work commitments on behalf of some aspirants — the sum total of which is a decline in traditional values and an increase in the amount of **stress** placed on individuals. Conflict also may be the result of newcomers infiltrating the power structures and land use traditions of a rural community. If part-time farming is an agent of adjustment, then all the consequences associated with change, both good and bad, will follow. Such is the importance of understanding the **motive** and **locational** context of part-time farming.

NOTES AND REFERENCES

1 Mage, J.A., (a) "A Typology of Part-Time Farming": Guelph Report I.

2 The five types of part-time farming are: small-scale hobby, large-scale hobby, persistent, aspiring, sporadic.

3 The Guelph micro-level surveys on part-time farming in different regions of Ontario (selected from the macro-level overview) were conducted between 1972 and 1974. Together with personal surveys the Rural Research Group have data on part-time farming in the following areas: Dufferin County, Waterloo County, Lambton County, Huron County, Hastings County and Rainy River District. In collecting and processing the data on over 500 part-time farmers in the province, the author wishes to recognize the efforts of L. Archdekin, W. Bamlett, R. Benson, J. Galloway, D. Gibbons, W. Hodgson, and E. Webster: all geography graduates of the University of Guelph.

4 In Ontario there tends to be a separation of part-time farming types by area. The distribution of dominant types and some of their associated characteristics are discussed in the macro-level overview and shown in the atlas of part-time farming in Ontario. Mage, J.A., (b) Part-Time Farming in Ontario: A Macro-Level Overview, Guelph, 1975; Mage, J.A. and Fuller, A.M., An Atlas of Part-Time Farming for Ontario, 1971, Guelph, 1975.

5 Bunce, M., "The Contribution of the Part-Time Farmer to the Rural Economy", Scarborough College, University of Toronto; paper *in absentia*, First Guelph Symposium on Rural Geography, June 1975.

6 Time, recorded as the number of days spent in off-farm work (10 categories), has been the chief measure for data cross-tabulations in the Canadian Census of Agriculture since 1951.

7 The measurement of the "one man work year" varies from country to country; for example, in the United Kingdom it is 271 days. In Canada it is assumed to be approximately 250 days, calculated by deducting all weekends and eleven days of holiday.

8 When a measure was taken of land quality for all part-time farms (including land rented), on the basis of adjusted acres, an average of fifty-three acres per farm was calculated, with only fourteen of 114 samples having over 100 adjusted acres. In 1965, 130 adjusted acres were considered the **minimum** necessary to operate a viable farm in Eastern Ontario. Noble, H., "An Economic Classification of Farms in Eastern Ontario," Report, Farm Economics, Cooperatives and Statistics Branch, O.D.A.F., Toronto, 1965.

9 Mage, J.A., and Fuller, A.M., op. cit.

10 See p. 10.

11 Custom work is that labour provided by a farmer and his machine for which a formal payment is made by the recipient farmer. Much of the off-farm work described as "agricultural" in the Agricultural Heartland of Ontario is custom work. (Mage, J.A., (b), op. cit.)

12 A scheme for outlining necessity and choice orientated decisions has been suggested by Fuller (Part-Time Farming: A Scheme for Geographers," Proceedings, C.A.G. Annual Meeting, Manitoba, 1970, pp. 121-126) and tested in his work with Italian farmers ("Towards a Typology of Part-Time Farming: A Conceptual Framework and the Case of the Val Nure, Italy," Proceedings I.G.U. Commission on Agricultural Typology, Verona, 1974).

13 See particularly, Fuguitt, G.V., "Part-Time Farming and the Push-Pull Hypothesis," **American Journal of Sociology,** vol. LXIV, no. 4, 1959, pp. 375-379.

14 In the Guelph regional surveys it was possible to cross-check the general validity of this conclusion by matching the family income structure with the operator's self-perceived image of his financial situation.

15 The use of discriminant analysis was in its simplest form, that is to assess the relative contribution of several factors to intergroup variability. For a more complete statement on the method and the subject matter see, "A Preliminary Report on Part-Time Farming in Hastings County," Rural Research Group, Department of Geography, Guelph, 1975.

16 When inter-correlated the seven factors produced a strong association (.0500 level of significance) between efficient dairy operation, high farm work requirement and low off-farm job commitment.

17 This was demonstrated in Hastings County by the fact that 77 per cent of the eighty-three samples in the Persistent group had dairy operations in 1967, a figure which was reduced to 36 per cent by 1973.

18 Galloway, J., "The 'Persistent' Part-Time Farmer," paper submitted for the C.A.G. Regional Conference, Ottawa, 1975.

CRITIQUE: "A TYPOLOGY OF PART-TIME FARMING"
(J.A. Mage) and
"THE PROBLEMS OF PART-TIME FARMING CONCEPTUALISED (A.M. Fuller)

Glenn V. Fuguitt

I would like to say first that I am very pleased to have been asked to participate in this conference on part-time farming. It has been stimulating to return to the literature in this field after a lapse of more than ten years. In North America, at least, interest in this subject has seemed to follow a twenty year cycle, the first major group of studies coming in the mid 1930s, and the second in the 1950s. Today I think it is fair to say there is little evidence of activity in the field in the U.S. and Canada with the notable exception of the group at Guelph. Their work represents, however, the most ambitious single project yet undertaken on part-time farming on this continent. I hope that soon their efforts will inspire others, and perhaps this conference will serve as a catalyst for a third cycle of widespread interest and activity.

The two papers we have just heard reveal the broad scope of activities going on here: careful conceptual development, empirical work to generate and to test typologies at both the macro and micro level, and attention to policy implications.

I want to begin by making some observations about the definition of a part-time farmer as discussed in both papers, then review the empirical work of Mage, react to the work of both on part-time typologies, and say a few words about policy.

The review of part-time farming definitions by Mage is interesting and useful. I was glad to learn that Canada, after employing a definition like that of the U.S. Census for some years, adopted a simpler off-farm work definition in 1971. I hope that the U.S. Census will soon follow their lead. Data are available in the U.S. Census of Agriculture on number of days worked off the farm for all farm operators, but the basic definition, as was reported by Mage, is limited to farmers with value of farm products sold under $2,500. This definition has led to unnecessary confusion and restricted many tabulations to only a portion of those working off their farms. In the United States in 1969, census part-time farms were about one-half of all farms with operators working off-farm 100 days or more, and less than 40 per cent of operators working any days off the farm.

In this connection, I found the distinction made by Fuller between part-time farms and part-time farmers helpful for my thinking. If one considers farms with low gross income to be, by and large, part-time farms in the Fuller sense, then the U.S. Census definition is an attempt to identify the intersection of the set of part-time farms and the set of part-time farmers. I think most of us would agree that this definition is too restrictive, and preference would be, as in the empirical work of Mage and Fuller, for a more inclusive part-time farmer definition.

Yet when interest focuses on policy issues relating to poverty and low farm income, it may be more reasonable to study instead the set of part-time farms, distinguishing between those operators or families that supplement their income through off-farm work, or through pension cheques or welfare payments.

The definition of part-time farming involves the nature of the commitment to farm and non-farm work, and this leads to concern about the decision to change status at any given time. Fuller suggests making a distinction between **necessity** and **choice** in deciding whether to combine farming and non-farm work, with choice describing behavior based on more than subsistence income considerations. Yet we know that subsistence level is a subjective matter. One person may feel forced to supplement his income, whereas another in the same circumstance may be willing to subsist. Nevertheless, this distinction, though very difficult to make, is important in the policy area. For example, if people are leaving rural areas and moving into cities by choice, because they would rather live there, that is one thing. If they are moving because of the necessity to find jobs but really prefer living in rural areas, that could be an argument for programs to make more jobs available in rural areas. In this connection, some full-time farmers may believe it necessary to supplement their income, and be faced with the choice of getting out of farming and perhaps moving to the city, or becoming a part-time farmer. Similarly, a suburbanite moving to the country may have a choice of suburban tract living, or purchasing a small farm to engage in part-time farming. We need to understand more about these types of decisions, and the characteristics of people who tend to go one way or the other.

Both Mage and Fuller allude to the family definition of part-time farming — that is, a part-time farm is one in which some family member works off the farm — but they do not pursue this avenue. Neither did I in my earlier work, but I think someone should. After all, a family farm is an economic unit, and traditionally a work unit in agriculture. Thus there is a family division of labour, and at least according to the popular press, wives have been expanding both their managerial and their labour input into farm operations.[1] The decision of a farm operator to work off the farm may depend on the willingness of the wife or children to take up much of the on-farm responsibility. Similarly, income from the wife's off-farm work might enable the husband to continue farming full-time. Research using family units would be much more complicated, particularly because of differences in family structure, and so cannot supplant concern with individual family members. Yet I fear we are inconsistent if we point to the importance of the farm family as a social and economic unit in rural society, and do research only on the farm operator.

Now I would like to turn to the empirical work of Mage. Generally, I am not too enthusiastic about the use of factor analytic techniques for empirical induction with a large number of variables. In Mage's macro-analysis, however, the results of the factor analysis followed by multiple correlation of the factors were interesting to me. I did not expect farm size and economic scale of farming to come out as separate factors, but this is consistent with the fact that part-time farming is not just associated with low farm income, but also with intensive agriculture.

58

The inductive approach makes for difficulties in conceptualization, however. At least I have trouble with the most important factor — the combination of age of operator and scale of sales. Evidently counties with low farm income have a higher proportion of older operators, but what does this combination factor mean? As a next step I would like to see a multiple regression using carefully constructed measures of age, size, scale, and type of enterprise, and allowing for interaction terms.

The hierarchical grouping technique in the macro-analysis identifies nonoverlapping groups of counties which dominate in characteristics already found to be associated with part-time farming. These groups include only twenty-two of the forty-one Ontario counties studied, but nineteen of those counties having more than one-third of their farmers part-time in 1966.

At the micro level, the hierarchical grouping technique results in groups that correspond to a reasonable typology based on career considerations. My concern here, however, is with the sample size. The number of cases represented by the six groups in Table 7 are 15, 12, 10, 6, 3 and 1 respectively, or 47 in all. Certainly more respondents are needed before one can make firm generalizations about types of part-time farmers in this Ontario setting.

I am intrigued by the proportion of part-time farmers (one fourth) who aspire to become full-time in Mage's study. I found a similar situation in my Wisconsin study of 1957, where about four out of ten part-time farmers, in both the former farmer and the former non-farmer groups, said they wanted to stop non-farm work and continue farming in the future. Only 5 per cent said they wanted to stop farm work. One of my students, Randall Jobnson,[2] used state income tax data to follow up on these respondents seven years later. He found that about 20 per cent had succeeded in shifting to full-time farm work, but 16 per cent had stopped farming. Yet Metzler's typology, cited by Mage, does not include the group going from part-time to full-time farming. Fuller chooses to concentrate his attention on the more "permanent" part-time farmer, but this emphasis is supported by a recent study in Illinois which found most all part-time farmers to be in the "permanent" group.[3]

One of Metzler's three groups was a transitional phase from full-time farming to non-farm employment. Mage did not identify such a group, and my data suggest this is not important as an intended route out of farming. A study of Iowa farm operators who quit farming, however, found a good proportion of these had had part-time farming experience.[4] We need to give more attention to these transition types in which part-time farming is a route into or out of agriculture, and try to explain why their importance may vary from area to area.

This brings us to the larger issue of typology construction. Mage gives us a career typology (Figure 9) and though its generalizability is limited due to the small number of cases, I think this is a worthwhile contribution. Among other things it graphs the tendency for types to be similar in amount of off-farm work commitment, locale of the non-farm job, and reasons for the part-time situation. Fuller in his paper considers the career, and shifts in status into and out of part-time farming, by developing the concept of adjustment time.

I believe that the logical extension of this is to a career-work history orientation, including potentially all those who are or have been involved in farming and allowing for multiple job commitments. In considering mobility into and out of different types of occupational arrangements, we need to take into account the fact that shifts may have different meanings and interpretations not only in terms of those statuses which have come before, but also in terms of the time in which they were made and in terms of the respondent's age and life cycle stage.

In demography there has been considerable methodological and substantive development in the study of fertility in the last thirty years by means of considering "cohorts" groups of women classed according to their age and followed over time.[5] The approach has been applied to migration through obtaining retrospective life history data, and a few years ago a study by Karl Taueber[6] appeared which traced the migration over time of farm-born cohorts classified by year of birth. The analysis of such data can be complex, and the costs of obtaining the number of cases required might be prohibitive. Nevertheless, I think that adopting the research orientations of such studies, even in the analysis of simpler data, would pay important dividends.

Making projections of part-time farming into the future, for example, would require some knowledge of the extent and type of movement out of agriculture, which can be obtained only through interviewing a cross-section of non-farmers (some of whom used to farm), or following a number of farmers, both part-time and full-time, over a time interval. Also, shifts into and out of part-time farming, and into and out of non-farm work will have different meanings and different probabilities at various stages of the life cycle, so projections should be made taking specific ages into account.

Another illustration of the advantages of this orientation is provided by the comparison of three groups made by Fuller. You will recall that Group A are former full-time farmers, part-time less than six years; C are former non-farmers, part-time less than six years; and B are part-time farmers more than six years. From a career perspective B includes the survivors of earlier Groups A and C, but undifferentiated as to farm or non-farm origin. Members of Group B should differ from A and C in tending to have longer work histories, and this might effect differences obtained. I would argue that B should more appropriately be compared with two groups probably not available in the study as designed — those part-time farmers six or more years ago who later became full-time, and those who subsequently left farming. A further breakdown by origin (farm, non-farm) and some control for number of working years or life cycle position also would be desirable. In making this three group comparison, I would also suggest giving attention to the respondent's desires and satisfaction with present status. One should not assume that a person not changing is satisfied, or that a person changing is doing so out of necessity.

Finally, I would like to make a few observations about part-time farming and two main areas of concern for rural development in the United States. The first is concern about structural changes in agriculture. Major changes have, of course, included the combination of increased total production with the decline in the number of farms and people directly employed in agriculture. The decline in

60

the population base has often been cited as the root of the rural development "problem" in the United States, but few have challenged the desirability of the technological changes leading to more farm production. If it can be assumed, however, that part-time farming does not have a significant negative effect on total production, then the promotion of this activity would seem to be a worthwhile way to try to achieve the rural development goal of stabilizing or increasing rural population. The research of Fuller and Mage, and hopefully the results of future more extensive typological comparisons, should be useful in designing programs to support viable part-time farming as an alternative to leaving the area, or possibly even as an encouragement for persons to move in. I am curious as to why I found almost no reference to this possibility in United States rural development literature. There is concern about, and some programs for, low income farmers, and perhaps a problem is the confusion of these two groups.

The second area of concern in rural development I want to consider is the continuing attractiveness of rural areas and farming activities as part of a life style deemed preferable to urban living. There is, of course, an element of nostalgic romanticism in this, but nevertheless, rural development programs have been justified in part because it is believed that people want to live in rural areas. Indeed, in the United States there has been a continuing flow of people from urban to rural areas, and this along with increased retention of ruralities has led to a situation in the United States where for the first time non-metropolitan areas are growing faster than metropolitan areas and the specific sub-areas of growth are not all located adjacent to metropolitan centres. This non-metropolitan growth has been associated with industrial development, retirement, and recreation, and undoubtedly part-time and even full-time farming is part of the picture. I understand that in Wisconsin, county agents and state extension people often get letters from city people asking for information about going into full or part-time farming. Should such activity be encouraged under certain conditions? It could lead to more rural citizens, but what would be the consequences? Should specialized extension assistance be provided for part-time farmers, in addition to that for all farmers, or for low income farmers? These are issues that should be faced in some parts of the United States, and I suspect in Canada as well. Hopefully the work of Fuller and Mage, important in its own right, will serve as a catalyst to generate increased attention to problems of the part-time farmer.

NOTES AND REFERENCES

1. Lublin, Joann S., "The Rural Wife: While Keeping House, Donna Keppy Ranks as a Partner on Farm." **Wall Street Journal** 55 (June 2 1975): 1, 10.

2. Johnson, Randell A., A Study of Mobility and Career Patterns of Part-time and Full-time Farmers. Unpublished Master's thesis, University of Wisconsin — Madison, 1967.

3. Spitze, R.G.F., Economic Analysis of Off-farm Earnings as a Factor in Improvement of Low Income Farmers. U.S.D.A. Cooperative States Research Work Unit/Project Abstract, Current Research Information System, CRIS No. 424850, 1974.

4. Kaldor, Donald R. and William M. Edwards, Occupational Adjustment of Iowa Farm Operators Who Quit Farming 1959-61. Iowa State University Agriculture and Home Economics Experiment Station, Special Report No. 75, March, 1975.

5. Ryder, Norman B., "Cohort Analysis." Pp. 546-550, Vol. 2, in David L. Sills (ed). **International Encyclopedia of the Social Sciences.** New York: The Macmillan Company and the Free Press, 1968.

6. Taeuber, Karl E., "The Residential Redistribution of Farm-born Cohorts." **Rural Sociology** 32 (March 1967): 20-36.

QUESTION PERIOD

H. Crown (Ontario Ministry of Agriculture and Food)

Professor Mage made reference to a classification of about 32% of what he calls hobby farmers. For the purpose of this discussion the hobby farm group, a very large group, should really be discounted from the point of view of agricultural policy. They have no effect one way or the other, either on production or on problems in a rural area. The main concern I think, from a government point of view, is related to land use problems and whether or not these people occupy good agricultural land which can cause problems in the demand for such land. From the point of view of whether we consider them as part-time farmers, I think that most people look upon them as having nothing to do with part-time farming. Only from a census point of view are they classified as farmers. It would simplify things just a little if that group called hobby farmers really have no part in farming agricultural policy. Their interest in agriculture from a commercial point of view is very minimal — their effect on agriculture is even less.

One brief comment on A. Fuller's paper. I was surprised that he considered that the group in the middle (Group B — persistent part-time farmers) was dynamic or transitional. I was of the opinion that there must be a large group there that are part-time farmers as a way of life and not moving one way or the other and, as Professor Fuguitt said, this was a group that may be quite stable.

J. Mage (Geography, Guelph)

Since you addressed yourself to the typology phase in the first part of your question, I will answer that. You asked why we include so-called hobby farmers in any discussion here. The major session — the initial session — was to identify who the part-time farmers are, and if we had some well constructed preconceived notion of part-time farming, and part-time farmers, then there would not be any need to have a session identifying these people because we would already know who they are. The purpose was to present the fact that part-time farming is not a homogenous phenomenon. There is a wide spectrum of situations ranging from the rural resident who dabbles in farming to the farmer who is very close to full-time farming. Perhaps for policy-making purposes involving agriculture directly, where one is looking at production economics, these people do not produce the equivalent of what they embrace in terms of land use and so on, and they should of course be left out. I think I have called them pseudo-farmers. However, based on criteria of income alone, one-third of full-time farmers in Ontario, as I will discuss tomorrow, should also be excluded from policy making. I am sure that you would not advocate that.

There are difficulties in an initial session of identifying precisely who our subjects are and we may decide that the hobby group is not a part of the agricultural policy-making thrust. It is, however, a very important component of the rural area. There will be two papers this evening to follow up this topic and to illustrate that we have programs to encourage people to enter agriculture perhaps through the hobby farming route. There is always the possibility that the hobbyist may in fact become a full-time farmer sometime in the future. That problem, however, can be easily reduced or removed if you simply re-define a census farm, and I think that is beyond us here. We have to, for data collecting purposes, define a farm and that happens to be 1 acre and $50 of sales per year. Not all the hobbyists, incidentally, work in the 1 acre, $50 category.

A. Lerner (Agricultural Economics, Guelph)

I would like to make just one minor comment on this question of hobby farmers. There are people who could be described as hobby farmers because their major occupation is elsewhere or their major income is from elsewhere. We should remember, however, that some of the greatest advances in agriculture throughout European and North American economic history have been made by hobby farmers who did not depend upon the farm for their living.

A. Fuller (Geography, Guelph)

A quick response to Mr. Crown's second point. If we have a group of people who were formerly full-time (Group A), and a group who have come into part-time farming from outside (Group C) then the dynamism of Group B is **before** they become members of Group B. They are aspiring to be full-time farmers, they are building up their operation, they are changing their ambitions, and so on. But once they arrive in Group B after six years (we feel that if they have not made it after six years they are Group B) then they become, as you say, a very stable, easily defined group. So the dynamism that I talked about, or the change which I talked about, is while they are members of Group A or C. But once they arrive at B the majority of them do tend to be relatively stable. So it is in the intervening six years that they are changing their ideas and changing their operation.

G.E. Jones (Rural Development, Reading)

I think we are at the usual problem of definition where you can make it whatever you wish it to mean at any time. I would just like to make two very brief comments which I think are pertinent to the papers we heard this morning and perhaps to ask one quite specific question. The first thing is although quite naturally one is thinking predominantly of Canada, of Ontario, and of the North American scene, this is an international symposium, and I think we have to remember that in different cultures the whole concept of part-time farming becomes something again very different. I think A. Fuller would be very conscious of the difference of the part-time farmer in Italy, compared to Britain, compared to here. The culture in a sense has to be a basic part of the initial definition. Secondly, I would like to suggest, particularly to J. Mage, that it might be very useful to extend further some sociological implications of the types that he is finding. At the moment they are largely in descriptive-cum-economic terms with some implications as to the status postitions, but I think there are some very interesting and important sociological implications within these types and similarly within the three types identified by A. Fuller.

The one very specific question: I think all the time it has been suggested that the part-time element is concerned with off-farm work. Should it not also concern on-the-farm work which is of a non-agricultural kind. Somebody could be a part-time farmer in this sense. We have already heard the case of a person who might have a job in his home which is on the farm, as a salesman, or something of this kind. I am thinking of Europe, particularly where much part-time farming income is being derived from non-agricultural enterprises on farms: from things like farmhouse tourism, craftwork, and pony trekking for example. Would that sort of enterprise also be included in one's definition?

J. Mage (Geography, Guelph)

We do in fact consider work done on the farm by the operators as part of the off-farm work. I think in reading the papers this morning we both neglected to state this, but, we recognise that saw milling operations on the operator's farm, for example, would be counted as "off-farm work".

G. Fuguitt (Rural Sociology, Wisconsin)

I might say you can also add the converse. For example, the problem of the situation where the farmer does custom work off the farm, so his off-farm work is farming.

I. Vogeler (Geography, Northwestern)

One of the things that struck me about the last paper and also your comments that there seem to be two approaches that are articulated. The one approach relates to the individual and the kind of response people make to their total environment. Your comment is that rural sociologists were studying that kind of thing. Then there is the other perspective that culture somehow is the causal mechanism which explains why part-time farms are where they are, and how many there are. It seems to me a third approach, which is a surrogate, may in fact be more fundamental that is, one which takes a much more structural approach to understanding the kinds of pricing mechanisms we use to pay farmers for their products, so that the farmer who is working a third of the year on his farm may be a full-time farmer if the price of commodities would be 2 or 3 times as high as they are now. It really appears that the individual is responding to a whole series of institutional mechanisms. To study the decision-making is to study the effect rather than the cause. We may not be really understanding the nature of part-time farming by using the two earlier approaches — culture, or individual decision-making — but rather we should use a structural approach.

P. Hackman (Agricultural Economics, Helsinki)

I think that A. Fuller has, to my view, started off by taking up the motives of part-time farmers as a starting point. I am not sure why he has not tackled the problem of the life cycle of the farmer and the farmer's spouse. What you see when studying the life cycle of the farm family is that, at about 25 years of age, the farmer and his spouse have rather small economic needs. These economic needs will increase heavily over time and will peak when the farmer is about 40 years of age. At the same time, the working capacity of these people is increasing and partially because of the variation of jobs they do not need time for leisure in the way other workers do.

A. Fuller (Geography, Guelph)

I am very glad you brought up the question of the family cycle and its effect on the decision to farm part-time. In my work on Italian agriculture I concluded that many decisions to seek off-farm work were directly related to household position in the family cycle (see, Fuller, A.M. "Towards a Typology of Part-Time Farming: A Conceptual Framework and the Case of the Val Nure, Italy"). However, to date in Ontario, I have found very little evidence that the same is true, although I will pursue the subject in our further research.

PROBLEMS ASSOCIATED WITH PART-TIME FARMING
—ECONOMIC MARGINALITY

CHAIRMAN: R.R. KRUEGER (Geography, Waterloo, Canada)

PAPER: G. STOCK (Rural Development Counsellor, Alberta, Canada)
                   "Off-Farm Work by Small Scale Farmers in Ontario"

PAPER: P. McLEAY (Geography, Wolverhampton, England)
                   "Part-Time Farming Among Statutory Smallholdings
                   in South Staffordshire, England"*

DISCUSSANT: A. LERNER (Agricultural Economics, Guelph)

*Paper read by G.E. Jones (Reading, England) in the absence of
P. McLeay.

OFF-FARM WORK BY SMALL SCALE FARMERS IN ONTARIO

George E. Stock

The relationship between small scale (non-commercial) farming and part-time farming has until recent years been overshadowed by a myth that all small scale farmers are part-time and conversely all part-time farmers are small scale. For instance, Higbee described small scale farmers as factory workers who are part-time farmers or farmers who are part-time factory workers, ". . . and just plain unemployed most of the time."[1] Similarly, Shepherd stated that non-commercial farms were "only country residences for city people with urban jobs or other sources of income."[2] Unfortunately, this myth was even evident in the Canadian Census definition of "part-time farm" in 1951, 1956 and 1961, wherein a maximum farm sales criterion of $200 was applied. Thus, the commercial farm operator was by definition excluded from enumeration as a part-time farmer.

Although the assumption that commercial farmers do not work off the farm has more recently been refuted,[3] small scale farming and off-farm work are very closely related. The following paper attempts to describe this relationship and to examine the characteristics of off-farm work as it applies to small scale farm operators.

DATA

Economic class of farms, based on the gross value of agricultural sales, is taken to be the most appropriate available indicator of the scale of farms. Statistics Canada has made available from the 1971 Census of Agriculture a wide variety of published and unpublished data cross-tabulated by economic class of farm.[4] Included are social, economic and production variables. With regard to part-time farming no definition of "part-time farm" was applied to the data. Rather the census division-level data cross-tabulated by economic class include the distribution of farms by days of work off the farm. Also applicable are cross-tabulations by total days and total numbers of operators reporting days of off-farm work for each of sixteen off-farm work types.

Further insight regarding the socio-economic characteristics of operators reporting off-farm work is facilitated through analysis of recently published province-level data retrieved through linkage of the agricultural and population censuses.[5] These include such variables as age, schooling and income cross-tabulated by economic class of farm and by off-farm work indicators. Unfortunately, these data were compiled from samples and many totals, distributions and definitions do not agree with those from the agricultural census. One such discrepancy is the total of 17,285 operators in Ontario who reported zero days of off-farm work but had off-farm employment income.[6] Another problem of these data relates to their credibility. For example, 115 operators reported farm sales of less than $2,500, a total income exceeding $10,000 and per cent of income from farming

68

of at least 75 per cent.[7] Either this is an instance of improper reporting and editing or of inadequate data description. Because of such problems, these data were not relied upon to any great extent. The following data unless otherwise noted are from the Census of Agriculture and were made available by the University of Guelph Department of Geography.[8]

SMALL SCALE FARMS AND FARMERS

There is little concensus regarding the definition of small scale. Small scale farms occupy the lower end of the value of sales continuum and are here operationally defined as census farms where the reported value of agricultural sales is less than $5,000. Much of the literature tends to treat small scale farms as an undifferentiated group of poverty holdings on which meagre agricultural incomes are supplemented by off-farm work. This "poverty" or "marginal farm" approach has merit in that a sales total of $5,000 per year is seldom sufficient to provide an acceptable family income, to usefully employ a man's labour or to yield adequate rates of return to the resources which must be employed to produce at such a level.

In a very general sense, a small scale farming situation can be thought of as a situation where the quantity, quality or balance of inputs (land, labour, capital and management) is limited in such a way as to reduce the productive capacity of the farm. In this regard small scale farms tend to be smaller in acreage and less capitalized than their commercial counterparts.[9] Furthermore, they are relatively more numerous in marginal areas characterized by poor soil and remoteness. Land use and capital composition characteristics of small scale farms indicate lack of a production orientation. In relation to other inputs, labour supplied by the small scale farmer and his family is fixed and under-employed.

Given the limited potential for producing an adequate farm income from the small scale farm and the relative oversupply of labour available to such farms, the adjustment of human resources to non-farm employment seems obvious. However, certain characteristics of the small scale farmer limit such possibilities. Small scale farmers tend to be relatively more numerous in the youngest and oldest age categories and in the level of schooling category representing those with less than fifth grade education; factors which limit their demand in the non-farm labour market. Strong ties to the home community, traditional values and low aspiration level are other limiting characteristics attributed to some small scale farmers.

OFF-FARM WORK BY SMALL SCALE FARMERS

Small scale farms in Ontario accounted for almost 45 per cent of all farms in the 1971 census. However, over 70 per cent of the total off-farm work days reported in the province were accounted for by small scale farm operators. Such a comparison indicates the very significant contribution that small scale farmers make to provincial off-farm work totals. Over one-half of all small scale farmers report off-farm work days as compared to less than one-third of commercial operators. A further 18 per cent of small scale operators apparently report off-farm employment income but report no off-farm days.[10]

The provincial distribution of small scale operators by days reported is indicated in Table 1. Only 15 per cent report between one day and 156 days of off-farm work. Over 31 per cent report greater than 228 days of work off the farm (full-time off-farm work).

The distribution of days and farmers reporting for sixteen different types of off-farm work is shown in Table 2. "Processing occupations" (factory jobs) account for the most off-farm work days (29 per cent). The second highest is "construction trades" and third is "truck or bus driver" with 13 and 10 per cent respectively. With less than 1 per cent of the total days each are "food and beverage preparation", "lodging and personal services", "fishing, hunting and trapping" and "transport and related equipment operation".

Table 1

**Small Scale Farm Operators
by Days of Off-Farm Work,
Ontario, 1970**

Days of Off-Farm Work	% Small Scale Farmers
0	43.2[1]
1-12	1.5
13-48	3.4
49-96	4.0
97-156	5.8
157-228	10.9
229+	31.2
	100.0

Source: Unpublished Data, 1971 Census of Canada, Agriculture, Ontario.

1 Among those reporting zero days are a further 18.1 per cent of all small scale farmers who report no off-farm work days but do report income from off-farm work.

Table 2

Participation Rates and Distribution of Off-Farm Work Days and Farmers Reporting Off-Farm Work by Type of Off-Farm Work, Small Scale Farmers, Ontario, 1970.

Type of Off-Farm Work[1]	Days Reported at Job as % of Total Days Reported	Farmers Reporting Job Type as % of Total Reporting Off-Farm Work	Average Participation Rate[2]
Agriculture	5.2	11.8	89.9
Fishing, Hunting and Trapping	0.1	0.2	111.0
Logging, Lumbering and Forestry Work	1.7	3.4	113.1
Operator of Road Maintenance or Construction Equipment	5.8	7.1	167.1
Lodging & Personal Services	0.7	0.8	178.4
Construction Trades	13.4	15.5	179.3
Truck or Bus Driver	9.7	11.0	181.7
Food & Beverage Preparation	0.7	0.7	201.5
Transport & Related Equipment Operation	2.7	2.6	209.1
Other Occupations	4.8	5.1	211.1
Service	5.2	5.0	211.4
Clerical and Related	3.7	3.6	211.6
Technical, Social and Cultural	6.1	5.6	221.0
Sales	5.9	5.5	221.6
Managerial and Administrative	5.0	4.5	222.7
Processing Occupations	29.3	26.7	224.4

Source: Unpublished Data, 1971 Census of Canada, Agriculture, Ontario.

1 Types of off-farm work are listed in order of participation rates.

2 Participation rate is taken to mean number of days reported in the type of off-farm work category per farmer reporting a job in that category.

The average participation rate of small scale farmers in off-farm work is indicated by the average number of days of off-farm work reported per small scale farmer reporting off-farm days. The Ontario average is 205 days. On Table 2, the participation rates are shown for the various types of off-farm work. Relatively full-time jobs of small scale farmers appear to be those in the classifications, "managerial and administrative", "technical, social and cultural", "sales", "clerical and related" and "processing", all of which are secondary or tertiary occupational categories. These account for over 46 per cent of the total days reported and for 42 per cent of the small scale farmers reporting off-farm work days. Jobs in the primary sectors, "agriculture", "logging, lumbering and forestry" and "fishing, hunting and trapping", are apparently seasonal. These account for only about 7 per cent of the total days reported but represent over 15 per cent of small scale operators reporting off-farm work days.

SPATIAL VARIATION IN OFF-FARM WORK CHARACTERISTICS OF SMALL SCALE FARMERS

Time and space do not permit the presentation of the spatial distributions of the many appropriate individual measures relating to the characteristics of off-farm work by small scale farmers. Therefore, principal components analysis was employed to reduce the number of independent factors which were entered into a hierarchical grouping analysis (without a contiguity constraint). The resulting groups represented classes of census divisions which are similar in off-farm work characteristics and are thus suitable as a basis for the discussion of these characteristics as they vary across Ontario.

The final input into the principal components analysis consisted of thirteen variables and over fifty-three observations (census divisions). The thirteen variables are listed on Table 3 and include three variables reflecting the distribution of small scale farm operators by the number of off-farm work days reported (participation) and ten variables which indicate the distribution of off-farm work days by off-farm work type.

The principal components analysis resulted in five factors explaining 80 per cent of the variance in the data. Significant factor loadings from the varimax rotation are presented on Table 3. The five factors were interpreted as follows (the individual per cent variance explained follows each in brackets):

1) Factor I.   Full-Time Farmers (25.1).
2) Factor II. Contrasts in Type and Duration of Off-Farm Work (18.2).
3) Factor III. Urban Professions (16.8).
4) Factor IV. Construction Work (11.4).
5) Factor V.   Service Occupations (8.8).

Table 3

Variables and Factor Loadings: Analysis of Off-Farm Work Characteristics of Small Scale Farmers, Ontario, 1970

Variable Number	Variable	Factors[1] I	II	III	IV	V
	Per Cent Small Scale Farmers by Days of Off-Farm Work Reported:					
1	% reporting 0-12 days	-0.89				
2	% reporting 13-228 days		+0.71			
3	% reporting 229 days and over		-0.80			
	Per Cent of Total Days of Off-Farm Work Reported by Type of Work:					
4	% days agricultural work	-0.75				
5	% days logging, lumbering and forestry work		+0.71			
6	% days truck or bus driver		+0.71			
7	% days operator of road maintenance or construction equipment		+0.71			
8	% days managerial and administrative work			+0.73		
9	% days technical, social and cultural work			+0.83		
10	% days sales work			+0.73		
11	% days service work					+0.98
12	% days processing occupations		-0.65			
13	% days construction trades				-0.94	

1 Factor I: Full-Time Farmers
  Factor II: Contrasts in Type and Duration of Off-Farm Work
  Factor III: Urban Professions
  Factor IV: Construction Work
  Factor V: Service Occupations

All five factors were considered to be significant and were entered into the grouping analysis.

Analysis of the within-group variance plot from the grouping resulted in the selection of a cut-off at the six-group level. The groups are mapped in Figure 1. Few of these groups form contiguous regions. Rather the groupings represent types of areas based on off-farm work characteristics. Interpretation of each of the six groups is facilitated through analysis of the factors for which there are many relatively distinctive scores. Such significant factors are listed on Table 4. The six groups were interpreted as follows:

1) Group A. Areas of Full-Time Off-Farm Workers
(12 divisions)

2) Group B. Areas of Full-Time Farmers
(23 divisions)

3) Group C. Areas where Off-Farm Work in Services is Distinctive
(7 divisions)

4) Group D. Areas of Part-Time Off-Farm Work and Rural Occupations and Construction Work
(5 divisions)

5) Group E. Areas of Part-Time Off-Farm Work
(3 divisions)

6) Group F. Areas of Urban Professions
(3 divisions)

Following is an analysis of the characteristics of each of the six groups. Because of the reliance of the classification technique on relative similarities and differences, the classification is supplemented in Table 5 by various "hard" statistics relating to the off-farm work characteristics of the six groups.

Group A: Areas of Full-Time Off-Farm Workers

A dozen census divisions dispersed in small groups in the Niagara area, the Southwest, the Northeast and in Central Ontario are characterized by relatively large percentages of small scale farmers participating full-time in off-farm work (i.e. greater than 228 days per year). The divisions of Group A vary from specialized crop and horticultural areas in Niagara and the Southwest to dispersed pockets of marginal agriculture in the Northeast.

Processing occupations account for over two-fifths of the small scale off-farm work days in Group A. This is consistent with the association between full-time off-farm work participation and processing occupations in Factor II (see Table 3). This very high commitment to processing occupations helps to explain the distribution of Group A members, all of which are near medium to large cities such as Windsor, Hamilton, St. Catharines, Sudbury and Sault Ste. Marie where medium to heavy industrial activities are important.

74

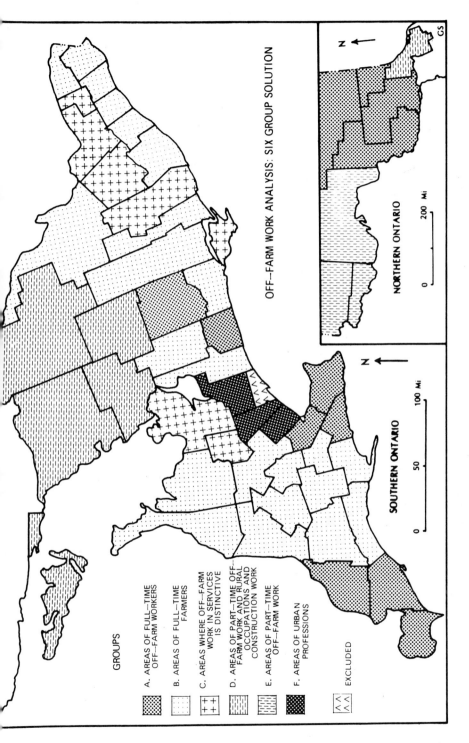

OFF–FARM WORK ANALYSIS: SIX GROUP SOLUTION

GROUPS

A. AREAS OF FULL–TIME
   OFF–FARM WORKERS

B. AREAS OF FULL–TIME
   FARMERS

C. AREAS WHERE OFF–FARM
   WORK IN SERVICES
   IS DISTINCTIVE

D. AREAS OF PART–TIME OFF–
   FARM WORK AND RURAL
   OCCUPATIONS AND
   CONSTRUCTION WORK

E. AREAS OF PART–TIME
   OFF–FARM WORK

F. AREAS OF URBAN
   PROFESSIONS

EXCLUDED

NORTHERN ONTARIO

0   200 Mi

SOUTHERN ONTARIO

0   50   100 Mi

Figure 1

75

Table 4

Analysis of Common Group Characteristics:
A Listing of Factors with Significant Scores on Most Members of a Group

Group	Factor	Sign	Interpretation
A Areas of Full-Time Off-Farm Workers	II	-	Full-Time Off-Farm Work
	III	-	Urban Professions Absent
	I	+	Full-Time Farmers Absent
B Areas of Full-Time Farmers	I	-	Full-Time Farmers
C Areas where Off-Farm Work in Services is Distinctive	V	+	Service Occupations
D Areas of Part-Time Off-Farm Work and Rural Occupations and Construction Work	II	+	Part-Time Off-Farm Work and Rural Occupations. Construction Work-
	IV	-	
E Areas of Part-Time Off-Farm Work	I	+	Full-Time Farmers Absent
	II	+	Part-Time Off-Farm Work and Rural Occupations
	IV	+	Construction Work Absent
F Areas of Urban Professoions	III	+	Urban Professions

Table 5

Indicators of Off-Farm Work Characteristics
of Small Scale Farmers, Ontario, 1970

Type of Area[1]

Indicator	A	B	C	D	E	F	Ontario Total
% Farms Small Scale	47.3	39.9	52.1	72.0	63.9	50.8	44.6
% Small Scale Farmers Reporting Off-Farm Work Days	60.7	54.2	57.7	59.7	69.5	56.5	56.8
Average Participation Rate[2]	201.7	199.0	207.3	162.3	190.3	224.1	204.6
Multiple Job Ratio[3]	1.08	1.08	1.15	1.17	1.26	1.05	1.09
Selected Off-Farm Work Categories: % total days reported							
Agriculture	4.6	5.8	4.2	3.8	2.5	4.9	5.2
Rural Occupations[4]	14.9	18.8	16.8	28.2	35.9	10.8	17.2
Urban Professions[5]	14.3	17.4	18.7	9.9	13.8	33.3	17.0
Processing	41.8	27.4	20.2	17.8	23.0	21.2	29.3
Construction Trades	13.6	13.4	14.7	19.9	8.7	9.7	13.4
Services	5.2	4.7	7.4	5.5	5.5	4.0	5.2

Source: Unpublished data, 1971 Census of Canada, Agriculture, Ontario.

Table 5 (cont'd)

1 A   Areas of Full-Time Off-Farm Workers
  B   Areas of Full-Time Farmers
  C   Areas where Off-Farm Work in Services is Distinctive
  D   Areas of Part-Time Off-Farm Work and Rural Occupations and Construction Work
  E   Areas of Part-Time Off-Farm Work
  F   Areas of Urban Professions

2 The "average participation rate" is the average number of days of off-farm farm work reported per farmer reporting off-farm work days.

3 The "multiple job ratio" is the average number of reportings of off-farm work types per farmer reporting off-farm work days.

4 "Rural Occupations" includes "logging, lumbering, and forestry work", "truck or bus driver" and "operator of road maintenance or construction equipment".

5 "Urban Professions" includes "managerial and administrative", "technical, social and cultural" and "sales".

Group B: Areas of Full-Time Farmers

Group B consists of twenty-three divisions dispersed across Southern Ontario. With exception of a few counties in Central Ontario, the Group B divisions comprise some of the best agricultural divisions in the province. With fertile soils and proximity to markets, over 60 per cent of the Group B farms are commercial. Group B accounts for almost half of Ontario's small scale farms. Thus, small scale farms in these divisions play a proportionally small role but are most numerous in absolute numbers. Farmers reporting little or no off-farm work are relatively distinctive in Group B. Surprisingly, the average participation rate differs little from that of Group A where full-time participation in off-farm work is distinctive (see Table 5). Although agricultural work accounts for less than 6 per cent of the off-farm work days in the group, it is the only off-farm work type distinctive to the group. Due partially to the large numbers of small scale farmers, the characteristics of off-farm work in Group B, as illustrated on Table 5, approximate those of the province as a whole.

Group C: Areas where Off-Farm Work in Services is Distinctive

Factor V (service occupations) scores highly in all seven divisions of Group C. Like Group B, Group C characteristics are relatively similar to the provincial averages (see Table 5). A slightly higher proportion of days in services and a much lower proportion in processing accounts for its differentiation from other groups. As portrayed in Figure 1, divisions which are members of Group C are somewhat dispersed. Cities such as Ottawa, Kingston, Belleville and Barrie appear to influence the distinctiveness of off-farm work in services.

Group D: Areas of Part-Time Off-Farm Work and Rural Occupations and Construction Work

Factor II (part-time off-farm work and rural occupations) and Factor V (construction work) appear to be significant in the divisions of Group D. Agricultural work, urban professions and processing occupations are relatively insignificant (see Table 5). The predominance of rural occupations and construction work with low participation rates (recall Table 2) results in a very low average participation rate for the group (162 days per year). Accordingly, the multiple job ratio, the ratio of the total number of job type reportings to the number of farmers reporting off-farm work, is the second highest among the six groups. This high multiple job ratio reflects a relatively high rate of job change, a consequence of seasonality and lack of job permanence and security.

As indicated in Figure 1, Group D is relatively contiguous, being comprised of four divisions in northern Central Ontario plus the adjacent island district of Manitoulin. The group is characterized by physical marginality for agriculture. Consequently, the percentage of small scale farms is the highest of the six groups. However, the divisions account for only 3 per cent of the provincial total of small scale farms.

Group E: Areas of Part-Time Off-Farm Work

Like Group D, Group E is characterized by marginal agriculture. The three members of Group D are located in a contiguous block in Northwestern Ontario and are affected by poor soils, harsh climate and remoteness to markets. Agricultural work and construction work are distinctively absent from these northern districts. The proportion of off-farm days devoted to rural occupations exceeds one-third of the total off-farm days. This represents the largest proportion in this category among the six groups. Consequently, the average participation rate in the group is low. It is, however, higher than Group D, largely due to more multiple off-farm job-holding. On the average, every fourth farmer reporting off-farm work in this group reports work in more than one type category. Off-farm work is a relatively common form of adjustment among small scale farmers in Group E, almost 70 per cent reporting off-farm work days. The group, however, accounts for less than 2 per cent of Ontario's small scale farms.

Group F: Areas of Urban Professions

In three counties surrounding Metropolitan Toronto, high percentages of days in prosperous and prestigious urban professions reflect a distinctive hobby or residential farm element among small scale farms in the metropolitan area. Rural occupations, processing jobs, construction trades and work in services are proportionally underrepresented in Group F. Having the highest average participation rate (224 days per year) and the lowest multiple job ratio, the small scale farmers of Group F have relatively secure year-round off-farm jobs.

Summary of Grouping Analysis

The spatial distribution of small scale off-farm job types as indicated in the grouping analysis tends to reflect the patterns of job opportunity. Urban professions, processing occupations and service jobs tend to be near cities where these respective types of employment are plentiful. Rural-oriented patterns also reflect the availability or lack of availability of the various categories of work. Where farming can be relatively prosperous, especially in Eastern and Western Ontario, full-time farming and off-farm work in agriculture are relatively important. In the North, small scale farmers tend to work at a variety of resource extraction and rural-oriented tertiary occupations. Here, opportunities are relatively limited; there is a tendency for jobs to be insecure and seasonal. Because of the lack of agricultural opportunity, a high proportion of the farms are small scale and farmers turn to off-farm work to supplement meagre farm incomes. Although the problems appear to be most acute in the marginal areas, they account for few small scale farmers in absolute numbers.

CONCLUSIONS

Various data discrepancies and definitional problems make it difficult to arrive at a precise measurement of the importance of off-farm work to small scale farmers. Most certainly, the majority of small scale farmers participate in off-farm work (perhaps as high as 75 per cent) and the majority of off-farm work in Ontario is accounted for by small scale farmers (probably over 70 per cent). Some 57 per cent of small scale farmers have no farm income or lose money farming as compared to about 30 per cent of commercial operators.[11] Despite this difference, the comparative average total incomes are respectively $5,600 and $6,400. Thus, off-farm work, whether in a permanent or temporary situation, is a major and successful form of supplementation of low farm income and of adjustment out of agriculture of redundant labour resources. To fully evaluate the success of this type of adjustment, more data are necessary relating to the need for employment among small scale farmers and to their employability.

In relation to the agricultural and especially the urban areas of the province, the most significant problems faced by the small scale farmer appear to be in the marginal areas where there are few alternatives. Agricultural potential is limited not only by the marginal physical resource base but also by remoteness to markets and agricultural services. Moreover, the meagre farm resources often have little value for any viable alternative productive use. The possibilities for human resource adjustment through off-farm work are not encouraging. The proportion of small scale farmers reporting off-farm work is large, but the low time participation and the high average number of job types reported indicate lack of secure year-round off-farm employment.

NOTES AND REFERENCES

1 E. Higbee, **Farms and Farmers in an Urban Age,** The Twentieth Century Fund, New York, 1963, p. 12.

2 G.S. Shepherd, **Farm Policy: New Dimensions,** Iowa State University Press, Ames, 1964, p. 82.

3 See for example, J.A. Mage, "Economic Factors Associated with Part-Time Farming in Southern Ontario and Waterloo County," in **Proceedings of G.I.R.M.S.,** Vol. 3, 1972-73, pp. 17-39.

4 Published source: Statistics Canada, **1971 Census of Canada; Agriculture; Selected Data for Census Farms Classified by Economic Class, Ontario,** Catalogue 96-731 (AA-14), Statistics Canada, Ottawa, 1973.
Unpublished source: Microfilm photocopy of "100" series data, Statistics Canada.
Because the published sources always include "institutional farms, etc." in the small scale class, the unpublished sources were normally used. The statistics refer to farm operators' off-farm work characteristics for 1970.

5 Statistics Canada, 1971 Census of Canada; Agriculture; **Farm Operators by Economic Class of Farm Showing Such Characteristics as Sex, Age, Income, Schooling, Off-Farm Employment, Canada and Provinces,** Catalogue 96-734 (AA-17), Statistics Canada, Ottawa, 1975.

6 Statistics Canada, Catalogue 96-734 (AA-17), Table 7.

7 Statistics Canada, Catalogue 96-734 (AA-17), Table 2.

8 Agridata, Rural Research Group, Department of Geography, University of Guelph, Guelph, 1971.

9 The various generalizations in the paper regarding the characteristics of small scale farms are drawn from research recently completed by the author:
George E. Stock, **The Geography of Small Scale Farming in Ontario,** unpublished M.A. thesis, Department of Geography, University of Guelph, 1975.

10 Statistics Canada, Catalogue 96-734 (AA-17), Table 2.

11 Statistics Canada, Catalogue 96-734 (AA-17), Table 2.

PART-TIME FARMING IN BRITAIN —
A STUDY OF STATUTORY SMALLHOLDINGS
IN SOUTH STAFFORDSHIRE

Peter McLeay

It has been suggested that part-time farming is a transitional stage in the process of agricultural adjustment that takes place as a society ceases to be agrarian and becomes increasingly industrialized. It is contended here that in Britain part-time farming and farmers have been an important group within the farming population since the 1840s at least. At this time in Yorkshire, for example, a group of Keighley weavers began to develop the Yorkshire or Large White pig which was to sweep the board at the Royal Show from 1848 to 1850 and achieve a world reputation for its high quality. In 1928, a representative pre-depression year, 30% of the agricultural holdings in England and Wales were classified as part-time.[1] Garratt offers a definition of the part-time farmer as being a farmer who has some other source of income. He later concludes that "... the part-time holding is likely to be a permanent feature of our agriculture." That this has been so, is well supported by the considerable amount of work published on the topic in the last two decades. This work ranges from the short accounts of individual part-time operators, for example, Clarke (1966)[2] to the more extensive regional and national studies of Harwood Long et al. (1958)[3] and Ashton and Cracknell (1961).[4] Furthermore, government awareness of the special nature of part-time farming is supported by the publication in 1966 of the "Report of the Working Party on Part-Time Farming."

It is interesting to note that one of the earlier writers on part-time farming was a geographer, Ifor Davies (1953).[5] In his work on urban farming in Birmingham he contributes to the continuing discussion of the problem of definition by suggesting the following:

1) A part-time farmer is a person in some other occupation besides farming, but where farming is the main source of livelihood.

2) The spare-time farmer has some full-time or nearly full-time employment other than agriculture, but farms in his spare time to supplement his income.

3) The hobby farmer farms for a motive other than profit, such as pleasure or amenity, and he is not, therefore, dependent on agriculture for a living.

Attention is drawn to this paper for two reasons. Firstly, it is one of the few written by a geographer on this topic, and secondly, it anticipated by some years the regional findings of Harrison (1966)[6] and Gasson (1967)[7] for the South East, Harwood Long et al.[8] for Yorkshire, and the national findings of Ashton and Cracknell.[9] From this more recent work it is possible to discuss the suggestion that there is a positive correlation between certain types of part-time farmers and urban areas.

The present work derives its impetus from a desire to consider further this relationship and to analyze the decision-making process with reference to these relationships. In selecting the study area cognizance was made of the need to work in an area that was essentially on the urban fringe and also one that had a high proportion of part-time holdings in a significant number of parishes. The South Staffordshire area is on the fringe of the second most prosperous conurbation in the U.K., and has a high proportion of part-time holdings (55%, with a range from 40% to 87% by parishes).[10]

It would seem, therefore, that in the forty-four years since Garratt's work there has been an increase in part-time holdings, as the national average is over 40%, compared to 30% in 1928. Has this increase also occurred in South Staffordshire? And if so, why?

In order to answer these questions a two-part survey is being conducted on the part-time farmers in the area. Part One consists of a postcard questionnaire designed primarily to distinguish between part-time and full-time farmers. Although the prime purpose is to define the population of part-time farmers,[11] other questions were included to provide additional back-up data to inform the ultimate category selected.

Initially, both the Ministry of Agriculture, Fisheries and Food (MAFF) and the National Farmers Union (NFU) were approached for lists of farmers in the area. As these were unavailable it was decided to use the rating valuation lists as a source for the required mailing list. It is possible to identify agricultural holdings from these lists because they are not rated. This is indicated by an "A" next to the address of the property. In order to test the feasability of the method, a pilot study was carried out on selected urban parishes, as the number of such properties was manageable. Some 112 cards were posted and only twenty-one returned. This represents a sample of 19% and was considered too small to be statistically sound. As a result the method was discarded. Furthermore, it was found that the rating list was not accurate due to the time lag between data collection and publication of the list. For example, in parts of Wolverhampton, areas that had been indicated as being agricultural holdings were in fact being used for playing fields and one was the site of a new school.

As a result of this experience, it was decided to consider an alternate means of obtaining a suitable sample for study. Accordingly, the County Land Agent was approached for a list of the county smallholdings. This had the advantage of being a known population of 130 farms ranging in size from four to 106 acres. The return on these questionnaires after a follow-up letter was raised to 55%. It is clear from the above that the problem of identifying who the part-time farmers are still existed even after these two surveys had been concluded.

A second approach was made to the NFU in an attempt to find a more effective way of obtaining the required number of farms. This met with some success in that they undertook to circulate the new card to those members of the union in the study area. The number of farms involved was one thousand. A 25% return on this circulation was obtained. These returns divided into the following three groups:

1) full-time farmers;

2) part-time farmers;

3) a group largely composed of ex-farmers and non-farming members of the union.

Although this survey provided, in numerical terms, enough farmers for the main interview survey, it would have been an unacceptably biased sample. However, as a result of the publication of Directive 161 of the European Commission and its implications for part-time farmers, a fresh approach was made to the Ministry. This promises to be more satisfactory in that an offer was made to circulate all the holdings under 275 standard man days (SMDs). This will mean that for the study area some six hundred holdings will be circulated when the project is set up. It is hoped that from this a valuable return will be obtained.

Although the results obtained so far have not been considered suitable as a basis for the major part of this study, nevertheless they do give some insight into the problems of identifying part-time farmers. The results presented are those obtained from the County Smallholdings survey.

STATUTORY SMALLHOLDINGS

Historically, these smallholdings were created by Act of Parliament in 1892 to provide displaced cottagers and farm labourers with an entry point into farming. This was later extended through the Smallholdings Colonies Act of 1916 and the Land Settlement (Facilities) Act of 1919 to provide holdings for ex-servicemen wishing to enter farming and also to improve home food production.

The majority of these holdings are now considered in the same way as any privately owned or tenanted farm would be, with certain significant differences. Firstly, they represent for many, the only opportunity to enter farming. Secondly, competition for such a holding is so fierce that the County Land Agent can be highly selective in choosing tenants, the most important prerequisite being that of proved farming ability. Thirdly, due to the size range of the holdings in some areas, it is possible for a tenant to progress from a twenty-five acre holding through to a one hundred acre or more holding as his capital and managerial skills permit.

The contemporary legislative position with regard to statutory smallholdings is described in the Agricultural Act of 1947, with amendments as a result of the Agriculture (Miscellaneous Provisions) Act of 1954. Both of these Acts established the size of a smallholding as being larger than one acre and smaller than fifty acres. In the Wise Report (1966)[12] evidence is presented to support the need for the removal of the upper size limit. This was accepted and discretion given to the Smallholding Authorities to exceed this limit because such a limit was not considered realistic for full-time holdings.

In the report two types of smallholdings were identified: the full-time holding already mentioned, and the part-time holding. In 1964 the latter group represented 44% of all smallholdings. Of these, some

92% were less than twenty acres. Over half of these holdings are located in six counties of Eastern England where high fertility has permitted intensive cultivation. Thus, size is of less importance than the intensity of cultivation. In other areas where less intensive enterprises prevail size becomes more significant.

The number of smallholdings in Staffordshire is less than in the areas mentioned above. For example, in 1964 there were 307 smallholdings in Staffordshire compared with 1,300 and 1,168 in the Isle of Ely and Norfolk, respectively. At the same time the number of part-time holdings in each of the three areas was 112, 1,028 and 494, respectively. By 1974 the total number of smallholdings in Staffordshire had declined to 236, of which eighty-one were part-time holdings. Their distribution, shown as smallholding estates, is illustrated in Figure 1. From this distribution it can be seen that many of these holdings are located close to the urban fringe where competition for land is at its highest. Land values of £800-£1,000 per acre are commonplace, whereas the national average for 1972 was £680. The location and high cost of land make any possible increase in holding size dependent on the amalgamation of existing holdings rather than through county council purchase of additional land for smallholdings.

When compilation of the mailing list for this survey was taking place, advice was sought from the County Land Agent. As a result, 130 holdings were circulated, sixty of which were adjudged to be part-time holdings on the basis of the 275 SMD criterion. From the questionnaires returned it has been possible, by using the three methods of classification,[13] to identify thirteen holdings that are part-time. The analysis of the returns from these holdings has involved three lines of investigation. They are:

1) the farm size factor;

2) the enterprise combination;

3) the nature of the holdings based upon questionnaire and interview material.

The Size Factor

A suggested diagramatic representation of the role of size in the decision to farm part or full-time is shown in Figure 2. The range of size of the holdings lies between four and forty-nine acres. There are two holdings over forty acres, three between thirty and forty, two between twenty and thirty, three between ten and twenty and two less than ten. This produces a mean of twenty-three acres per holding compared with forty-three acres for full-time and part-time holdings combined. It is clear that in this case there is a significant difference between the two groups on the basis of actual size. A further means of analyzing the size factor is by means of the SMD criterion. The county office has its own SMD classification of these holdings and thus it is not only possible to allocate each holding to a category, but also to compare the official classification with the farmers' classification. The county classification is as follows:

Class A =   275 SMDs = less than 1 full-time labour unit
Class B = 275-599 SMDs = 1-2 full-time labour units
Class C = 600-899 SMDs = 2-3 full-time labour units

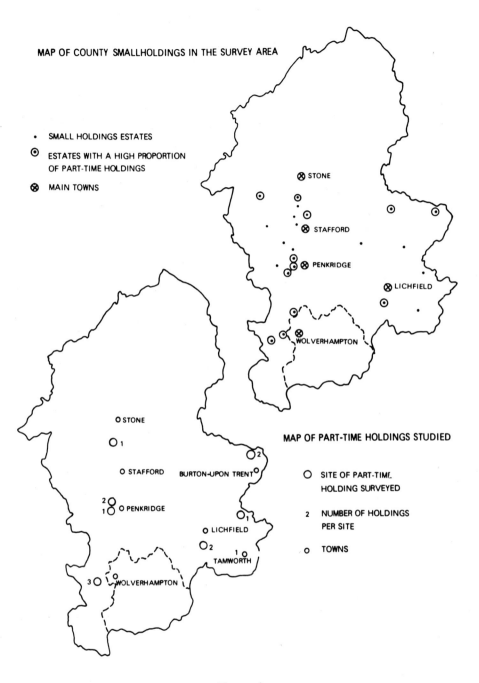

MAP OF COUNTY SMALLHOLDINGS IN THE SURVEY AREA

- SMALL HOLDINGS ESTATES
⊙ ESTATES WITH A HIGH PROPORTION OF PART-TIME HOLDINGS
⊗ MAIN TOWNS

⊗ STONE
⊗ STAFFORD
⊗ PENKRIDGE
⊗ LICHFIELD
⊗ WOLVERHAMPTON

○ STONE
○ 1
○ 2
○ STAFFORD   BURTON-UPON TRENT ○
2 ○
1 ○ ○ PENKRIDGE
○ 1
○ LICHFIELD
○ 2
1 ○
TAMWORTH
3 ○ WOLVERHAMPTON

MAP OF PART-TIME HOLDINGS STUDIED

○ SITE OF PART-TIME HOLDING SURVEYED
2 NUMBER OF HOLDINGS PER SITE
○ TOWNS

Figure 1

87

A SUGGESTED DIAGRAMMATIC REPRESENTATION OF THE RELATIONSHIPS BETWEEN THE
VARIABLES ASSOCIATED WITH THE ANALYSIS OF THE SIZE FACTOR IN PART-TIME FARMING

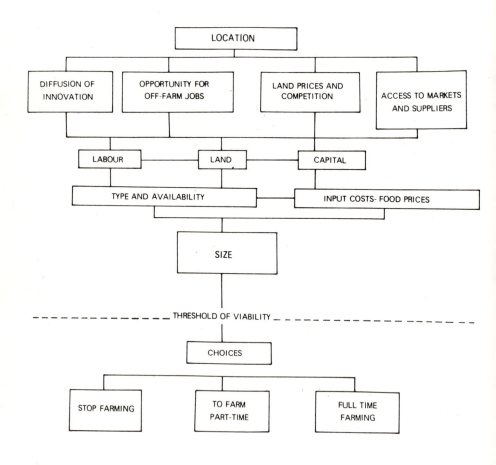

Figure 2

Table 1

THE TOTAL NUMBER OF COUNTY HOLDINGS
PER SIZE GROUP

	SMDs	No. of Holdings
Class A	<275	81
Class B	275-599	70
Class C	600-899	81
Class D	900+	4

	Acres	No. of Holdings
Class A	<20	68
Class B	20-50	104
Class C	50-100	60
Class D	100+	4

On the basis of this classification there are eight Class A holdings with an average range between four and thirty acres, two Class B holdings (twenty-five acres and thirty-six acres) and three Class C holdings with ten, forty-eight and forty-nine acres. Of those four in Class A who answered this question, only one considered himself to be employed full-time on the holding. The others were well below the 275 SMD figure, as was one of the B class. One member of the three in the class replied. In SMD terms this was a large holding requiring 900 full-time labour units. For a study of this size there is a positive correlation between the county office classification and the farmer's view of himself in SMD terms.

Enterprise Combinations

When considering the enterprise combinations of these holdings it is of value to refer to the size factor and also to appreciate that the Wise Report recognized that enterprises such as milk, pig, poultry and vegetable production could be described as intensive, whereas cereals and general cropping could not (Figure 3). Livestock rearing lies between these extremes. Given these premises it would be expected that dairying would head the list in terms of SMDs and possibly acreage. This is certainly true of three out of the five holdings with dairy enterprises. Of the other two, one holding is thirty acres with a 150 SMD input, but this is due to the fact that this particular farmer is in the process of building up his holding from which he derives 80% of his income. The remainder is from off-farm work on another farm. He hopes to be employed full-time on his holding within two years. The second is truly a part-time farmer in that his holding is seventeen acres with 90% of his output in milk and 10% derived from a beef enterprise. This contributes only 30% of his income; the remainder has been obtained from off-farm work as a joiner. He is now retired and thus supplements his income with his old age pension. Seven of these farmers have a livestock enterprise, three of which developed out of the dairy enterprise where livestock con-

TO SHOW THE ENTERPRISES WITHIN EACH SIZE GROUP AS A PERCENTAGE OF THE GROUP OUTPUT

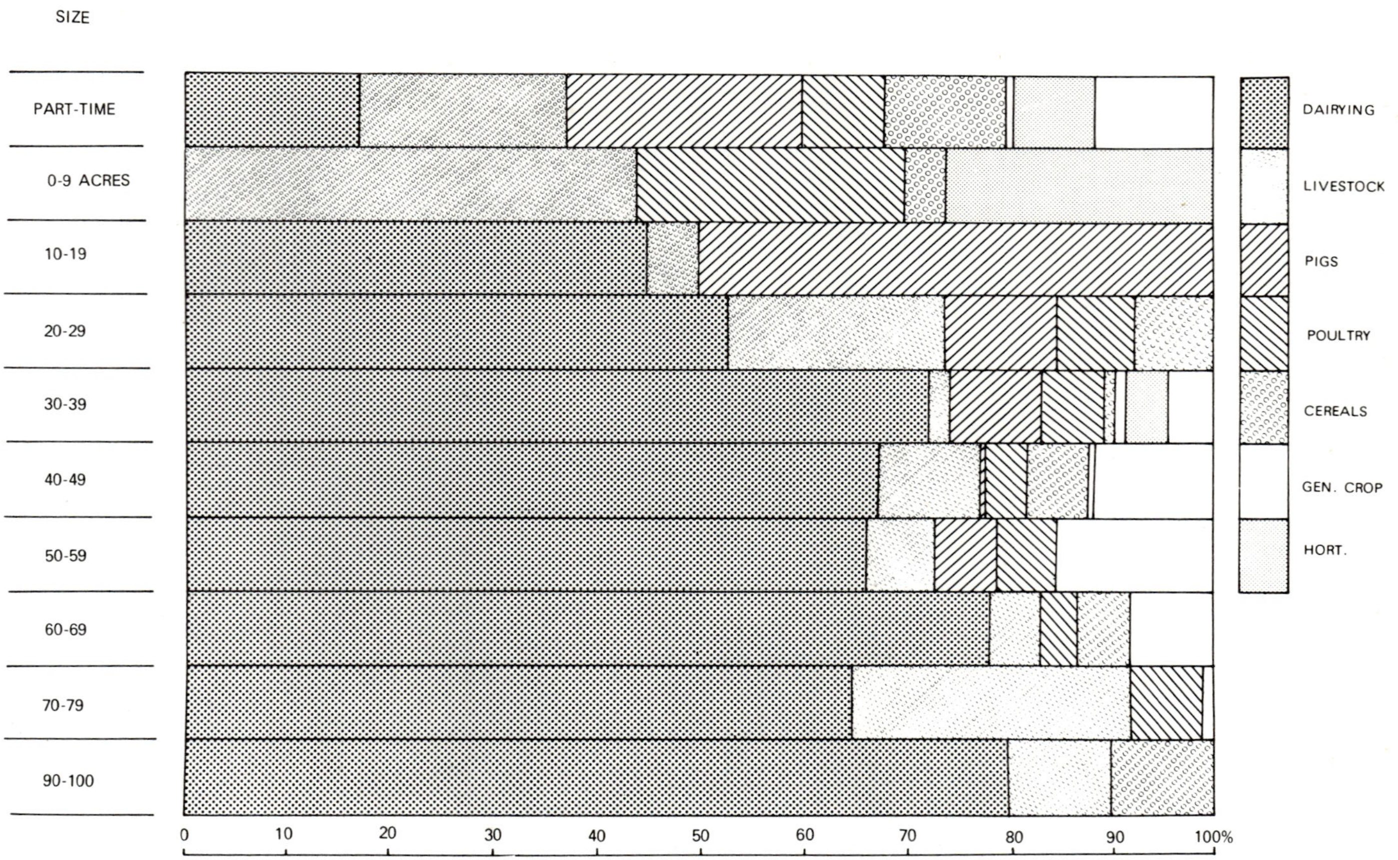

Figure 3

tributes no more than 20% of the output. For three of the four remaining farmers this enterprise is the main one contributing between 50% and 90% of the output. Livestock contributes only 5% of the output for the fourth farmer. Where livestock is the main enterprise the size ranges from a forty-eight acre Class C holding to a four acre Class A holding. On this latter holding there are two other enterprises — poultry and horticulture — which contribute 20% of the output. However, all three enterprises only provide 10% of the income. Where the other 90% comes from was not disclosed. The other farmer in this group had a Class A, seven acre holding and supplemented his farm income with a pension (Figure 2).

For three of the holdings, pigs constitute the main enterprise and is for one the only enterprise. All three are Class A holdings between eleven and thirty acres. The two large ones have cereal enterprises. The smaller holding is building up a very intensive enterprise with a recently installed swill sterilization plant costing £3,500. It is hoped that the tenant, who has been ill for some time, will be able to provide more of the labour input as he recovers. This explains the fact that he considers himself a part-timer although he derives 100% of his income from the holding.

Poultry is another intensive enterprise and is present on two holdings. The size of these holdings is Class C, nine acres; and Class A, four acres. The nine acre holding has a SMD rating of nine hundred and has a carrying capacity of fourteen thousand birds. Technically, this cannot be described as a part-time holding. However, it has been included because the tenant considers himself to be part-time even though he is not, according to standard criteria.

Cereal enterprises are less intensive and therefore are to be expected on larger holdings. This is supported by the data, that is, of the five such enterprises, three are on holdings of at least twenty acres. Equally, the labour input is lower on all but one and this can be accounted for in terms of a poultry enterprise on the holding. Of the others, three Class A and one Class B, on only one do cereals constitute the main output of the holding. General cropping is only present on one holding which is a twenty acre A Class where it contributes only 5% of the output. This holding is particularly interesting because pigs contribute 55% and cereals 40% of the remainder of the output. The entire farm output is only 40% derived from a twenty acre Class A holding.

Horticulture forms the main enterprise in one holding and plays a smaller role in one other. Both have low acreages, less than B, and are Class A holdings.

From the foregoing and the data shown on Table 1, it is clear that the pattern of enterprise generated by this sample is complex and while size is significant, it is only one of the factors involved. For example, if a comparison is made between the enterprise combinations of the part-time and the full-time farmers from the same location, it is found with few exceptions that they are similar even though the average size of the part-time holding is 50% less than that of the full-time holding.

Because many of the sample farmers are operating near the margin of economic viability, they are generally more prone to the effects of external changes than larger and more highly capitalized holdings. This is supported by the fact that one tenant, whose agricultural income is derived from pigs, has been forced to take an off-farm job as a lorry driver. He is located within the urban area and is therefore able to supplement his income in this way. In more rural areas such employment is not so readily obtained. Two others in similar positions (i.e., where agricultural income became insufficient) had to take less well paid work on other holdings. At least two others are dependent on their pensions and another on national assistance. This latter case is important because the tenant is a widower with a large family. His holding, of under fifteen acres, does not produce enough to pay the rent. It is clear in this instance that size is a crucial factor in terms of economic viability. The need to make a living was uppermost in the minds of many of those interviewed. This usually took the form of seeking an increase in acreage either by moving to a larger holding or renting additional land which would allow the farmer to discontinue off-farm employment. Only two of those interviewed seemed happy with their two jobs.

Several of the interviewees mentioned the smallholdings system as being an important means of entry into farming, particularly for the ex-farm worker. It appears that this group was generally more successful than others who entered farming this way. Two further points were made in connection with this topic. First, the majority felt that the size range of smallholdings should be retained to allow progression up the ladder. This is also the view of the Staffordshire County Smallholdings Committee, who made a case to the government for not implementing the recommendation of the Wise Report that there should be a progressive reduction, through amalgamation, of part-time holdings. Thus it is found that whereas the percentage of part-time holdings went up between 1954 and 1964 (the Wise Report data year) from 32% to 36%, in the post Wise period there was a slight reduction in the proportion of part-time holdings from 36% to 34%. From this it is reasonable to claim that the Smallholdings Committee has been successful in maintaining the bottom rungs of the farming ladder. The value to the community to be derived from off-farm employment undertaken by part-timers was also recognized.

It would be fair to comment that in the case of Britain, part-time farming is a permanent feature of the agricultural structure, even if individuals pass through such a phase into or out of full-time farming.

CONCLUSION

It is perhaps permissible to pose questions for discussion and make suggestions for further work. Much debate has been centered on the problem of definition. It may well be that by adopting and applying the typology suggested by Fuller (1974)[14] some resolution of this problem may be achieved. There remains, however, the need for further work on the concept of size as a factor in the decision to farm part-time. It is one of the aims of the research from which this paper is derived to consider further such questions as the nature of size. In this paper it has been defined within the parameters of acreage, SMDs, and income, but this is not enough. As was said by one interviewee, "...you cannot be a full-time farmer with a dairy enterprise on less than thirty acres," and yet many smallholders farm full-time with less land. Clearly there is a need to consider the notion of a threshold of viability. Such a threshold will vary between enterprises and between holdings. It is contended here that until this work is done, the significance of size, however defined, as a factor in the study of part-time farming, will not be fully understood.

NOTES AND REFERENCES

1   Garratt, G.T., **The Organization of Farming.** Heffer, 1930.

2   Clarke, G.J., "Part-Time Cereal Farming," **Agriculture** 73(5), 1966.

3   Harwood Long, W., Butler, J.B., Wynne, A.J., and Edith Wright, **The Small Farms of Industrial Yorkshire.** University of Leeds, Department of Agriculture, 1958.

4   Aston, J. and B.E. Cracknell, "Agricultural Holdings and Farm Business Structure in England and Wales," **Journal of Agricultural Economics** 14(4), 1961.

5   Davies, I., "Urban Farming: A Study of the Agriculture of the City of Birmingham," **Geog.** 38, 1953, pp. 296-303.

6   Harrison, A., "The Farms of Buckinghamshire," Misc. Stud. No. 40, Department of Agricultural Economics, Reading, 1966.

7   Gasson, R., "Part-Time Farming and Farm Size," **Sociologia Ruralis** 7(2), 1967.

8   Harwood Long, et al., **op. cit.**

9   Ashton, J. and B.E. Cracknell, **op. cit.**

10   The definition applied here is the one of less than 275 SMDs used by the MAFF.

11   This was done by means of three questions, relating to size in SMD terms, amount of income derived from the farm, and lastly a question requiring the farmer to assess whether he is a part or full-time farmer.

12   Wise, M.J., "First Report of the Departmental Committee of Inquiry into Statutory Smallholdings," **MAFF,** H.M.S.O., 1966.

13   See footnote 11.

14   Fuller, A.M., "Towards a Typology of Part-Time Farming: A Conceptual Framework and the Case of the Val Nure, Italy." Paper presented to the I.G.U. Commission on Agricultural Typology, Verona, Italy, 1974.

DISCUSSION OF THE PAPER BY
G. STOCK ON OFF-FARM WORK BY SMALL
SCALE FARMERS IN ONTARIO
Arthur Lerner

This paper attempts to describe the relationship between small scale farming and off-farm work and examine the characteristics of off-farm work as it applies to small scale farm operators.

Stock uses the available statistics in a workmanlike manner and makes some perspicacious observations about some shortcomings of the agricultural and population census linkage. I might point out, however, that it is possible to work off-farm and earn no money, or even lose some, and also to earn money off the farm without devoting enough time to it to make its declaration worthwhile.

Less than $5,000 of Gross Sales is taken as the most appropriate indicator of small scale farms, which comprised almost 45% of 1971 Census farms. He departs from the official terminology in calling farms with sales over $5,000 "Commercial Farms", instead of the standard usage of over $2,500, and the reader accustomed to the standard usage must be careful not to get confused.

The analysis of the main types of work performed by these farmers is clearly described and the use of principal components analysis to classify the areas where different types of off-farm work are most prevalent clearly links the type of work to the proximity of urban work opportunities. This is something which should be borne in mind by policy makers and planners, because the predominance of non-urban types of off-farm work in certain areas may be linked to a lower overall opportunity for off-farm work by farmers who need it and whose continued presence in a rural area may be socially beneficial. This leads me to take issue with Stock's judgements in his last page. The development of off-farm work opportunities in remote or infertile areas can keep some resources in agriculture, rather than aid in their removal. Such retention would be socially useful, especially where "the meagre farm resources ... have little value for any viable alternative productive use." Government program aid to prevent the depopulation of such areas would not only help those areas but also reduce the pressures on Megalopolis.

DISCUSSION OF THE PAPER BY P. McLEAY
ON PART-TIME FARMING AMONG STATUTORY
SMALLHOLDERS IN SOUTH STAFFORDSHIRE
Arthur Lerner

This paper begins by pointing out that part-time farming has been important for over a hundred years and cites Garrett, who defines a part-time farmer as one with "some other (unspecified) source of income", concluding that "the part-time holding is likely to be a permanent feature of (British) agriculture." This sets the ground nicely for a continuance of the widespread confusion among writers on part-time farming between a farm which does or does not warrant the labour of a full-time operator and an operator who does or does not himself work full-time on the farm. It is disappointing to see an author, who gives A.M. Fuller as a major reference, neglect this important distinction.

The research is said to derive its impetus from a desire to consider the relationship between certain types of part-time **farmer**[2] and urban areas and to analyze the decision-making process with reference to these relationships. South Staffordshire is chosen because it is on the fringe of a prosperous conurbation and has a high proportion of part-time holdings. There follows an announcement of a two-part survey being conducted on part-time farmers in the area, to answer the questions: "Has the increase in part-time **holdings**[2] (to 40% from 30% in the U.K. since 1928) also occurred in South Staffordshire? And if so, why?" Part One, a postcard questionnaire, is described, but we are left to guess at the nature of Part Two. Three attempts at getting suitable returns from a postcard survey are detailed and a fourth attempt in the future, based on a Ministry promise to circulate all holdings under 275 standard man days (SMD), elicits from the author the hope of "a valuable return" from about six hundred holdings circulated, "for the major part of this study" which is presumably an interview survey, although no details of the intended interview questions are given.

The author goes on to say that "the results obtained so far ... nevertheless ... do give some insight into the problems of identifying part-time farmers". These results appear to have been obtained from the County Land Agent's list of 130 smallholdings in the area. Sixty of these were judged to be part-time holdings on the basis of the official County criterion of 275 SMD. However, the 54% response from the 130 smallholders circulated (which means seventy-one replies) enabled the researcher "to identify thirteen holdings that are part-time." How these identifications were made is not clear, however. What **is** clear is that only eight of the thirteen farmers showed the holdings as part-time on the 275 SMD criterion, although it is not made clear whether the SMD class of these holdings was the official County classification or was modified by the assertions of the seven out of the thirteen who answered the man-days question. One of these eight farms provided **all** the farmer's income and one provided 80-90%. Of the remaining five, two were in the SMD class requiring one to two full-time labour units, while three were in the class requiring two or three full-time labour units. Two of these last provided all the farmer's income, while one provided 80%. The discussion of the enterprises of each of these thirteen farmers indicates information that must have been obtained by interviews, but no statement of the interview survey method, or of the questions asked, appears. It is hard to see from all this what standards were used to determine that these thirteen holdings were "part-time", or whether the operators were part-timers employing additional labour, or whether the operation itself only warranted the employment of less than one full-time labour unit. The farm income is only shown as a percentage of total income and not in absolute size, and there is no indication of what percentage of off-farm income was from off-farm labour and from other sources.

Whatever criteria were used, the acceptance of thirteen out of seventy-one answers (14%), when sixty out of the 130 smallholdings in the area (46%) were judged to be part-time holdings, hardly suggests that they were representative of smallholdings in the area, any more than the 19% (twenty-one returned out of 112) of the first postcard survey, or the 25% return of one thousand cards from the National Farmers Union (NFU) members, both of which were discarded, the former as a sample "too small to be statistically sound," the latter as being "unacceptably biased".

The last three pages purport to be conclusions based on a study of this flimsy sample. These conclusions contain a number of desultory generalizations, such as, that enterprise patterns are complex; size, though significant, is only one of the factors; and part-time farming is a permanent feature of Britain's agricultural structure and may be a phase for individuals moving into or out of full-time farming.

Nowhere is there any attempt to satisfy the stated objects: to consider the relationship between part-time farmers and urban areas and to analyze the decision process with reference to these relationships, or to answer the questions posed for the research at the beginning, that is: Has the increase in part-time holdings apparent in the U.K. also occurred in South Staffordshire? And if so, why? Nor is there any suggestion of how the larger survey planned for the future can answer such questions without some historical data. As for the insight into the problems of identifying part-time farmers, which the results obtained so far are supposed to give, the personal remarks and conditions of a handful of farmers interviewed hardly adds to current knowledge.

Let us hope that some of these criticisms may result in some improvements in the structure of the future survey, justifying the author's hope that "a valuable return" will materialize.

NOTES AND REFERENCES

1. Discussant's insertion. Is a farmer who works full-time on the farm, but has investment income, a part-timer?

2. Discussant's underlining.

QUESTION PERIOD

W. Freeman (Statistics Canada)

Mr. Stock, in your presentation, on page 4, and your reference to the level of schooling of the small scale farmer, what is your source of data?

G. Stock (Alberta, Agriculture)

It was the Census of Canada Agricultural Population linkage. I am sorry, I should have given the source.

W. Freeman (Statistics Canada)

It seems from our calculations that operators with less than Grade 5 represent only 8 per cent of small scale farms, which is hardly a significant factor; operators with university degrees represent over 5 per cent.

G. Stock (Alberta, Agriculture)

As I remember there was no great difference between small scale and commercial except in the Grade 5 category; this is why I made that statement there. Education, in the literature, is something that has been consistently associated with sociological studies of small scale or low income operators. This problem always occurs; when you are talking about low income farm people are you really talking about small scale farmers or not? I say this because of off-farm work. Some of them are from the highest income classes in this society, doctors and lawyers and small hobby farmers, rural residents who happen to produce enough to come under the Statistics Canada definition of a farm.

W. Freeman (Statistics Canad)

I have other comments on your criticism of the Ag. Pop. linkage. Can you identify what definitions appear to be different between the census of agriculture and the population census.

G. Stock (Alberta, Agriculture)

This is more or less implied. I worked with the 1951 through 1966 census fairly extensively in one of my jobs and all that time I was under the impression that when I worked with farms reporting off-farm work that I was using the total farms reporting off-farm work, not those reporting off-farm days only. There is also confusion in the 1971 Census where they do not give a definition of a part-time farm, but only the distribution of those farms by the number of days of off-farm work reported and one is left to assume that if there are zero days reported that the farmer does not participate in off-farm work. When you get to the county level you have nothing to work with to tell how many people report income from off-farm work but report only days of off-farm work. I am surprised that Statistics Canada does not do something like assigning at least one day to anyone who puts down zero days; something that will not affect the averages but which will reflect that person as reporting off-farm work. Surely one must spend some time, off the farm, to earn the sort of money that some people are reporting.

W. Freeman (Statistics Canada)

The Ag. Pop. has identified that there are members who do not report these jobs but who are reporting income.

G. Stock (Alberta, Agriculture)

That is what I mean, it is very confusing in the census documents as they stand right now.

A. Lerner (Agricultural Economics, Guelph)

It must be remembered that this is a linkage and that inconsistencies are bound to occur.

W. Freeman (Statistics Canada)

This is in fact what the linkage has shown — that there is a discrepancy between those reporting off-farm income in one census (population) and the number of operators reporting days of off-farm work in the other (agricultural).

B. Proud (Statistics Canada)

The question I have is related to the previous discussion. All through the conference I have been wondering why we have this emphasis on 'off-farm'; days of off-farm work etc. I am a little concerned that we are overconcerned with this part-time farming terminology, I think the time element is something to be careful of. I like the definition that A. Lerner mentioned, I am not sure where he got it from because I have not had the opportunity to read all the papers. His definition of a part-time farmer was one who has earnings from non-farm sources. This gets away from the problem that G. Stock brought up about the doctor who perhaps in 10 hours off the farm can make anywhere up to $300.00 compared to a bus driver who in 10 hours off the farm can make an income of $30.00. Therefore, when we are talking about these transition stages, surely the person who has the potentiality of earning $30.00 or $40.00 an hour off the farm compared to the person who has a chance of perhaps $3.00 an hour off the farm is in a very different position regarding whether he is going to make full-time farming his occupation or not. Why are we not talking a little more about earnings on the farm and earnings from other sources, and why are we not talking far more about the family unit rather than the farm operator. We should be considering the earnings of the total family unit, both from on the farm and from non-farm sources. Here, we do come to rather a strange situation. I do not know how many census divisions or counties you (G. Stock) have listed as being full-time farmer counties. In 1973, from our calculations, there were in fact only 6 counties in Ontario where average net farm earnings were greater than average net earnings from other sources. Yet, you have shown rather more than 6 counties which you are suggesting are full-time. To me this is something of a conflict.

98

G. Stock (Alberta, Agriculture)

This confusion may be in regard to the technique used. Principle component analysis identifies areas which are relatively distinctive for a certain phenomenon and if everywhere there was zero of a variable, except in one place, and there was one there, then that area would be distinctive for that variable. For that reason you may notice that I said there are 16 types of off-farm work and that I ended up analyzing 10 of them. I threw 6 out because they represented less than 1 per cent of the total off-farm work days in the Province. I did not want to distort my data by keeping those in.

B. Proud (Statistics Canada)

But the point I am making is when you have an area where the farm income is less than the off-farm income, but it is designated as an area of full-time farming.

G. Stock (Alberta, Agriculture)

They still spend less time off the farm.

B. Proud (Statistics Canada)

This is the point I am trying to make. In many cases, incomes are not entirely made up from salaries and wages from off-farm work, but are made up from investment income, pension income and from other sources. Again this aspect has not been mentioned at all at this conference.

G. Stock (Alberta, Agriculture)

I would have been very happy to use income data at the county level if it had been available, but it was not. The only promise I had was that there was going to be available information at the provincial level which would not be any good for spatial analysis.

A. Fuller (Geography, Guelph)

Can I just reiterate that point. We would have been more than pleased to use income data if it were available.

W. Freeman (Statistics Canada)

It is available in Canada. On the Ag. Pop. linkage program.

A. Fuller (Geography, Guelph)

Unfortunately, much of what you describe, at the detail you describe, is not publically available and the Ag. Pop. linkage material at the Provincial level has only been out a relatively short time. Such knowledge is certainly interesting and we will get at it as soon as possible to see what can be done with it.

SOCIAL DETERMINANTS OF PART-TIME FARMING IN A MARGINAL REGION OF ITALY

Ada Cavazzani

THE "FIELD" OF PART-TIME FARMING

The subject of part-time farming is generally dealt with by students of agricultural problems, who therefore tend to overestimate the "agricultural" side of the question. This attitude is, by itself, insufficient to give a clear interpretation of the origin and of the principal reasons of part-time farming. The major part of the existing literature on part-time farming, while not omitting to emphasize the growing heterogeneity of the forms of part-time activity, centres the analysis on the farm unit. As agriculture cannot be considered an independent and homogeneous sector, since it includes very different productive and social realities, so we must distinguish, as precisely as possible, the various forms of part-time farming, particularly taking into consideration its specific functions in relation to the phase of development of society.[1] These functions do not only depend on the structural characteristics of agriculture but, in certain phases of social development, depend mainly on external factors. For the present phase, the influence determined by the processes of industrialization and urbanization has been widely recognized in the studies.[2] Therefore, if part-time farming is not a phenomenon that can be explained only with reference to economic and productive problems, we must adopt adequate theories and methods of observation, which do not take the farm unit as the fundamental object of analysis.

At least two other elements appear essential to explain the causes of part-time farming: the decentralization of branches of industries and the dynamics of the labour market. As regards the tendency to decentralization, part-time farming represents a favourable external condition, as it ensures the availability of labour easy to "recall" and control.[3] As regards the labour market, at a point where the principal contradictions of the social and economic structure are most evident, part-time farming has a function of reducing the level of under-employment and of checking the negative effects, socially dangerous to the stability of the system, of the growing proletarianization and pauperization of small peasants.

Therefore, it is clear that part-time farming has mainly a function of "service" as to the needs of the industrial productive system as well as to the political system. These remarks are closely connected with the analysis of a line emerging in Italy in the last few years, but they confirm as well a trend brought to light by studies conducted in other countries concerning the growing economic marginality of part-time farm units.[4] This tendency is obviously influenced by the processes of rationalization in agriculture which force the unit to choose between increasing productivity, by enlarging the volume of production and reducing costs, or being pushed towards a definitive marginality. Even though theoretically part-time operations could strengthen the structure of farm units, in practice it works only in keeping the peasant's family on the land. Part-time farming is, for the family on a marginal farm unit, merely a solution to its income problems.

These preliminary remarks merely emphasize the limitations of analyses which assume as central factor "physical marginality". The contribution which such analyses give may be valid only if we consider it **partial** and we use it to integrate wider interpretative models and to deepen the level of knowledge. It is in this light that I shall deal with the theme proposed by the organizers of the Symposium, adding a few notes about the concept of marginality.

THE CONCEPT OF "PHYSICAL MARGINALITY"

If we consider part-time farming a phenomenon which has to be related both to agriculture and industry, we have, then, to give a new definition of the concept of "physical marginality" with reference to parameters relative not only to the farm business but also to the industrial structure of the area. From the former point of view, "physical marginality" is defined by natural factors which limit productivity, even though these limits are not fixed once and for all but may be modified by human actions. Parameters such as the physical and chemical characteristics of the soil, the lie of the land, the exposure to the sun, the climate and the availability of water supplies are employed by regional planning to define "homogenous" areas. The zones classified according to altitude (mountain, hill, plain) may be considered a large "homogeneous" area defined according to much simpler criteria. The degree of marginality of a geographical region depends on the value of those "parameters" which principally influence production and the possibilities of exploiting resources, when natural resources are combined with artificial ones.

From the latter point of view, that is, with reference to the industrial structure of the area (from which commuting develops) and to the distribution network (which sustains home work[5]) "physical marginality" must be considered in connection with other "parameters" relative to the structure of the territory and its organization.

As far as the Marche is concerned, commuting has developed within a system of low-lying strips parallel to each other and perpendicular to the sea. These strips make up a network of roads which meet the arterial road at the valley bottom along the coastline. Commuting has also developed inland, in a hilly and mountainous area, around industrial zones which are also meeting points for another road network.

Since 1950 a great number of "métayers"[6], moving along this road network, have left the farms in the mountains and have settled on farms in the hills or in the valley bottom, near the industrial zones. As a consequence the family units working outside the farm can reduce the time-space of commuting and the farmer, being still a "métayer" or having obtained the ownership of a small piece of land, has the possibility of farming a more productive holding.

The areas where occupational activities take the form of home work are the most typical in comparison to the areas where commuting is more frequent, and are relatively independent of the road network. In fact these areas develop in relation to the need of labour and to the managerial ability of intermediaries. Consequently, during a period of economic growth, even the most isolated farm households become involved in this kind of work. In the case of a wide area of coverage, the distributive tasks are attributed to the *gruppista* (group-work organizer); a new kind of middleman who puts in touch the traditional intermediary and those who produce at home.

The parameters of "physical marginality" which we have taken into consideration up to now define subregional areas. The "physical marginality" of some regions in comparison to others — even though it depends on the original structure of the area where the value of raw materials is based on natural motive power and on a natural system of communication — is, in industrialized countries, less important than all the other factors which, from the historical point of view, have caused the industrial structure of a particular country to be regionally unbalanced. The same ideas apply, to some extent, to agriculture, whose natural resources can be better exploited thanks to new technologies.

"MARGINALITY" IN THE MARCHE

This paper presents the first results of a survey made in the Marche in 1973. Not all data are available yet. The survey concerned a sample of 1297 farms, operated directly by the owner of the farm *(conduizone diretta)* or by a "métayer" *(mezzadria)*. The sample accounts for 1.3 per cent of the total number of farms below 50 hectares in the region. The data collected through direct interviews concerned the farm structure, the type of farming, raising and breeding, as well as the single items of the balance sheet of the farm. Moreover, the survey took into consideration all the family units that were in one way or another connected with the same farm, and in particular the work done both on the farm and outside the farm (even if the work was not continuous) by the single members of the households. In the region, the farms below 50 hectares account for 98.7 per cent of the total number of farms and cover 75.3 per cent of the total area. The remaining area is mainly occupied by capitalist farms which are not well developed in this region.

The "marginality" of the region, as far as agriculture is concerned, depends on the relatively high degree of frequency of "métayage" (in 1970 32.4 per cent of the total number of farms were run according to this form of land tenure and they concerned 32.3 per cent of the total agricultural land of the region). During the last twenty years a lot of "métayers" have become owners of the land or have emigrated. "Métayage" — in 1950 this form of land tenure concerned 69.1 per cent of total agricultural land — is connected with the absenteeism, of the owner of the land, who did not invest money in the farm. Consequently, the growth rate of agricultural output in the Marche is the lowest in Italy. The inadequate utilization of the resources of the region — they are not plentiful but they are not scarce either — makes it possible for "economic marginality" to create "physical marginality" insofar as the degree of "under-utilization" of the available resources becomes higher and higher.

The "marginality" of the region with reference to its industrial and commercial structure depends on the relative isolation of the Marche from the rest of the country. Only towards the end of the sixties was the region linked to the rest of the country by means of a toll-motorway which crosses the region from North to South. Rail communications are slow and inadequate; communications by air and sea practically non-existent.

The Marche is in central Italy and lies on the Adriatic slopes of the Appenines, at the same latitude as Tuscany. The "marginality" of this region is not defined in relation to the whole country but to the industrial areas of the North. During the years of the economic "boom" craftsmen and small "entrepreneurs" started producing for markets which were not far away and whose demand for manufactured goods was increasing. Moreover, the region could offer abundant labour force to the medium sized industries of the adjacent regions and to the larger industries of the North that were beginning a process of diffusion over the country. Small and medium industrial plants were set up along the coast, better equipped and organized, and inland along the regional communications network described previously. The main feature of this development has been a high degree of specialization of the valleys in different branches of production (clothing, shoes, furniture, electronic and mechanical engineering). In all these sectors the decentralization of the production is possible, down to the level of home work. Thanks to the development of these industrial activities, the region began to come out of the condition of marginality in which other regions in Central and South of Italy still remain. However, the industrial structure of the region is still weak and at times shows its weakness here and there even though on the whole the industries of the region produce not only for the home market but also for foreign markets.

Farms and families in the region

The main problem of our study of part-time farming concerns the way in which this new form of reltionship between agriculture and industry influences the structure of production in agriculture.

In the fifties the families of the producers who owned and farmed the land and of the "métayers" anticipated the farming crisis of the following ten years. In fact young members of the family, who were under-employed on the farm, left the land without causing any decrease in the levels of production, thanks to the more intensive work of those who remained on the farm. Nevertheless, in the sixties farming itself got involved in the crisis, due to the need of capital to be invested in machinery, fertilizers and seed in order to keep on with the increasing average levels of productivity. Emigration and urbanization continued mainly because of two effects: a "pushing effect" away from agriculture and a "pulling effect" towards industry. However, the diffusion of part-time farming was the main **new factor** in this situation. According to the Census of 1970, there are in the

Marche 100,000 farms, 6,000 of which are capitalist farms. There are 50,000 heads of family who work mainly or only on the farm; 28,000 farmers working mainly or only on the farm who are not heads of family or who are retired heads of family; lastly, about 22,000 farmers work mainly outside the farm (see Table 1).

Within this framework, which refers to the whole of agriculture in the region, there are different situations according to the altitude of the land. Passing from the mountainous internal areas to the coast there is a decrease in the proportion of farms, where either the operator is mainly employed in activities outside the farm, is not the head of the family, or is a pensioned head of the family. From these data we can see that the peasant families who remain on the land have a tendency to consider the farm as a central source of income, so that they assign at least one labour unit to the operation of the farm (80 per cent of the cases). Nevertheless, the personal characteristics of this unit change to a large extent, as does the help that other members of the household give to the operator of the farm.

In the mountains over a quarter of the operators are more than sixty-five years old and over 40 per cent of them are over sixty. In the hills these values are respectively 15 per cent and 27 per cent. In both areas young men under thirty-five years are relatively few. These data confirm that the operation of the farm is generally left to the oldest members of the family, who remain active even after retirement. This situation is more evident in the mountains than in the hills. A similar process of aging can be noticed for all the labour force active in agriculture, if we compare it to the age classes of workers in other branches of production.

The labour of the operator is the principal resource, in terms of manpower, of the farm unit, when the operator is mainly or exclusively engaged on the farm. The contribution of family labour becomes important when the operator works outside the farm. On the whole, the family members give an average of 1.4 working days for every working day of the operator. But this proportion varies noticeably according to the size of the farm unit, the altitude of the land and the form of management (Table 2). The contribution of family labour increases with the size of the farm up to 20-30 hectares; after this level the contribution of hired labour becomes determinant. The number of days worked by family members, compared to those of the operators, is higher in the hills than in the mountains, and on farms managed by "métayers" than on farms directly operated by the owner.

Within a family unit, whose size varies from an average of four persons in the mountains to five members on the coast, family labour devoted to farming amounts to an average of 1.5 units. It is possible to evaluate that 80 per cent of family labour in the mountain farms is formed by women, while this proportion reaches 88 per cent in the coastal areas. These data confirm the large contribution to the farm of female labour both in the mountains, where labour is becoming scarce, and in the coastal area, where the farms are larger size and where female work on the farm "frees" the man labour force for non-farm occupations.

105

TABLE 1

FARM OPERATORS ACCORDING TO POSITION IN THE FAMILY AND WORK ON THE FARM

(per cent)

	Operators heads of family mainly or exclusively working on the farm[1]	Operators not heads of the family or heads retired, mainly or exclusively working on the farm[2]	Operators, heads and family members mainly working outside the farm[3]		Total (%)
			Agricultural Sectors	Other Sectors	
Mountain	35	36	5	24	100
Internal Hills	55	23	6	16	100
Coastal Hills	61	17	6	16 ˙	100
TOTAL	54	23	6	17	100

1 Persons classified by the Census of Population 1971 as heads of family and independent workers in agriculture.

2 Difference between farm operators mainly or exclusively working on the farm (Census of Agriculture 1970) and number of heads of family independent workers in agriculture (Census of Population 1971).

3 Operators classified according to work outside the farm (Census of Agriculture 1970).

TABLE 2

WORK DAYS OF FAMILY LABOUR AND HIRED LABOUR EXPRESSED AS A PROPORTION OF OPERATOR'S LABOUR

Farm Size (SAU)	Family Labour	Hired Labour
Up to 3 ha	0.88	0.10
3 to 5 ha	1.17	0.10
5 to 10 ha	1.58	0.15
10 to 20 ha	2.23	0.33
20 to 30 ha	2.40	1.13
30 to 50 ha	1.89	2.84
50 to 100 ha	1.42	6.38
over 100 ha	0.65	18.55
Altitude		
Mountain	1.17	0.19
Hill	1.40	0.25
Form of Management		
Ownership	1.17	0.10
Métayage	1.66	0.05

PART-TIME FARMING AS A "MARGINAL" SOLUTION TO THE FAMILY FARM CRISIS

The relationship between the family and the farm seems to be the most important element for the analysis of part-time farming in the Marche. This problem will be discussed with reference to the first results of the research conducted in the region in 1973 (Tables 3, 4, 5).

At first, we notice that part-time farms, amounting to 47 per cent of the sample, bear a demographic charge higher than full-time farms. This situation is directly linked with two joint phenomena. First, family size of part-time farms is always larger, on the average by 0.7 per unit, even if we compare part-time and full-time farms according to altitude, form of management and size of the holding, although the size of part-time farms is lower, on the average by 2.1 hectares, in comparison with the types and locations of full-time farms.

The higher demographic charge per unit of arable land determines a sharp reduction of standard income per unit, produced by the farm operation: 266 thousand liras compared to 371 thousand liras of full-time farmers. From these figures of gross income, yet three or four times lower than the national average, we must deduct the share of rent owing to the owners of the land. In addition, it has to be made clear that we do not count any return of farm capital nor, obviously, of family labour (hired labour is almost non-existent).

To assert that the **demographic charge per unit** is crucial to explain the reduction of income to a level difficult to sustain, implies an evaluation of other factors that could be important additional causes of the phenomenon. These refer to the structure of farm production. As a matter of fact, a comparison between part-time and full-time farms, according to the altitiude of land, form of management and farm size, does not show relevant differences as to the operation of the farm. On the contrary, the gross marketable output per unit of cultivated land is, on the average, slightly higher in part-time farms. This may result from a higher use of labour, contrary to expectations, on part-time farms: the average is 133 days per arable hectare compared to 122 days in full-time farms. However, this is only an hypothesis that must be checked, because the higher use of labour might result from a lower productivity of labour itself due to some particular elements (age, sex). In fact, while on the average of full-time farms labour is composed of 2.1 full-time units and 0.5 units working only partially on the farm (housewives, old members, schoolchildren), on part-time farms there are 1.4 full-time units, 0.4 irregular family labour and 0.5 part-time units. Another factor that seems to influence the level of gross output per unit is the type of enterprise. In part-time farms crops are more frequent than livestock, and subsistence output, which covers more than one quarter of the gross output of crops, is higher in part-time farms, especially in the mountains and on holdings of under 3 hectares, where 37 per cent of the land output is consumed by the family.

TABLE 3

MAIN FEATURES OF PART-TIME AND FULL-TIME FARMS IN THE MARCHE

	Part-time	Full-time
FAMILY		
Family members n.	4.8	4.1
Full-time inside n.	1.4	2.1
Other labour inside n.	0.4	0.5
Part-time n.	0.5	—
Full-time outside n.	0.5	—
Not working	2.0	1.5
FARM MANAGEMENT		
Arable land, ha.	4.6	6.2
Gross output x ha.	419	373
Crops gross output x ha.	183	164
Labour days x ha.	133	122
Capital productivity (1)	1.19	1.25
Subsistence crops (2)	28	25
Agrarian capital x ha.	393	364
Machinery value x ha.	139	124
Scorts value x ha.	254	241
Land capital x ha.	1607	1465
Land improvements x ha.	142	98
STANDARD INCOME		
Farm income x unit	266	371
Additional income x unit	295	—
Total income x unit	561	371
INVESTMENTS (LAST 5 YEARS)		
House	518	378
Farm (x ha.)	251	197
TOTAL CASES	609	677

+ All the values are expressed in thousand Italian Lire

1. Land capital/Added value
2. Proportion subsistence output/gross output (only for crops)

TABLE 4

MAIN FEATURES OF PART-TIME AND FULL-TIME FARMS IN THE MARCHE BY ALTITUDE

	Mountain		Hill	
	Part-time	Full-time	Part-time	Full-time
FAMILY				
Family members n.	4.4	3.6	5.0	4.5
Full-time inside n.	1.2	1.7	1.6	2.3
Other labour inside n.	0.4	0.7	0.3	0.4
Part-time n.	0.5	—	0.5	—
Full-time outside n.	0.5	—	0.5	—
Not working	1.6	1.2	2.1	1.8
FARM MANAGEMENT				
Arable land, ha.	4.6	7.0	4.6	5.6
Gross output x ha.	315	256	488	492
Crops gross output x ha.	120	100	223	229
Labour days x ha.	116	92	145	153
Capital Productivity (1)	1.20	1.37	1.18	1.19
Subsistence crops (2)	37	31	25	23
Agrarian capital x ha.	308	278	448	450
Machinery value x ha.	110	92	157	156
Scorts value x ha.	198	189	291	293
Land capital x ha.	1006	896	2000	2044
Land improvements x ha.	72	46	189	152
STANDARD INCOME				
Farm income x unit	229	328	291	402
Additional income x unit	353	—	265	—
Total income x unit	582	328	556	402
INVESTMENTS (LAST 5 YEARS)				
House	650	350	431	401
Farm (x ha.)	161	169	310	225
TOTAL CASES	241	309	368	368

+ All the values are expressed in thousand Italian Lire

1. Land capital/Added value
2. Proportion subsistence output/Gross output (only for crops)

TABLE 5

MAIN FEATURES OF PART-TIME AND FULL-TIME FARMS IN THE MARCHE BY MANAGEMENT

	Ownership		Métayage	
	Part-time	Full-time	Part-time	Full-time
FAMILY				
Family members n.	4.5	3.8	5.5	4.8
Full-time inside n.	1.2	1.8	2.1	2.5
Other labour inside n.	0.4	0.6	0.3	0.4
Part-time n.	0.5	—	0.4	—
Full-time outside n.	0.5	—	0.4	—
Not working	1.9	1.4	2.3	1.9
FARM MANAGEMENT				
Arable land, ha.	3.7	5.5	6.9	7.8
Gross output x ha.	390	354	447	395
Crops gross output x ha.	173	155	191	174
Labour days x ha.	141	118	121	127
Capital productivity (1)	1.18	1.27	1.25	1.26
Subsistence crops (2)	30	27	26	22
Agrarian capital x ha.	356	344	429	387
Machinery value x ha.	154	136	115	104
Scorts value x ha.	203	210	313	282
Land capital x ha.	1516	1423	1684	1500
Land investments x ha.	146	102	134	92
STANDARD INCOME				
Farm income x unit	202	320	265	299
Additional income x unit	328	—	233	—
Total income x unit	530	320	498	299
INVESTMENTS (LAST 5 YEARS)				
House	657	506	188	112
Farm (x ha.)	353	282	116	71
CASES	428	457	181	220

+ All the values are expressed in thousand Italian Lire

1. Land Capital/Added value
2. Proportion subsistence output/Gross output (only for crops)

The more intensive use of labour and the higher proportion of subsistence output in part-time farms might be interpreted as a sign of marginality of the farm. In trying to face the competition of full-time farms by such an intensive use of the resources its future development will be seriously damaged. However, on the contrary, several indicators show that not only the management is competitive, but so also is the structure of the farm, at least as far as the total amount of capital is concerned. Both the agrarian capital and the land capital, per hectare of arable land, are 10 per cent higher in part-time farms. In particular, the machinery value and the supplies value are higher, on the average. The highest level is reached by capital investments for land improvements, first of all for vines which in part-time farms are 45 per cent greater than in full-time farms. Finally, the relation between agrarian capital and added value, which can be used as a productivity index, is higher in part-time farms.

The half unit (0.5) working part-time inside and outside the farm and the other half unit (0.5) working full-time outside the farm make the standard gross income per unit increase from 266 to 561 thousand lire per year. This level is still only one-half of the national standard income per unit in 1972, and it shows how precarious and under-rewarded occupations outside the farm still are. Of these occupations, 80 per cent is covered by dependent work, 13 per cent by craftsmanship and 7 per cent by home work. Through this exploitation by the decentralized industrial structure, the farm family seems to be willing to save itself and the farm as well, even if the latter remains absolutely marginal within the agricultural system of production.

In this framework we can explain the fact that the average amount of investments for home improvements in the last five years, although modest, is 37 per cent higher in part-time farms, and investments on the farm are 27 per cent higher than in full-time farms. On the other hand, the larger size of farm and the smaller size of family of full-time farms, seem to indicate an alternative answer (that probably prevailed in the recent past) to the crisis of the family-farm unit of production, that is, the expulsion from agriculture of some active members of the family through migration towards industrial areas. This was probably the only solution available at that time, in a situation of absolute marginality of the region, not yet invested by the diffusion of industrial activities.

NOTES AND REFERENCES

1 See the paper presented *in absentia* to this Symposium by G. Sivini, **Some Remarks on the Development of Capitalism and Specific Forms of Part-Time Farming in Europe.**

2 To mention only a few, see Loomis (1965), Gasson (1967), Lacombe (1968), Harrison (1969), Fuller (1974).

3 See, for theoretical aspects G. Sivini, **art. cit.;** for empirical data L. Frey (ed.), **Lavoro a domicilio e decentramento dell'attività produttiva,** Milano, Angeli, 1975, pages 1654.

4 This fact is confirmed by all Western countries, with the only exception of Great Britain. Gasson and Harrison found some part-time farming associated with modern forms of investments in agriculture in areas which are within the influence of Greater London. For Italy, see G. Mottura and E. Pugliese, **Agricoltura, Mezzogiorno e mercato del lavoro,** Bologna, Il Mulino, 1975, pages 327.

5 **Home work** (also written **homework**) refers to manufacturing done in the home using materials furnished by an entrepreneur who pays for the work by the piece.

6 "Métayage" is a system of land tenure in which the farmer pays a proportion (usually a half) of the produce, as rent, to the owner, who furnishes the stock and means of production or a part thereof.

PART-TIME FARMING IN A PHYSICALLY MARGINAL AREA OF NORTHERN ONTARIO

Richard C. Benson

INTRODUCTION

In the last half-century there has been a growing awareness of, and interest in part-time farming as a form of agricultural activity. Geographers, economists, sociologists and others have attempted to increase our knowledge of this agricultural phenomenon by examining a multitude of characteristics generally describing the subject. In recent years the studies concerning part-time farming have become more specific, examining such attributes as farm operation differences, operator and family characteristics and social relationships affecting the nature of the part-time farmer and the part-time farm. Much of the interest in part-time farming has been generated through studies examining the subject in excellent farming areas and areas proximate to or within the sphere of influence of large urban centers. However, an examination of the distribution of part-time farmers in Ontario (Figure 1) clearly indicates that very high intensities of part-time farmers also occur in the Canadian Shield — a physically marginal area of the Province. Thus it can be proposed that part-time farming is, in many instances, spatially associated with the degree of physical marginality in an area such as Ontario or Canada.

The Rainy River District Study

In the summer of 1973 I visited the Rainy River District of Northwestern Ontario to conduct a field survey to examine the nature of part-time farming in that region. The area shown in Figure 2 was chosen for two reasons. First, the Rainy River District had the highest incidence of multiple jobholding[1] in the province (65.5 per cent of all farmers were multiple jobholders) and secondly, the area is physically marginal.

Farming in the district is carried out on a clay plain developed on the clay and silt deposits resulting from the processes of sedimentation during the time of glacial Lake Agassiz. The soils are generally fertile (with the exception of large tracts of muskeg and organic soils) but the area is rendered physically marginal by its moderately harsh climate. Summer temperatures average 60° Fahrenheit and although the growing season is about 170 days, the frost free period is only 110 days. The cool temperatures and mean annual growing degree days[2], ranging from 2,500-2,700, limit the production of certain feed and cash crops such as winter wheat, grain, corn and soybeans.

The Field Study

During the summer of 1973, 116 randomly selected farms were visited in the Rainy River District and a questionnaire designed to examine full-time and part-time farming characteristics was administered to each. The data gathered included variables of the following:

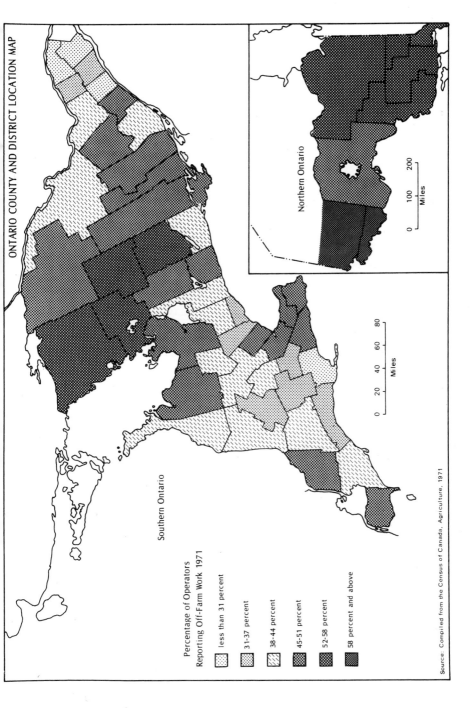

ONTARIO COUNTY AND DISTRICT LOCATION MAP

Northern Ontario

Southern Ontario

Percentage of Operators
Reporting Off-Farm Work 1971

less than 31 percent

31-37 percent

38-44 percent

45-51 percent

52-58 percent

58 percent and above

Source: Compiled from the Census of Canada, Agriculture, 1971

Figure 1

RAINY RIVER DISTRICT LOCATION MAP

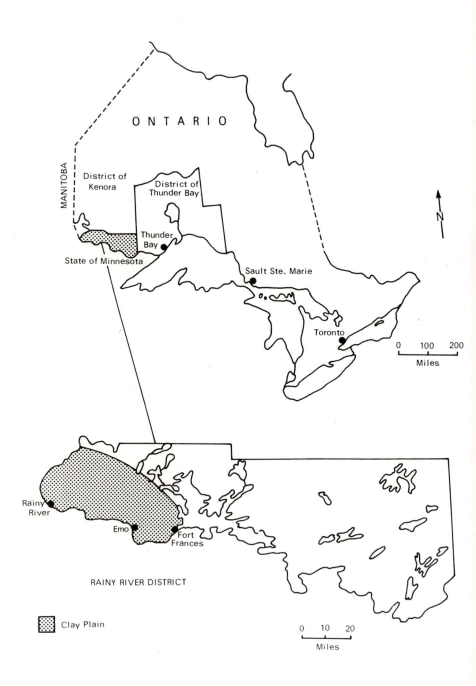

Figure 2

1) Farm Enterprise Characteristics
2) Inputs and Outputs of the Farm Operation
3) Social Characteristics
4) Off-Farm Work Characteristics

The study was divided into two parts, the first being a comparison and synthesis of full-time and part-time farming, and the second, an examination of the nature of the off-farm work situation and the sub-types of part-time farming.

The Full-Time and Part-Time Farming Comparison

Of the 116 farms visited, 35 were full-time operations while eighty-one were part-time farms. Because of the large number of variables gathered for the study, factor analysis and discriminant analysis were employed to reduce the data matrix to the key under-lying factors and help differentiate the characteristics of the two groups. The analysis indicated that the major differences between the two groups existed in terms of inputs and outputs of the farm operation and especially in the intensity of farm inputs. Generally the full-time farms were much more intensively operated than part-time units, having higher labour inputs and a greater number of crop and livestock units. In terms of the actual farm enterprise, the major difference existed in the emphasis on dairying found on the full-time farms. Of the farms visited, only one part-time farmer had a dairy operation while over 60 per cent of the full-time units were dairy. Table 1 lists some of the average characteristic differences which existed between the two farming groups in the Rainy River District.

PART-TIME FARMING IN THE RAINY RIVER DISTRICT

General Characteristics

In general terms, the part-time farmers of the Rainy River District operated farms having moderate herds and producing crops including hay and some grains to be used as forage. These farmers focussed much of their activity toward off-farm work as the average part-time farmer spent 158 days per year off the farm. This non-farm work was the major income producing activity of the farmer as the group average for off-farm income was $5,897 per year while the net agricultural income on the same farms was $1,414 (only 23 per cent of the total).

The major finding of the study, and the major thrust of this paper is that part-time farming is a long term, persistent, and his-torically evolved response of farm operators who combine and utilize the agriculture and forest resource base of the region. In this century the focus of farming activity has evolved to create a symbiotic relation-ship between agriculture and the pulp and paper industry of the Rainy River District.

Forest-Farm Relationships in the Rainy River District Survey

Of the eighty-one part-time farmers interviewed in the 1973 survey, forty-five per cent were in some way directly involved with the forest industry. This involvement took place at two levels:

117

Table 1

Average Full-Time and Part-Time Farming
Differences in the Rainy River District

Investment Type	FT Farm	PT Farm
Land	$23,114	22,246
Buildings	24,085	14,196
Machinery & Equipment	14,942	11,808
Livestock	27,980	14,086
Total Capital Value	90,271	62,407

Type of Sales		
Livestock	$ 7,362	5,167
Crop	40	191
Milk	12,628	246
Poultry & Eggs	760	14
Other	93	0
Total Sales	20,793	5,620

Labour Input (hours per year)		
Operator	3,404	2,068
Wife	529	375
Other	2,242	657
Total Hours	6,176	3,100

Land Use		
Total Acres Operated	478	460
Total Improved Acres	220	176
Total Cropland Acres	154	119
Acres of Hay	129	99
Acres of Grains	25	20

Livestock and Poultry		
Total Beef Cattle	50	52
Total Dairy Cattle	32	1.6
Total Milkers	22	Less than 1
Total Pigs	4	Less than 1
Layers	110	Less than 5
Total Poultry	123	Less than 5

Family and Social Characteristics		
Operator Age	50.8	47.9
Years as an Operator	22.0	27.5
Number in Household	5.0	4.2

Farm Intensity Differences		
Total Capital Value/Improved Acre	$ 442	$ 415
Total Sales/Improved Acre	98	35
Net Income/Improved Acre	37	8
Net Return/Hour of Labour	1.39	.52

1) There were fourteen farm operators working at a secondary industrial level, being employed by the Pulp and Paper and Kraft mills in Fort Frances.

2) Thirty-one operators were engaged at the primary industrial level, cutting pulpwood (through contracts with the mill) in the forest regions of the district.

Those farmers engaged in secondary industrial employment are termed "Residential Part-Time Farmers." They are virtually full-time non-farm employees as they averaged a total of 253 days per year in off-farm work. Because of their large non-farm time commitment and the fact that they are organized union employees, their non-farm earnings were quite high, averaging $9,571 per year. These farmers tended to operate their farms as a hobby, having a relatively small scale of operation and averaging only $2,950 of gross sales per year.

Those operators engaged in primary industrial cutting operations in the woods are termed "Bush Farmers". These farmers are engaged in a number of situations. Of the thirty-one bush farmers, fifteen are engaged only in bush work while the remaining sixteen do bush work and other non-farm work as well. Those working only in the bush average sixty-nine (eight-hour) days of off-farm work, earning an average $2,887 per year. However, they have fairly large farm operations as they averaged $6,673 gross farm sales per year. The remaining sixteen bush farmers (who have more than one non-farm job) average 125 days of non-farm work and earn $5,560 off the farm. These operators average $4,973 worth of gross farm sales in addition to their non-farm earnings.

Bush Farming — A Unique and Important Part of the Rural Economy of the Rainy River District

Traditionally, and in the 1971 Census of Agriculture, the cutting and sale of wood products has been considered part of the farm operation. Nevertheless, forest related income is not only earned from farm holdings and cannot be included as agricultural income. The Rainy River District provides a unique opportunity in examining the importance of an ancillary resource base to agriculture and also illustrates how bush activities are divorced from agriculture. For example:

1) In most instances the areas of cutting are not on the farm lot on which the operator resides but on a lot bought or leased specifically for the production of wood products.

2) Many operators cut on both their own purchased woodlots (deeded lands) and on Crown Lands for which they pay stumpage fees.

3) To cut pulpwood for sale, the farmers must obtain cutting contracts from the Boise Cascade Mill which works in conjunction with the Ministry of Natural Resources for the establishment of contract sizes, species to be cut and cutting areas.

4) Many farm operators have geared their income earning activities away from the farm operations through capital investments in expensive machines such as "tree farmers," trailer and semi-trailer pulpwood trucks, hydraulic lifts such as "timberjacks" and other equipment designed for bush work rather than farming.

In each case the operator is engaged in bush activities peripheral or not related to the production of crops and/or livestock. The wood cut in the district is found in natural stands, not those planted specifically for wood production and therefore not an agricultural resource for the purpose of this study.

The importance of the income which comes from pulpwood sales cannot be ignored when examining farm income structures of the district. It is difficult to estimate the number of farmers who utilize the opportunities afforded by the availability of forest resources for producing supplemental income but one could estimate that at least 40 per cent[3] of the farmers in the district are bush farmers. In terms of actual income, Table 2 illustrates the various categories of income divisions for Rainy River farmers from 1968-1974. As illustrated, pulpwood sales represented 36.7 per cent of the 1974 total income found on the Rainy River District farms. Forest products were the most important single income producing commodity for the farmers in the district that year (1974) and in the last seven years the sales of pulpwood ranked first or second in importance six times. The pulpwood sales from deeded farm lands in 1974 totalled $267,045 and sales from cutting permits on Crown Lands (for which stumpage fees were paid) were $1,112,708 while other timber products totalled $75,000.

The Evolution of the Forest Farm Relationship

The economy of the Rainy River District has always been dependent on the natural resources of the region, beginning with furs and later including the mineral, forest and soil resources. However, the district did not begin to grow as an economic region until a pulp and paper mill was built in Fort Frances at the turn of the century. With the development of a fairly sound economic base, the district started to grow in population. Farmers began homesteading the area, determined to earn a living supplying the woodsmen and urban residents with agricultural products. However, the thick pine and spruce forests, the harsh climate and other frontier problems posed many difficulties in the establishment of a farm. As a result, most farmers were forced to become woodsmen before they could farm. In many instances this proved to be an advantage for the farmers as they had a ready market for wood products in the pulpmill and the many sawmills of the district. The farmers could cut pulpwood in the winter (while clearing their own land) and sell the logs to mills, or, work directly in the bush camps operated by the various wood companies in the area. In many instances, the money provided through wood sales or bush work could be applied to the purchase of farm equipment or livestock. In some instances the opportunity provided by the forest was detrimental. The ready market for wood products

Table 2

Sales Categories of the Rainy River District Farmer
1968-1974 (in thousands of dollars)

	Forest Products		Dairy Sales		Livestock Products		Other Income		Total Sales Income
	Total	%	Total	%	Total	%	Total	%	Total
1968	780	31	729	29	928	36	111	4	2549
1969	1080	34	886	28	1094	34	122	4	3184
1970	1185	37	824	26	1088	34	112	3	3210
1971	1039	33	832	26	1169	37	111	3	3185
1972	1136	30	925	24	1616	43	122	3	3800
1973	881	23	1020	27	1661	44	230	6	3794
1974	1454	36	1437	35	974	24	198	5	4065

Source: Art Hamilton (Agricultural Representative OMAF for the Rainy River
District) Yearly Report, Agriculture

attracted "bogus settlers" or timber pirates, whose only desire was to strip the land of merchantable timber and then move on. Also, many settlers who, having come to the area to farm, later abandoned the farms for more lucrative jobs in the forest industry, leaving much land idle and useless. However, with stricter legislation[4] concerning cutting rights on agricultural lands and the developments of forest and farming policies, a balance was established between forestry and agriculture which halted much of the timber piracy. Nevertheless, the forest was still, important to the farmers. Once farm operators became used to receiving income for pulpwood or bush labour it was difficult for them to stop and as a result the farming-forestry work situation has become a sustaining feature in the agricultural scene of the Rainy River District.

PERSISTENT PART-TIME FARMING IN THE RAINY RIVER DISTRICT

As emphasized in the 1973 survey data and the evolution of forest-farm relationships, wood resources have become an integral part of the farming activities in the region. This evidence has also indicated that part-time farming is of a persistent nature having its beginnings in the first settlement of the area. For the purposes of this paper, a persistent part-time farmer is one who has been in a multiple jobholding situation for at least a 10 year continuing period.[5] Figure 3 illustrates the length of tenure and work status of the bush oriented part-time farmers in the 1973 survey. Overall, 73 per cent of the bush oriented operators can be termed persistent, with one half of the resident part-time farmers and 83 per cent of the bush farmers engaged in long-term multiple jobholding. Table 3 shows the tenure averages for each of the part-time farming groups.

Table 3

Average Years of Farm and Non-Farm Activity of the Bush Oriented Farmers

	Resident PTF	Bush Farmers Total	Bush Only	Bush plus Other Job
Number Persistent	7	26	14	12
Percentage Persistent	50	83	87	80
Years of Farming (Average)	23	23	24	22
Years Holding a Non-Farm Job (Average)	19	23	25	22

This table indicates that those farmers who have worked in a multiple jobholding situation for more than 10 years have done so on a long-term basis. These farmers have committed themselves to a part-time farming lifestyle whereby they engage in farming and non-farm activities continually.

122

LENGTH OF TENURE AND WORK STATUS OF THE BUSH ORIENTED PART-TIME FARMERS

Figure 3

Further information concerning the long term resource relationships between agriculture and forestry can be drawn from the family work history of each part-time farmer. In order to illustrate that this particular form (persistent) of part-time farming has evolved with the history of the district, each part-time farmer's family history was examined. Overall, 75 per cent of the bush oriented part-time farmers had fathers who were farmers and 54 per cent of these had fathers who were also part-time farmers. More specifically, Table 4 shows the historical farm and non-farm activities of the persistent part-time farmers of the District.

The table indicates several facts. First, the resident part-time farmers do not have a definite history of farming or part-time farming in their families. This could indicate that these individuals are generally "hobby farmers" who have moved from Fort Frances or another center because of the amenities of rural life and have established small

Table 4

Part-Time Farming History in the Families of the Bush Oriented Survey Farmer

	Resident Part-Time	Bush Farmers with Other Job	Bush Farmer Only
Percentage whose father did not farm	36	33	0
Percentage whose father was a farmer	64	67	100
Percentage whose father was a part-time farmer	7	53	75
Percentage whose father was a "Bush Farmer"	0	40	69

farm operations. Secondly, the farmers who work directly in the bush have both a history of farming and multiple jobholding in their families. More specifically, 85 per cent of the families with a history of multiple jobholding had operators who were also engaged in bush operations. This evidence indicates that part-time farming is a persistent lifestyle with its origins imbedded within the history of the Rainy River District.

CONCLUSIONS

The facts presented in this paper provide substantial evidence that part-time farming in the Rainy River District is a long-term "persistent" situation which has evolved as a symbiotic relationship between agriculture and forestry. The physically marginal conditions resulting from the climate and soils of the area have prevented a majority of the farmers (especially non-dairy) from establishing viable commercial operations. As a result, these farmers have been forced to seek off-farm employment as a supplementary means of securing a livelihood. The result has been the evolution of a fairly sophisticated situation of farm and non-farm work relationships in the district. Better modes of transportation and roads have increased the boundaries of the forest tracts. The use of highly sophisticated machines has made cutting practices more efficient while increased controls of contracts, prices and cutting areas have all benefited and reinforced the forest related activities of the farmers in the Rainy River District.

The implications of a study such as this are many. It has been shown in this paper that bush work is a major factor contributing to the continuance of farming in the Rainy River District. The physical constraints of low productivity and a harsh climate in the district make the area marginal for agriculture, and bush work (and its related returns) has provided the income necessary for helping many of the farmers earn a satisfactory living. In a large proportion of farming areas the winter season proves to be an idle period (in terms of total farm labour inputs) on most beef cow-calf operations. Although this is true in the Rainy River District, this long winter season is utilized effectively by the farmers who increase their overall income through cutting wood on Crown Lands. Those individuals who combine farming with winter bush work illustrate how part-time farming can successfully overcome low income farming problems in a physically marginal area.

Although a discussion of policy implications and part-time farming is not the purpose of this paper, this factor cannot be ignored. Because of the importance of the forest relationships and farming in the district, a program of well developed forest management policies for Crown Lands, A.R.D.A. holdings and deeded lands could provide the impetus for the maintenance of a well developed agricultural economy in the Rainy River District.

NOTES AND REFERENCES

1 These are farmers reporting any off-farm work for income. The term multiple jobholding is synonymous with the term part-time farming for the purpose of this study.

2 Calculated by adding the number of degrees above 42 degrees for all days between the dates of occurrence of 42 degrees.

3 This figure was calculated from examining contract records with management personnel in the Boise Cascade Mill in Fort Frances and from figures taken from the Census of Canada, Agriculture, 1971.

4 Legislation such as "The Revised Regulations Governing the Cutting of Pulpwood on Settler's Lands in Ontario," July 19th, 1928 (Department of Lands and Forests, Ontario) regulated the amount of pulpwood cut by setting contract limits dependent on the length of residence on the farm and the amount of land cleared that year.

5 This ten year period should remove those farmers who look at part-time farming as being a transition into or out of agriculture. A failure to achieve the transition in ten years or less will most likely reinforce the existing multiple jobholding situation as a continuing way of life for the farmer.

DISCUSSION OF THE PAPER BY
A. CAVAZZANI ON SOCIAL DETERMINANTS OF PART-TIME FARMING IN A MARGINAL REGION OF ITALY

V. Safvestad

I will comment only briefly on both the papers here, beginning with Professor Cavazzani's paper, I agree that, as agricultural economists, we have in the past overestimated the "agricultural side" of the problem. Now that geographers and sociologists are studying part-time farming, I hope that they do not make the mistake of going too far in some other direction. We need team work in this very difficult question of part-time farming. You spoke of external factors being of prime importance in the Italian context. This is true also in my country, Sweden. We have, in addition, a very important internal factor. In Sweden the number of farms is decreasing. New techniques and machinery create a surplus of labour — a process which should continue into the future with obvious implications for part-time farming. You mention the fact that in Italy part-time farming represents a "service" to the needs of the industry in the city. This is not true of my district in Sweden where many operators of small farms have become craftsmen and entrepreneurs situated right on their farms. This situation has also influenced small industrial plants to move into the district — a phenomenon specific to my area but well known in Europe. So we have the opposite direction of movement here.

DISCUSSION OF THE PAPER BY
R. BENSON ON PART-TIME FARMING IN A PHYSICALLY MARGINAL AREA OF NORTHERN ONTARIO

V. Safvestad

I now turn to Mr. Benson's paper the subject of which is more familiar to me. With respect to the "bush-farmers", you present no specific definition of a part-time farmer. Does "any" off-farm work qualify a farmer to be a part-time farmer? What about the family cycle? Does this influence a farmer's ability to acquire off-farm work in different periods of the cycle here in Canada? When discussing the economic conditions of part-time farming, have you considered the cost of travelling to the off-farm job? Here one has an obvious cost. Similarly there will be a cost involved if a farmer resides in a town for a period of the year. One should consider these alternate costs.

Both papers neglected to state part-time farming trends in the respective areas. Specifically in Canada, will mechanization in the forest industry result in fewer job opportunities for bush-farmers in the future? It appears to me that for the farmer it is a question of farm resources available. It would be interesting for both papers to discuss the relationship between land, labour and capital allocation at both the micro and macro level. What happens for example, to the size of farm area operated when some labour is removed and more capital is acquired (via the off-farm job)?

I found both papers to be very interesting and I should have liked to present a deeper analysis at this time.

QUESTION PERIOD

I. Vogeler (Geography, Northwestern)

Professor Cavazzani — you mentioned that originally some agricultural regions were so poor that people were leaving farms. However, with rural industrialization and job opportunities did individuals become part-time farmers because of low wages paid by industry and lack of unions? That is, was there a reverse case of people getting involved with some farming in fact subsidising industry and is it a mechanism that society uses to exploit the farmers?

A. Cavazzani (Sociology and Political Studies, Calabria)

I think that this is the effect because now, while some people are working for industry they do need this "subsistence" farming to supplement their incomes.

I. Vogeler (Geography, Northwestern)

But are industry and agriculture equal partners in promoting rural development? Many people in this country feel that by locating industry in a "poor" rural area one can promote a better harmony between the two sectors. It appears that in your example the benefits are unequal.

A. Cavazzani (Sociology and Political Studies, Calabria)

Yes, the benefits are not equal.

L. Reeds (Geography, McMaster)

Mr. Benson, I would like to know how many of your bush-farmers would be cutting their own woodlots? In that case it would not be "part-time" but rather part of the farm operation.

R. Benson (Ontario Ministry of Housing)

If you consider the traditional Southern Ontario situation with the woodlot comprising only a small portion of the farm area and providing occasional "farm" income from timber cut, then what happens in the north is quite different. Woodlots are acquired specifically for wood cutting purposes and may be quite apart from the farm proper. The practice of cutting wood on one's own farm was more prevelant in the past than it is now.

T. Usher (Natural Resources Branch)

Mr. Benson's paper appears to reflect the basic type of agriculture occurring on the Canadian Shield. We heard this morning that part-time farming is a funciton of the choice of the operator to do or not to do off-farm work in addition to farming. Does the bush-farmer actually have much of a "choice".

R. Benson (Ontario Ministry of Housing)

Traditionally, the bush work was part of the farm operation. In the early days wood harvesting equipment was relatively unsophisticated consisting of the axe and the saw and teams of horses to haul away the logs. Today however many farmers consciously invest much money in complicated bush cutting machines and it therefore does depend on the decision to enter this type of operation. Tradition does, of course, play a large part and many farmers simply accept the dual occupation as part of farming in this area.

M. Troughton (Geography, Western)

Professor Cavazzani — is the trend toward part-time farming in Southern Italy sufficient to retain people in the south?

A. Cavazzani (Sociology and Political Studies, Calabria)

No. Part-time farming appears as a short run solution in the total economic development scene.

SPECIAL SESSION

CHAIRMAN:	J.A. MAGE (Geography, Guelph, Canada)
PAPER:	D. GALAJ (Director, Institute of Rural Development, Warsaw, Poland)*
PAPER:	M. MUSZYNSKI (Institute of Rural Development, Warsaw Poland) "Part-Time Farming in Poland: Conclusions and Prospects"

*Paper read by M. Muszynski in the absence of D. Galaj
The main papers appear in the "Papers In Absentia" section.

PART-TIME FARMING IN POLAND —
CONCLUSIONS AND PROSPECTS

Marek Muszynski

Part-time farmers constitute almost 30% of the total employment in the non-agricultural sectors of the national economy. In such sectors as transport, construction and agricultural services, their proportion is considerably greater. The labour potential actually represented by the peasant-workers in Poland is very great. Taking into consideration the somewhat lower average productivity of this population (due to the diverse occupational structure, lower skill levels, etc.), it can be estimated that the part-time farmers produce 25-28% of the national income. Many prognostications indicate that, even in the future, the role of this group, though relatively reduced, will still be very important in the development of the national economy. The permanence of such a significant role for the peasant-workers in the sphere of material production was, and is, possible in Poland for several reasons:

First, by calculating the approximate productivity of both part-time farmers and workers on the job and also the productivity of peasant-worker farms up to a certain size, it was demonstrated that a two-fold increase in the employment of peasant-workers had a positive or neutral effect on productivity. Only after crossing the spatial threshold does the productivity of the peasant-worker fall, both on the job and on the farm. The same can be said about the length of the trip to the place of work: the shorter the trip, the more productive the work.

Second, the extremely high cost of obtaining labour very frequently increases the number of peasant-workers because it is more advantageous to employ the manpower reserves from the rural areas than to create the conditions for their permanent migration from the village to the city.´

Third, the dual occupation population is characterized by high mobility in both time and space.

Fourth, the objective and subjective difficulties of expanding apartment construction and the social infra-structure for the peasant-workers have played a basic role here. In the concrete situation of our country, which meant a reliance upon agrarian overpopulation, an abundance of manpower and a lack of investment funds, it was easier to offer employment to the part-time farmers and expand the means of transportation for them. The actual calculations indicate that the costs of transportation to average-size Polish cities from a 20 km. radius are lower than the costs of apartment construction, and this is the zone of residence preferred by the peasant-workers. However, the majority of peasant-workers commute from a greater distance, and thus, the cost analysis will have to be revised to take into account the future spatial structure of the hub city and the settlements of the part-time farmers.

Fifth, in the past, the relatively slow growth of real wages, especially in the case of unskilled workers, retarded, or ruled out, permanent migration and the uni-directional orientation to work.

In regard to the continued evolution of their employment and work, in regard to the necessity of their completing their education, one cannot give a uniformly positive evaluation of the various groups of part-time farmers. Even if their positive role in past concrete conditions in Poland did not evoke reservations, the practice of two primitive occupations cannot be recognized as desirable in the future. In this connection, a program is now being worked out in Poland for the gradual alleviation of this problem by the diminution of the numbers, the internal transformation, and the displacement of this population to cities, or special settlements surrounding the cities, which employ the part-time farmers.

The problem of the peasant-worker population cannot be solved by **one** economic manoeuver. This problem, as an object of suitable state policy, must be solved gradually. The well-founded opinion exists that this policy cannot set as a goal for itself the final liquidation of this phenomenon, but must undertake the means which would give it the form and dimensions corresponding to the interests of the entire national economy and to the development of the social relations of the rural and urban population. Generally speaking, the solution to the problem of part-time farmers in Poland must also provide the basic part of the process for the socialist reconstruction of the village and agriculture. For portions of the dual occupation population, and also for portions of the presently purely agricultural population, it is necessary to make possible their final departure from agriculture and the village. For this purpose the following, among others, would be relevant:

1) to create the conditions and stimuli for the gradual passing of the dual occupation population to one occupation, mainly outside agriculture;

2) to increase the possibilities of absorption of the rural population by the centers of growth (cities) through the expansion of apartment construction;

3) to ensure differential forms of moving from the village to the city, or its suburbs, adapting them to the preferences of the population shifting from agricultural to non-agricultural jobs;

4) to assist the dual occupation population residing in the distantly situated settlement units of the lowest rank (villages) in the exchange of their place of residence and in their transfer to neighbourhoods of their place of work.

Limitation of the growth tendency of the rural dual occupation population and acceleration of the process of passing from the position of farmer to the position of employee in a socialized enterprise ought to be the basic goal of a complex program for solving the problem of securing manpower from agriculture for non-agricultural occupations. A measure of significance of this problem is the following numerical data. If, in the five year period 1971-1975, total employment in Poland grew by approximately 1.8 million people, then in the years 1986-1990 the increment of workers reaching productive age will increase total employment by about 300,000 persons annually. The village will then be the basic source of manpower reserves, which is why the plan for the solution of the peasant-worker question is taken under consideration today.

131

This plan must be both an integral part of the plan for the spatial management of the country and its various regions and also the ordering of the networks of rural and urban settlements. In this matter the main concern is meeting the desire of the rural dual occupation population wishing to own their own house, garden, or plot. In this regard, various possibilities are presently being discussed for changing the place of residence of this population, such as:

1) an apartment of the urban, high-rise type;

2) an apartment of the urban, high-rise type and the ownership of a separate garden plot in or near the city;

3) a private, single-family house in high density areas, with or without a garden plot in or near the city;

4) a private, single-family house in a settlement of peasant-workers of low density and with a garden plot.

In addition, there are opinions that it is necessary to admit the possibility of the peasant-worker family keeping its residence in the village and conveying its land to the State Land Fund. On the one hand, this would favour the emergence of a group of workers residing in the village, and, on the other, would favour the creation of a healthier agrarian structure. It is this form which is to be preferred in areas a short distance from work (5-7 km.). This assumes that the transportation network will permit relatively convenient commuting to work by private or public means.

The principles of apartment allocation (or private houses in the city or in peasant-worker settlements), the principles of payment, the size of garden plots, the city planning design of these settlements, the social infra-structure, the employment of peasant-worker family members, etc., are all problems requiring penetrating studies adequate for both the present and future conditions of projected solutions. Even at this moment, however, agreement can be found on the necessity of observing the preferences of some groups of this population in order to keep the development of this process in the desired direction. These preferences ought to take into account the interests of the general public, those of the non-agricultural work establishments and service institutions, the interests of agriculture and spatial aspects. This means that the program for solving the part-time farmer question should, above all, concern itself with:

1) farmers and peasant-workers from distantly located settlement units, for the purpose of reducing the social costs connected with transporting them to work;

2) farmers and peasant-workers from settlement units who are included in the population proposed for relocation, such relocation limited to the ordering of the settlement network and adapting it to new settlement configurations;

3) farmers and peasant-workers from settlement units forecasted for liquidation in the plans for spatial management of rural regions;

4) farmers and peasant-workers whose departure from the village is favourable to an improvement of the agrarian structure and better land management, that is, those farmers from undeveloped farms which are evolving in the direction of kitchen gardens;

5) peasant families containing several children and several generations from which several members have already taken or can easily take up wage work outside agriculture;

6) young farmers wishing to permanently move to the city and have no future interest in taking over or running their own farm;

7) peasant-workers whose relocation to the vicinity of their work is advisable considering the type and nature of their practiced profession.

The relocated groups of the rural population ought to be entitled to the right of priority in the shift of residence and also to material and financial assistance from non-agricultural establishments and the state. The type, scope and form of this material and financial assistance ought to:

— be consistent with the general principles for the socio-economic and cultural development of the country;

— accelerate the tempo of transformation of the peasant-worker groups into a population with a uni-directional occupational orientation;

— stimulate the selection of variants more economical in terms of the cost of transforming the dual occupational population into single occupational.

The system of priorities ought to be sufficiently differentiated so that it might ensure the achievement of the goals mentioned above in regard to particular groups of farms and particular regions of the country. Specific priorities are required for those peasant-workers who give up running the farm and, for example, transfer the land to the state treasury, but remain in the village, continually commuting to work. For the older farmers in this group it would be likewise necessary to create a retirement priority, even if their term of work in socialized work establishments is relatively short. In such situations, the basis for obtaining pension rights also ought to be work on their own farms in the period prior to undertaking work outside agriculture.

Thus, the program presently being prepared in Poland for solving the part-time farmer question has to equally take into account the needs of the general public, the concrete stage of the economic and socio-cultural development of the country, and the needs resulting from the necessity for the socialistic reconstruction of agriculture. It has also to take into account the concrete situation, both economic and socio-cultural, in which the peasant-workers today find themselves and in which they will find themselves in the future when the level of Poland's development is considerably higher.

QUESTION PERIOD

Question

If the government does buy the land will it then be rented back to another more prosperous or more efficient farmer? Or what happens to the land once the government has acquired it?

M. Muszynski (Institute of Rural Development, Poland)

Fifteen per cent of the land in Poland belongs to the government. We have very new and modern big farms belonging to the government but the cost of such farms is much higher than the cost of private farms.

The farms belonging to the government are wonderful but the government, that is society as a whole, must pay for them. Such agriculture, although costly, is necessary in Poland if we are to make the step forward. These are the farms of the next century.

I. Vogeler (Geography, Northwestern)

Is there any attempt to encourage those people who own very small parcels of land to be among the first to offer their land for sale?

M. Muszynski (Institute of Rural Development, Poland)

Peasants in Poland are very close to the earth and it is very difficult — even if they only subsist — to create something new, to change the mentality and to tell an older farmer who may farm many tiny parcels of land that he should amalgamate his parcels into one. At the present we do not want to interfere too much with the old structures.

P. Brasher (Tiny Tay Planning Board)

What would be the population of the average village that you are planning?

M. Muszynski (Institute of Rural Development, Poland)

We would like to have not more than about 5,000 people in a village. But this is not a strict rule. The size of the village will depend on the size of the factories which may employ up to 10,000 people. So the size of the city will be as big as is necessary.

Question

The conditional approach in Poland and all socialist countries in Eastern Europe appears to have been that you put people in the city as a more advanced stage economically and socially. Your smaller villages seem to be an attempt to make your cities a little more "human", but do you think that as Poland becomes more advanced that you will have the situation that we have here — that is, well-educated and high income people who want to go back to the land and leave the cities?

M. Muszynski (Institute of Rural Development, Poland)

What we would like to do is take the next step. We do not want the situation of people coming to big cities and then leaving them. We would like to study the situation that is here in Canada and that is why I am here. We found that after a period of time, and after some process of industrialization, people leave the town to live in the country. They buy farms similar to your hobby farms as I discovered today. So we would like to take the steps faster. We want to have the small villages with land around them for people to farm. We know it is a very serious problem because, for example, in Russia 30% of the meat is produced on small holdings. We understand the problem and we want to move forward today.

M. Troughton (Geography, Western)

Does the housing stock in the existing cities and in the villages that will be built also belong to the state?

M. Muszynski (Institute of Rural Development, Poland)

All the houses in Poland built in big cities belong to people who are living in the houses. It means they are communities. A house which has 100 flats belongs to 100 families. The same applies to houses in the new villages. Of course there are some people who are not wealthy enough to buy the flats and in this case they are given the flats. For example, if there is a factory in an area requiring some engineers or some unskilled labour, housing will be provided for the workers. So part of the housing belongs to the government.

A. Cavazzani (Sociology and Political Studies, Calabria)

What proportion of food production comes from the private section of your agriculture ? Are you independent in food production, or do you import food?

M. Muszynski (Institute of Rural Development, Poland)

About 80 per cent of the food is produced by the private sector. Generally, we are independent in food production and we export some agricultural produce. We import some wheat but we export meat. In the category of value, it depends on world prices so that we can have a net gain or loss.

SESSION II

PROBLEMS ASSOCIATED WITH PART-TIME FARMING — NEWCOMERS TO AGRICULTURE

CHAIRMAN: D.W. HOFFMAN (Centre for Resources Development, Guelph)

PAPER: M. TROUGHTON (Geography, Western, Canada)
"Hobby Farming in the London Area of Ontario"

PAPER: G. HUTCHISON (Continuing Education, Guelph, Canada)
"Educating the Novice Farmer"

HOBBY FARMING IN THE LONDON AREA OF ONTARIO

M. Troughton

INTRODUCTION

The so-called "hobby farm" has become an integral element of the rural-urban fringe of many North American cities. One might categorize "hobby farms" as a sub-set of part-time farming on the basis of certain economic and operational criteria; namely that only a small part, if any, of the owner's income derives from the farm, and that the labour input is part-time. However, "hobby farms" are characterized by other criteria — economic, social, behavioural — which make it appropriate, at least in this context, to distinguish them as a separate type.

"Hobby Farming" is specifically an urban-related phenomenon. Various types of exurban development (villa, estate, etc.) have been known for centuries, but today's affluence, mobility, and a status conscious society has produced a mass version of the "hobby farm" or rural estate. The "hobby farmer" is essentially urban based as to income and employment. The farm may be acquired for a number of reasons which may or may not include the farming component. The farm is rarely required to furnish substantial basic income. Although a definition of "hobby farm" has not been found, the following by Anderson of the (larger) estate farm is highly indicative:

> Estate farming is an agricultural activity engaged
> in by persons who have made their investment in
> farming from earnings made in non-agricultural
> occupations and who are interested in farming
> primarily as a hobby or for prestige[1].

The phenomenon, however, has its variations; with growth has come a widening of the traditional socio-economic groups engaging in "hobby farming", and a variety of sizes and styles of property are involved. Recreation *per se,* status, as well as privacy, rural amenity and life style are placed alongside some type of agricultural land use. Like any pattern of land tenure, "hobby farming", in a particular temporal and spatial setting, is the result of dynamic interaction between economic, social and institutional attributes. As with part-time farming, the "hobby farm" poses questions as to its form and function relative to structural change in agriculture, **and** to the processes of urbanization and repopulation of the countryside. Do "hobby farms", for example, contribute to or benefit agricultural land use or production? Do they preserve or enhance a rural life style or set of amenities, or are they essentially the vanguard of a more thorough urban transformation?

The empirical evidence to be noted will be that of studies in the London, Ontario area; a pilot study of two years ago,[2] and an ongoing enlargement which seeks to investigate the relationships between part-time and "hobby farming", and the urban-fringe

137

location. However, given the incomplete nature of those results and the belief that "hobby farms" merit consideration on a separate basis, this paper will attempt to broaden the discussion and look briefly at the following:

1) the antecedents to today's "hobby farms" — estates and the criteria they established;

2) the current frame of reference for "hobby farming" as a mass phenomenon;

3) the case for and against "hobby farming" and;

4) exemplification of the characteristics and relationships of "hobby farms" using the London area studies.

Antecedents

Although we are concerned with what is a current and primarily a North American phenomenon, certain characteristics associated with "hobby farms" have a long lineage, review of which provides a temporal and cultural perspective in which to view the contemporary situation and criteria.

Although a permanent rural/farm situation was the way of life for the global majority until very recently, there have been significant urban places since the second millenia B.C., and elements of an **urban to rural** movement can be discerned at an early date. In Alexandrian Greece (400 B.C.), Classical Rome (200 B.C.) and T'ang Sung China (150 A.D.) wealthy inhabitants of early cities had begun to develop a re-attachment to the rural life style as an adjunct and an antidote to city life. Western and eastern urbanites looked to the settled countryside to provide a pastoral and relaxed or garden-like and aesthetic counterpoint respectively, to the noise and stress of the city.[3] To furnish this **recreative** base, country estates or villas were established within access to the city. While in some cases the estates were ancestral homes and/or provided the income for city life, in many other cases the villas were independently established and other factors placed before their economic worth.

The estates were for **an elite minority,** but in Italy in particular every city has villas in the surrounding countryside which are links with Etruscan, Roman, Florentine, or Venetian city state systems. Elsewhere in Europe in the Middle Ages, in a less urban society, estates were virtually the preserve of royalty and a few nobles, which gave them even greater **prestige**. Royal preserves were often set aside as hunting forests rather than farmland, which may explain the concepts of "parkland" and of "the chase" widely associated with estate living. Fox-hunting, for example, was widely diffused in England by the 18th century, and appeared in association with estates in the United States in the 1880's, and has a long aristocratic, country-gentleman association.[4]

Membership in elite groups tied to specific pursuits, however, was less significant than **land ownership and status within a landed class.** In Europe at least, and in early colonial America, achievement and status were naturally rewarded with land (and title) as a

138

source of wealth. With the coming of the Industrial Revolution other sources of wealth emerged, and stronger distinctions between man and land developed. However the Industrial Revolution, which formed the basis for the major rural to urban migration and the attendant changes in post-feudal agriculture, also created a growing number of persons with capital derived independent of land.

In England the newly-rich industrialists created a new breed of "gentleman-farmers". Their estates were usually close to the source of wealth, but the object was physical and social separation from the industrial milieu. Often this was achieved by re-establishment of almost feudal relationships with the rural population. Despite a more egalitarian rural society, the rise of a similar concentration of estates associated with the large industrial cities of N.E. United States occurred in the 19th century.

The estate style, in practically every case, developed markedly **different land use patterns** from those of contemporary agriculture. Although some estate owners were renowned for their experimental and innovative farm practices, overall considerations of recreation and style were the main determinants. Where agriculture was carried out, the stress was on animal breeding of a prestigious type — purebred cattle and sheep, and thoroughbred horses. The latter, in particular, reflected the place of equine pursuits in upper-class rural society. Some of the most distinctive rural landscapes are found where a concentration of this type of specialist activity occurs, for example the Newmarket area in England or the Kentucky Bluegrass country in the United States.[5]

To summarize this brief review; a small, but significant reverse flow of urban to rural population and investment gave rise to various versions of the country estate. Commonly held characteristics included the urban origin, the exurban location, and the acquisition and development of land for primarily residential, recreational and prestige purposes, with agricultural land uses absent or in a subordinate role. In many cases estate farms were part of a process which tended to establish an elite society separate from both its urban roots and from indiginous rural society.

CURRENT CRITERIA

The dominant population movement in the twentieth century has been from farm to city. However, as cities attracted more people, their character has changed. Especially in North America there has been movement outward — dispersion, suburbanization — for which the three elements of automobile based mobility, rising general middle class affluence, and availability of land are generally held responsible.

In looking at the current situation therefore we find a gross distinction from earlier times, in that "hobby farms" are now part of, rather than distinct from a general population trend, that they form part of a tenure continuum stretching from the suburban lot to the large "estate". On the other hand there is surprising continuity in the set of values and criteria that seem to underly the type.

139

In England, the Gilchrist-Shirlaw provides the following description:

> The proximity of London has influenced the farming system in a rather interesting way; Surrey has long been regarded as the home of the hobby farmer and there are certainly quite a number of successful businessmen who travel to London each day and concentrate on farming in the evenings, at weekends, and during vacations. The holdings of these farmers often stand out because of the high investment in new buildings and other improvements — often higher than the natural fertility of the land would appear to warrant. The farms are usually devoted to the breeding and rearing of high performance pedigree cattle. Because of the demand for such farms, land prices are maintained at a higher level than for similar land in other parts of the country.[6]

Clearly the urban influence is strong. The businessmen are a particular group of persons who are making investment capital and for whom the hobby farm is also a useful tax deduction. The reference to land prices is supported by many observers of the "urban fringe" who have noted the development of economic rent structures to the disadvantage of conventional agriculture. Of special significance are the economic rent functions of demand peaking at the city edge for land for exurban residential, recreational and speculative purposes — each function associated with "hobby farm" investment.[7]

Fraser-Hart describes a similar "Gentleman-Farm Belt" which reaches its greatest extent in association with the Eastern U.S. "megalopolis". It reflects, he says, a mass escape from the cities of newly affluent urbanites seeking open space, recreation, and a residential setting long confined to the rich. This "urban fringe" is still associated with horses and hunting, and is closely linked to the wealthy suburban set of land uses — golf and country clubs, nurseries, private schools, riding stables, gift and antique stores. The larger "hobby farm" properties represent the epitome of prestige exurban living where large amounts of capital are being spent to fashion a quite distinct type of countryside in which the social and economic values are specifically non-commercial farm.[8] Other studies in the United States have described the transfer of farm properties into recreational-residential units[9], and the strength of the suburban equine and other "amenity agriculture" forms.

The broad attractions of exurban life and the development of rural estates or "hobby farms" has been noted in relation to many Canadian cities. "Hobby farms" have been acquired to provide "rural living", which includes freedom from the city and its "problems", private recreation space, or an investment, which may be pure speculation or a hedge against inflation. In recent years a number of people have bought farm properties which they may or may not continue to farm. Tax laws may make it advantageous to engage in agricultural activity but the required minimum may be attained at a very low level of intensity.[10]

140

Perhaps the best documented account of exurban development in which "hobby farming" has a strong role, is that of the exurban areas of Toronto by Punter for Central Mortgage and Housing Corporation.[11] This study reveals a general pattern consistent with the place of "hobby farming" in the urbanizing region, but also indicates how certain contacts can affect the resultant socio-economic and land use pattern.

Major exurban development began in the 1930s when wealthy Toronto entrepreneurs established estates north of the city in the classic mould, complete with hunting and fishing clubs and thorough-bred horses and cattle. In the 1940s and 1950s suburban expansion included some dispersed exurban, largely residential development, but in the 1960s lot size restrictions, zoning by-laws, and the willingness of farmers to sell, led to the purchase of many "hobby farm" lots from ten acres and up. Punter makes three very significant observations about the sequence of development: the establishment of first ten and then twenty acre minimum lot sizes encouraged a large residential estate or "hobby farm" lot pattern to develop; the more stringent the controls (i.e. larger minimum lots) the more expensive and exclusive the development; and the use of zoning is now being applied by the exurban (hobby) group to preserve a large-lot, rural elite situation. What has happened in Toronto's exurbia is the creation of a much more sharply segregated socio-economic "hobby farm" population. Land prices have been inflated and conventional agriculture has declined markedly. Other significant findings include the attraction for, and subsequent private alienation of, much of the best scenic-recreation land, especially associated with the Niagara Escarpment (land not particularly suited to agriculture); and everywhere a stress in terms of investment in such prestige elements as the residence, fencing, ponds, landscaping and recreational amenities.

Thus, despite the transformation of the exclusive estate into the mass "hobby farm" the carry-over of estate characteristics is remarkable and the urban linkage is dominant.

The "hobby farm" is strongly associated with the "urban fringe" whether that area is being developed in orderly fashion or on a piecemeal basis. The factors of sprawl, ribbon development, high land prices, non-conforming uses etc. that have been seen as so detrimental to conventional agriculture, do not seem to affect the demand for land by urbanites — rather one might even say that "hobby farming" is another characteristic of the "urban fringe" and a result of the processes at work creating that fringe zone.

Status and prestige are relative, but despite a spreading of wealth, no one driving through some of the "hobby farm" areas north of Toronto can doubt their presence in terms of some of the architecture and amenity investment. The "hobby farm" carries a strong connotation of being part of a private recreation, leisure oriented landscape.

Turning to definition in more conventional agricultural terms, i.e. land tenure, operation and income, some general characteristics may be noted, albeit with wide variation within the type. Land ownership seems to be largely of a private freehold nature, especially where the owner is a resident. In some areas group or partnership investment is encountered and may be associated with land speculation or with intensive agriculture via a farm manager. The distinction between resident and non-resident ownership is not well documented but is likely to have a marked effect on land use. Farm size is perhaps the most variable aspect of "hobby farms". Where one moves from residential lot to "hobby farm" is often problematic, and arbitrary cut-offs have been developed both statistically (e.g. Census) and on institutional grounds (e.g. Land Assessment). The operation of the "hobby farm" may reside in the owner, or in a manager or tenant. Often the owner's main interest is in the residence and amenity aspects and he may rent out crop or pasture areas. It follows that the labour input of the owner may vary, but an emphasis on custom operations has been noted.

Investment in the property is often very large. Initial prices tend to be above the market level for farmland. Heavy investment in the residence, special buildings, and amenities (e.g. fencing, ponds, tree planting, landscaping) is common. On the other hand the most clear-cut characteristic is a low return to investment and the fact that the farm rarely contributes a significant amount to the owner's income. The possible realization of capital gains and the contribution to tax deductions should not be ignored, however.[12]

None of the foregoing factors satisfactorily defines "hobby farms", nor do they separate them clearly from other part-time farms. It is the less tangible aspects of the urban association and life style that make the difference.

THE PROS AND CONS OF "HOBBY FARMING"

On the basis of the characteristics associated with "hobby farming", and particularly the association with urbanization and the relative decline of conventional agriculture, it is logical that sharp distinctions are made as to the value of "hobby farming".

The proponents of "hobby farming" cite the following as advantages. "Hobby farms", like other part-time farms, retain land either in agricultural use, or "banked" against future demand. They maintain a farming stock and may contribute something to food production. For conventional farmers they often provide a supply of cheap rental land in otherwise prohibitively expensive zones, and save him the costs of farm enlargement. They may also give employment through a demand for custom operations. In a few cases the "hobby farm" may be the means of entry into full-time farming. Most cited, however, is the role of the "hobby farmer" as a preserver of rural amenity and life style and the only person able to invest in that amenity. Fraser-Hart makes the point:

City people who use the countryside can do much to help maintain its beauty and prevent its deterioration by spending their money to keep it attractive, whereas most working farmers can no longer afford the luxury of doing so. Most city folk who own land in the country can do their bit, but by far the most impressive examples are the showplace gentleman farms ... The gentleman farmer likes to gaze out on well-kept fields and pastures and fine livestock. His ability to pay for what he likes has created some of the most beautiful rural landscapes in the United States.[4]

In a statement a few years ago Everett Biggs, commenting on "hobby farms in Ontario", made the distinction between the "small lot exurban" population who are generally undesirable elements in the rural landscape and those "hobby farmers" who have purchased larger holdings and who

> seem to be motivated largely by a desire to recapture, if only on a part-time basis — a rural **good** way of life, who invest heavily in farm improvements — encourage preservation — and sound land use planning to ensure the future agricultural nature of his holding.[13]

Biggs' arbitrary cut-off between "small lot" and "hobby farm" was ten acres, and his comments mask the variety of motive and operation that may occur at any size.

The detractors of "hobby farms" would discount much of the agricultural value attached by Biggs and cite the following disadvantages: that most "hobby farms" remove land from conventional agriculture either entirely or to the level of low intensity of use, and are thereby part of the process of loss of farms and productive farmland to urban uses. Further, that although the land may be held in an extensive situation, the prices paid for it induce farmers to sell, and the prices received upon conversion to intensive urban uses are speculative gains at agriculture's expense. In the wider sense in the exurban landscape, the "hobby farm" contributes to the alienation of land from public (especially recreational) uses through the buying up of attractive landscapes, and elsewhere is often undistinguishable as part of "urban sprawl" or "ribbon development". Lands fragmented into relatively small "hobby farms" can never be reassembled into working farms. Last but not least, "hobby farmers", although swelling a depleted rural population, are often accused of distorting rural values or of being part of elite societies which are alien to the rural tradition.

THE LONDON AREA

London, with a relatively small metropolitan area and population (ca. 250,000), is somewhat isolated from other urban influences, situated in the midst of agricultural land that is of optimum quality for Canada. In the surrounding municipalities over 90% of all land is Class 1 or 2 Capability for Agriculture and over 80% is cropland. Prosperous agriculture and relatively poor Recreational Capability (over 85% Class 6) might be expected to offset exurban development and "hobby farming".

Nevertheless an extensive "urban fringe" can and has been documented. In 1960 an "urban shadow" zone was delimited of twice the built-up area of the city. It extended into the adjacent townships, was marked by ribbon development, and included farmland for sale in non-farm uses and assessed non-farm.[14] Among the components of the "urban fringe" are increasing numbers of part-time farm operations, many operators taking advantage of the varied employment opportunities and ease of commuting in the locality. In addition, "fringe" uses such as riding stables, golf courses, sod farms, gravel pits etc., are well in evidence. Although there has been space for extensive suburban development in the city, especially since annexation in 1961, the population is affluent with a high proportion of managerial and professional persons capable of generating exurban demand and development.

No specific information on "hobby farms" existed prior to 1973. At that time the study by Hale was conducted in the six immediately adjacent townships.[15] Hale's study, from which most of the illustrative material presented here originates, focussed particularly on identifying the gross numbers of "hobby farmers", their occupations, locations, and the physical characteristics of the property units. A present study of an enlarged area of thirteen townships (to a perimeter of ca twenty-five miles) seeks to consolidate the earlier approach over a wider area, and to explore further characteristics of the "hobby farmers" (socio-economic, behavioural) and their relationships to other operators and to the processes at work in the urbanizing area. Among the "hobby farm" characteristics that are of most concern are the decision-making processes which underly the purchase, operation and disposal of the "hobby farm", the nature and potential of land uses on the farms, and the relative merits of "hobby" and other types of farm operations to serve the varying land use requirements of an urbanizing region.

A few of the hypothesized relationships concerning "hobby farms" may be noted, as follows:

1) — an increase in the number of "hobby farms" is paralleling that in part-time farming and the growth of the city;
 — "hobby farm" locations will be concentrated close to the edge of the city;
 — "hobby farmers" will show strong evidence of their continued urban attachment (employment, income, contacts) and will have a socio-economic profile markedly distinct from that of part-time and full-time operators.

2) — "hobby farmers" will show a locational preference for certain less agriculturally suitable land, evidencing a desire for recreational or scenic landscape amenities;
 — the majority of workable land held as part of "hobby farms" will be rented out to other full-time farmers;
 — "hobby farm" land use will evidence a preference for horses, pasture and woodland, and the labour and capital investment will be to those ends.

3) — the prime function and consequent values attached to "hobby farms" will be largely in terms of residence;
 — prices paid for "hobby farms" will be above those paid for normal farms;
 — the land holdings will generally be smaller.

4) — "hobby farms" will contribute very few persons to full-time farming;
   — agricultural production from "hobby farming" will be of little actual or potential value;
   — the income generated from farm activities by "hobby farmers" will be negligible.

5) — "hobby farmers" will expresss strong preferences for controls on land sales and land use zoning to preserve rural land use and amenity.

NUMBERS AND DISTRIBUTION

There are approximately four thousand census farms in the thirteen townships around London, and a considerably larger number of property units that carry the assessment designation of "farm". Hale's study suggested that "hobby farms" over ten acres in size accounted for ca. 18% of the census farms in the six inner townships. Taking into account an expected decline in numbers with distance from the city (below), but comparing the 1975 estimate for inner and outer townships, a figure of ca. 15% of census farms is suggested. More meaningful, however, is the count with respect to assessed property units, insofar as some "hobby farms" are included in census/commercial farms as rented parcels. In this case, preliminary figures suggest that some 10% of property parcels over five acres may be classified as "hobby farms". Hale noted, and the current study supports, considerable variation in relative density between townships. Several reasons could account for this: the existence of land particularly attractive for "hobby farms" (or unattractive for conventional farms), the presence of major access routes, or differential controls on sales of rural lots. No one reason can be advanced at the township level, although it is worth noting that Westmister with the highest incidence (24%), is the township which until recently lacked any sort of official plan or zoning bylaw.

"Hobby farms" occur as a scatter of individual locations around the city (Figure 1). Three locational relationships may be examined; the distance relationship to the city, the relationship to major access routes to the city, and location with reference to landscape variation about the city.

A plot of the distance of "hobby farms" from the centre of London (Figure 2), although inhibited by an absolute limit of ca. fifteen miles, suggests support for a preference for locations close to the city. The peak is reached at ca. eight miles from the city centre but generally within three miles of the edge. The decay function is strikingly similar to those proposed by Found to describe residential, recreational and speculative land demands outside the city. The proportions whereby the respective demands contribute to the overall curve is being investigated.

Each major access route to London (except Highway 401) has "hobby farms" located along it. However, preliminary measures fail to establish a significant proportion of "hobby farms" as highway located. It may be that the main highways are generally unattractive on the basis of ribbon residential and commercial development, and the consequent lack of scenic value. Overall the network of both

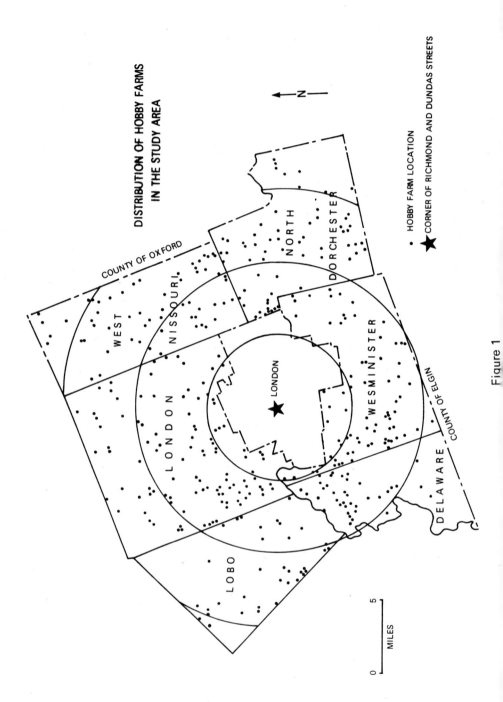

DISTRIBUTION OF HOBBY FARMS
IN THE STUDY AREA

N

• HOBBY FARM LOCATION
★ CORNER OF RICHMOND AND DUNDAS STREETS

COUNTY OF OXFORD

WEST

NISSOURI

NORTH

DORCHESTER

LONDON

LONDON

WESMINISTER

COUNTY OF ELGIN

LOBO

DELAWARE

0   5
MILES

Figure 1

CUMULATIVE TOTAL OF "HOBBY FARM" PROPERTIES BY DISTANCE FROM LONDON'S CBD

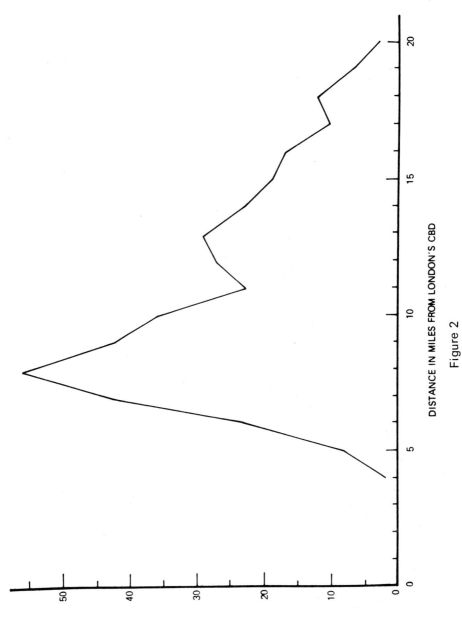

OCCURANCE OF "HOBBY FARM" PROPERTIES

DISTANCE IN MILES FROM LONDON'S CBD

Figure 2

paved and unpaved township roads is sufficiently dense to make access little problem. There is some suggestion, however, that location close to one of the dormitory villages is assuming increasing importance.

One of the most interesting relationships suggested for "hobby farmers" is that between location and landscape, in terms of postulated preferences for particular features. It has been suggested that among the landscape elements which would both attract "hobby farmers" from a scenic or recreational point of view, and possibly detract from use for conventional agriculture, are rough terrain, steep, wooded slopes, streams and ponds, and low capability agricultural land.

Initial comparison may be made between the "hobby farm" locations and assessments of the landscape in terms of single or multiple features. Two recent landscape evaluations have been prepared for the London area. In one Scott and Nelson used a modified version of the McHarg overlay technique to isolate areas of outstanding attraction in terms of accumulated natural and cultural features with potential for use as conservation of outdoor education centres.[16] Overlay indicates that each of the four areas chosen has a high density of "hobby farms". Another evaluation was that produced in connection with the assessment of the environmental impact of a Hydro Corridor through the area.[17] A wide variety of criteria were assessed on a 500 metre grid mesh with the aid of computerized data handling and mapping. Two maps in particular, "Natural Landscape Diversity", and "Recreational Impact" identify the physically more diverse and recreationally attractive areas. In each case there is a strong suggestion of "hobby farmers" having exercised locational preference for the areas depicted.

However, the London area landscape is subtle rather than spectacular, and a more refined examination of individual "hobby farm" locations in respect of soil conditions, presence or absence of water, woodland, etc. would be preferable. Hale went some way in this task. Comparing the overall occurrence of Class 1 soil capability and of physical limitations to agriculture, to "hobby farm" location, distinctions significant at the 99% level were found in each case (Table 1). Hobby farmers seem to avoid Class 1 land and to prefer features such as poor drainage and topography which downgrade land for agriculture. Hale was also able to find some indication that both water and topographic variation were preferred features. At present, plans are to digitise each hobby farm and compare the polygons to those for each physical feature and capability rating. In addition, a questionnaire asks for information as to whether physical features were influential at the time of purchase.

Socio-Economic Characteristics

A very wide range of characteristics have potential significance with respect to characterizing "hobby farms" and "hobby farmers". Many of these are only available through interview, but there is information on some and indications in further directions.

Table 1

Comparison of Acreages with Class 1 Capability for Agriculture or Acreages with Topographic Constraints to Agriculture with "Hobby Farm" Occurrence Within the Same Areas

(per cent)

	Total	West Missouri	North Dorchester	West-Minster	Delaware	Lobo	London
Total Percentage of ARDA Class 1 Agricultural Soils (Acres)	62	76	52	69	42	61	62
Occurrence of Sample on Class 1 Agricultural Soils	26	20	30	21	9	17	30
Total Percentage of Soils with Constraints to Agriculture due to Topography (Acres)	18	12	22	25	7	25	15
Occurrence of Sample Properties on Soils with Constraints to Agriculture due to Topography.	57	36	56	81	23	69	57

"Hobby farms", with some notable exceptions, are much smaller than the average census or commercial farm. "Hobby farms" average only slightly over fifty acres in size (median group twenty-six to fifty acres) compared to the average farm size in the London area of over 150 acres (70-129 acres median). This size distinction is not only statistically significant, but is strongly suggestive of the inability of "hobby farms" to function as commercial operations. Most management studies suggest that commercial operations, except for horticulture or broilers, require at least in excess of 100 acres (usually over 200 acres) to be economically viable. There are a few large properties (which are also located on better agricultural land), and there may be a significant distinction between those for which a commercial venture is possible and those for which it seems unlikely.

Tenure conditions with respect to "hobby farms" vary considerably. The majority of resident holdings are individually owned, but many of the non-resident properties (which Hale did not class as "hobby farms") are owned by groups or companies and there is a suggestion of speculation there. There is considerable evidence of rental of land, although no precise figures are available at this time.

"Hobby farmers" profess a variety of occupations and the significant facts are the predominance of certain groups, generally less well represented in either overall urban or rural populations. Hale identified two particular groups: the managerial, administrative and professional (30%); and the processing, machine and equipment operators, and construction trades (49%). The former incidence was expected; the latter a slight surprise. Present studies are tending to confirm the findings although the "blue collar" proportion is reduced somewhat if non-residents are included. Nevertheless these two groups dominate, and one must then ask if they reveal similar or divergent characteristics as to either properties or their operation and motivation. Preliminary evidence gives a slight suggestion that the professional group is more conscious of location with respect to landscape features.

To date there are no hard data on overall or farm generated income, except that the majority of owners belong to above average income occupation categories. In terms of investment, studies are being carried out with respect to prices paid for land. These seem to be well above average farm prices, but whether they are higher than land prices generally in the "fringe" area remains to be seen.

From the Assessment Rolls, Hale was able to suggest that "hobby farmers" were concentrating their investment in the residential aspect of property. Assessed values for land were comparable to other properties but those for buildings were high, and in most cases this was taken to mean the residence *per se*.

This last item returns us to the more subjective aspects of status and prestige. There have always been a few large "estates" in the London area, belonging initially to soldiers, latterly to successful businessmen. Several of them engage in purebred cattle breeding, with the operations under skilled management. There is also a fully-fledged hunt in London operating from an exclusive golf and country club, although how many "hobby farmers" are members has not yet been ascertained. Although London has nothing to match the

150

spectacular "estate" architecture north of Toronto, there are increasing numbers of substantial rural residences. There is some evidence that in some exurban locations, the residents have realized the collective amenity value of their property and are trying to control any further rural subdivision. There is also some evidence of their political influence used to block a major highway alignment.

However, the overwhelming evidence is of a mass phenomenon, of relatively small residential-recreational properties (with farmland rental) which represent an exurban extension of earlier suburban trends, and which coexist with more commercial and non-conforming fringe land uses. There seems to be a very marked contrast between "hobby" and full-time farmers, somewhat less with part-time farms in terms of size, but possibly very great with respect to income and aspiration. Part-time farmers, for example, resent any control on the price of land and their rights to dispose of their property. "Hobby farmers" are already trying to "preserve" the rural landscape.

CONCLUSION

While the foregoing paragraphs indicate that much remains to be clarified concerning "hobby farms", there seems little doubt that interest in them can be justified in relation to a number of major themes.

From the villas of the wealthy few to the burgeoning rural properties of a generally affluent society, the estate or "hobby farm" represents a contemporary urban response to the attractions of country life. It is significant in terms of both its effect on rural society, and as an element of urbanism.

In the present North American context, the "hobby farm" is a factor in the debate on regional planning and development. It is an element in the concern over the loss of prime agricultural land and the planning policies that might be needed. The position of the "hobby farm" vis a vis conventional agriculture, conservation, and rural social and land use amenity, is an ambivalent one, but there is no doubt that many "hobby farms" fall clearly into the dynamic land use zone of the "urban fringe". As Martin has indicated in a recent study of the "urban fringe", it is a zone of transition in which complex relationships exist between socio-economic, accessibility, and land use characteristics of the rural and urban systems.[18] Further study is obviously necessary and could be clearly rewarding.

NOTES AND REFERENCES

1   Anderson, J.R., **A Geography of Agriculture in the United States'**
    Southeast, Geography of World Agriculture 2, Akademiai Kiado,
    Budapest, 1973, p. 54.

2. Hale, P.R., An Examination of the distribution of "Hobby Farm"
    Properties in the six townships surrounding London, Ontario,
    unpub. B.A. Report, University of Western Ontario, London, 1973,
    81 p.

3   Tuan, Yi Fu, **Topophilia: A study of Environmental Perception,**
    Attitudes and Values, Prentice-Hall, Englewood Cliffs N.J.,
    1974, 260 p. (see chapter 8).

4   Hart, J.F., **The Look of the Land,** Prentice-Hall, Englewood
    Cliffs N.J., 1974, 210 p. (see chapter 11).

5   Anderson, J.R., Op cit., Ref. 1 pp 54-55, and Hart, Op cit.,
    Ref. 4 pp 185-7.

6   Gilchrist-Shirlaw, D.W., **An Agricultural Geography of Great**
    Britain Pergamon Press, Oxford. 1966, p. 157.

7   Found, W.C., **A Theoretical Approach to Rural Land-Use Patterns**
    Macmillan Canada, Toronto, 1971, 190 p., see p. 75-9.

8   Hart, J.F., Op cit., Ref. 4. p. 184-5.

9   Hart, J.F., The Three R's of Rural Northeastern United States
    The Canadian Geographer, Vol. 7 (1963), p. 13-22.

10 Ontario regulations until 1972 granted a 25% rebate over 10
    acres on municipal taxation to all properties assessed "farm".
    After 1972 a 50% rebate is in order for properties of all sizes
    that meet the requirements of a minimum gross income from
    agricultural activities of $2,000 per year.

11 Punter, J.V., **The Impact of Exurban Development on Land and**
    Landscape in the Toronto-Centred Region (1954-71) Report to
    Central Mortgage and Housing Corporation, Toronto, 1974, 480 p.
    + maps.

12 Hart, J.F., Op cit., Ref. 4, p. 185 gives specific U.S. examples:
    in Canada the Federal Income Tax Act (current 1973) is mainly
    concerned with the definition and amount of income and income
    losses from farming. On what might be termed "hobby" or
    residential farms, deductions against farm expenses include
    an initial $2,500 and 50% of any balance up to a maximum overall
    of $5,000. Other distinctions are made in terms of active versus
    undeveloped property and vis a vis rental income. The relevant
    sections of the Act include 31:1 and 248:1 (definition), 11:1c
    (deductions) and Transitional Section 37:6.

13   Biggs, E., Present and Future Demands for Land — as Influenced by Agricultural Developments, paper to **Ontario Soil and Crop Improvement Association Land Use Conference,** Toronto, 1972, pp. 4-5.

14   Gertler, L.O., and Hind-Smith, J., **A Pilot Study of the Impact of Urban Growth on Agricultural Land,** Conservation Council of Ontario, for Resources for Tomorrow Conference, Montreal 1961, 26 pages + maps.

15   Hale, P.R., Op cit., Ref. 2. See also P.R. Hale & M.J. Troughton, Some characteristics of "hobby farms" in the vicinity of London, Ontario. paper C.A.G. Ontario, London, 1974, 17 p.

16   Scott, S., and Nelson, J.G., **Outdoor Environmental Education in Canada: A Preliminary Study,** National and Provincial Parks Association of Canada, Toronto, 1973, 50 p. + maps.

17   Troughton, M.J., and Newkirk, R.T., Environmental Impact Assessment for Hydro-Transmission Corridor Delimitation, paper, C.A.G. Annual Meeting, Toronto, 1974, 20 p. + maps.

18. Martin, L.R.G., **A Comparative Urban Fringe Study Methodology,** Report to Lands Directorate, Environment Canada, Ottawa, 1975, 88 p.

EDUCATING THE NOVICE FARMER

Gary Hutchison

The Ontario Agricultural College at the University of Guelph is in the business of educating the novice farmer. We offer evening courses in applied agriculture in several metropolitan areas each fall and winter.

Why Guelph went into the business?

Because of its proximity to the golden horseshoe of Ontario and its reputation in agriculture, many city people, contemplating purchasing a farm, knew of the University and were within easy physical access to it. Consequently these people were arriving on campus unannounced. They were seeking assistance with their hobby or full-time farming dreams and the assistance they received on any given day depended on the directions he or she was given upon arrival on campus. Even if they happened to be steered in the right direction, the particular faculty member was sometimes involved in teaching, research or extension at the time and unavailable.

Some people were well looked after and quite grateful. However, the novice farmer was tying up faculty members on a one to one basis with no direct compensation to the member and/or the institution. Several of us exposed to this time consuming effort, but quite sympathetic to the requests, decided we could serve this clientele with a better product, and more efficiently from the college's standpoint, if we organized an educational program for these people. Thus was born the Night School Program for Novice Farmers. It should be mentioned at this time that the Ontario Agricultural College does offer several extension programs throughout the year at Guelph, but not in the other urban areas and they are commercial farmer oriented, but open to anyone. However no special overtures were made toward the novice to attend these daytime programs and unless a novice farmer was a part of the regular farm communication system, he or she may not have been aware of the programs even if time permitted him to attend them.

AIMS AND OBJECTIVES

It is not our goal to encourage or discourage part-time farming; it is, however, our objective to present the realistic technical and economic facts of farming to these people. Such facts will often discourage these people. If they still decide to continue with, or begin, farming it is our hope that they will be better equipped to cope with it.

Many of our students never intend to do any farming when they enrol, but they do live in the country and they would like to be able to understand and communicate with their neighbour who is farming. Our instructors are advised to outline the technology available to the commercial operator and then relate how it might or might not apply to small scale farming.

Another goal of our program is to teach these people the language of the science of agriculture and sufficient principles and technical know-how in order for them, hopefully, to be in a position to commun-

154

icate with the country extension people on a level that is not frustrating to either party. Many commercially oriented extension people have little sympathy or understanding of the part-time farmer and in many cases rightly so.

Types of Courses Offered

Introductory and specialized courses are available and six such courses offered in the past include: Introductory Agriculture, Beef Management, Crop Management, Horticultural Science, Engineering for the Farm, and Soil Management for Crop Production. Each course consists of ten, two-hour lectures offered one night per week and such courses as the Introductory and Beef courses include a Saturday visit to farms and beef processing facilities.

We commenced our program in the fall of 1972 with 180 people enrolled in the Introductory course in Guelph and two locations in Toronto, and reached a peak of 775 last fall with six courses offered in sixteen classes, including the Ottawa area, and sixty-four different lecturers. (The Kemptville College of Agricultural Technology has since assumed the responsibility for Eastern Ontario.) This fall we are offering eight courses in twenty classes in Guelph, Hamilton, London and Toronto.

Every attempt is made to allow a student to take any combination of courses at one time with no prerequisites. All courses are not offered each semester in each location, but rotate according to demand. Additional courses will be added over time to increase the options available.

Most of our students can consider farming because they have been successful in business, industry or a profession and they are also sharp enough to realize their knowledge of agriculture is minimal. Therefore, most are satisfied to start with the Introductory course. Consequently, it is the most popular course with 62 per cent of all households starting with this course. The Introductory course is a survey or general overview of a different subject area each evening. Although there are only two hours devoted to each subject, the sessions are "jam packed" with a rapid fire presentation using visuals and handout material.

Contrary to many educational programs wherein one instructor does all the lecturing in a given course, we have taken the approach of using a specialist in each subject area. Even the Introductory course has nine lecturers teaching the ten sessions and no one lecturer teaches more than four of the ten lectures in any one course. This may and does result in some overlap or deficiencies, but we think the exposure to many faculty and their ideas is more valuable than any shortcomings.

The following list of lecture topics in the Introductory course may give the reader some idea of the course content:

- — Understanding Soils
- — The Beef Industry at a Glance
- — Where do Sheep and Goats Fit In?
- — Swine in an Agricultural Production System
- — Horses for Everyone
- — Waterfowl
- — Woodlot Management
- — A Bird's Eye View of Field Crops
- — Horticultural Crops
- — Financing Farms and the Income Tax Angles
- — A Farm Visit

Part-time farmers need much the same technical information as commercial farmers in such areas as animal health or crop production. Consequently the novice farmer is receiving much the same technical information the commercial farmer is exposed to with one difference. We assume the student is completely unfamiliar with the field of study including the language of the science and thus we start at square one, whereas farm meetings usually assume some understanding although it varies considerably from subject to subject.

The Introductory course has been offered thirteen times in Toronto, five in Guelph, three in Ottawa and twice each in London and Hamilton for a total of twenty-five offerings with 1,406 students, or an average of fifty-seven students per course. The beef course has been offered eleven times with 590 students, or fifty-four per class. Soil management is highly specialized and beyond the interests of many, but with twenty-five per class we are satisfied to continue with it because it does contribute to the total educational program and as long as the total program is covering all variable costs, we can, and have lost money on individual courses in some locations.

Who are the lecturers?

The faculty members giving the lectures are selected for their understanding of agriculture in general and their appreciation of the needs of the novice. Several of the lecturers are part-time farmers themselves, but this is by no means a prerequisite to a good instructor. Although most of the lecturers are from the faculty, we do use farmers, personnel from government services, and faculty of other universities and colleges. We do not profess to have all the expertise, and in such areas as machinery operation and maintenance individuals such as the machinery manager of the research farms is an excellent choice. A farmer who is a graduate of the University and works closely with the college is the "answer to a layman's dreams", as one student put it. He teaches the "whys" and "wherefores" of seed bed preparation and harvesting methods. We also have a full-time fence builder teaching the lecture on fences.

Many of our campus persons can lecture to these people because of their experience with all types of on-campus students, many with no agricultural experience. Teaching experience is significant, but the most critical criterion is the ability to appreciate and relate to the interests of people who do not necessarily wish to maximize profits (although very few intend to lose money.) The students evaluate the study material and lecturers, and lecturers have been replaced or re-oriented based on the feedback. The best lecturer appears to be the generalist who has been exposed to teaching, extension and research; one who has been called upon to work with all types of agriculturally oriented groups.

Types of Students

No one is overlooked as a potential student of this program. The matronly looking librarian or the frail 55 year old secondary school English teacher is as much a part of our student population as the firefighter or robust truck driver attempting to return to the land. Several music teachers are advocates of our program, but engineers surpass all other individual professions in numbers followed by physicians. Approximately 50 per cent of the student population is from the professions followed by business and management backgrounds. Civil service, armed forces, policemen, social workers, housewives, and skilled tradesmen constitute the balance (Table 1). Again it must be emphasized that one cannot categorize students by occupation, age or social structure. The stylish wife of a general manager of a large corporation just may be the principal tractor driver or an actress may be the nursemaid to sick animals on a part-time farm. On the other hand we do have some young "hippie" types attempting to learn to be self sufficient on a "commune" type farm, although they are outnumbered by the "pin striped" businessman.

Wives are encouraged to participate in the courses even if it is only "hubby" who is really interested in farming. We would like the spouses to be aware of what their husbands are getting them into. Our statistics indicate exactly one half of the students in the Introductory course have participated as couples, and 36 per cent in all courses. Wives tend to lose interest when it comes to machinery and buildings, but in the horticultural area they represent 51 per cent of the student body.

Table 2 represents the number of males, females, couples and families participating in each course. Sixteen hundred and thirty-three different households have been involved in the program to date completing 3,018 courses. One hundred and ten females have participated in one or more courses with no male involvement in the program from the same address. This does not necessarily mean the husband is not interested in agriculture, but we know this to be true in some of the areas.

Accomplishments

We have certainly discouraged some people, not because we have taken a pessimistic approach to agriculture, but because we have presented both technical and economic factual information. Some are discouraged by the technical aspects of farming. For instance, a so-called beef enthusiast commented after the lecture "What else have you got, that's too complicated for me". Other people are actually astounded by the low potential returns.

157

Table 1

SELECTED PARTICIPANTS — INTRODUCTORY FARMING COURSE, UNIVERSITY OF TORONTO

OCCUPATIONAL STATUS	OBJECTIVE FOR JOINING COURSE (Participant Statement)
1. Automobile Mechanic	We desire to have our own beef farm in futu
2. Manager	To get the most out of our 100 acre farm.
3. Director of Food Services	
4. Supervisor	To see if we are cut out to be farmers. I own 100 acres near Peterborough.
5. Accountant	I have a 120 acre farm and would like to enter a cow-calf operation.
6. Financial Analyst	
7. Animal Nutrition Department	Increased knowledge will be beneficial in my occupational field.
8. Pediatrician part-time	My husband and I have 30 acres farming lan and want to use it properly.
9. Secretary, Livestock Branch OMAF	Better job appreciation
10. Secretary, Livestock Branch OMAF	Better job appreciation
11. Geological Engineer	Background to buying a farm. Owner of farm and part-time farmer.
12. Chemist	Part-time farming
13. Computer Operator	To own and manage a small farm
14. Manufacturing Executive	Retiring — plan to make use of 150 acre far
15. Mining Engineer	Part-time farming.
16. Housewife	Small mixed farm.
17. Civil Engineer	Second career.
18. Clerk	To operate own farm in future.
19. Stockbroker	General farming.
20. Home Economist	To start in part-time farming.
21. Telephone Clerk	Interested in taking farming as a career.
22. Chef	
23. Plastic Engineer	89 acres.
24. Child Care Worker	Hope to move to my 50 acre farm to manag this property economically & enjoyably.
25. Lawyer	Farmers at heart.
26. Builder	Owner.
27. Surgeon	Horse breeding.
28. Textile Sales Agent	
29. Machinist	Purchased 50 acres, part-time farming.

Table 2. NIGHT SCHOOL ENROLMENT

Course	Total Participation	Number Enrolled As Couples	Number Individual Males	Number Individual Females	Families	Family Participants	Courses Offered	Average Participation Per Course
Introductory	1,406	700	574	86	14	46	25	56
Beef Management	590	218	332	16	6	24	11	54
Crop Production	335	64	243	15	4	13	8	42
Horticulture	271	104	101	58	2	8	6	45
Engineering	293	62	212	8	3	11	5	59
Soil Management	123	30	75	8	3	10	3	41
Total	3,018	1,178	1,537	191	32	112	58	52

In other situations we have taken the shroud off a mysterious science and the participant's enthusiasm has increased. Many have become wary, but not discouraged because of our schools. The standard comment from those already farming is "I have run into some of the same problems mentioned and I will certainly be watching for the other things you covered." The starry-eyed twentieth floor occupant of a downtown apartment building is the hardest to convince of the perils of part-time farming. Most of those already in the country have faced some devastating experiences and they have their feet at least close to the ground.

An interesting side effect of this program is the attitude the participants have developed toward the commercial farmer. Many of these people have commented that they are fiercely defending the farmer from their cohorts at work or social functions. Such disciples must surely be welcome in agriculture's struggle for understanding and appreciation.

Finally, I cannot believe at least a few people will be less frustrated and humiliated from their experience with us. There is sufficient evidence in our files to indicate that many of the part-timers are finding country life much more rewarding, even if they did take our advice to give or rent their farm to a commercial farmer rather than try to farm themselves. One of the most rewarding things to me is the comments of several extension people. They have become more interested in, and less frustrated with, the "would-be" farmer. Full-time farmers have also commented that the "city" neighbour is now more realistic about such things as renting and fence repair.

Where to from here?

No doubt we will continue along the same pattern as in the past because even after twenty-five offerings of the Introductory course all three classes had their maximum of sixty participants this past semester. Not all courses presently available will be offered every semester and we will continue to rotate courses between cities with the possibility of offering courses in more centres than present, but not necessarily more distant from Guelph.

We expect to add more specialized courses such as Farm Income Tax and Reproduction in Farm Animals, but the offerings will depend firstly on the demand and secondly on the resources available. There is also a possibility we will break with the traditional ten lecture sessions and offer some subject areas in, for example, three evenings and one Saturday field tour. We think Swine Management or Maple Syrup Production could be handled in this manner, although the maple syrup enterprise could be a part of a ten week course in Woodlot Management. Field days could be exploited more fully if the resources are made available to organize them. I am convinced all costs of such an adventure could be covered wherein a bus tour of Beef Operations could be offered one Saturday, followed by Crops the next, and so forth. We are exploring this concept at the present time.

Although we may offer more courses and diversify our program, I have the feeling we should wean many of these people and let them participate with the full-time farmers in the regular extension programs. Many of them need the same technical information because of the scale they are operating on and many are committed financially not unlike the commercial operator.

CONCLUSION

The theme of the conference is Part-Time Farming — A Problem or Resource in Rural Development. Education of part-time farmers is a means to an end rather than the goal itself. However, I am satisfied that our educational program has in the past, and will continue to influence in some small way whether or not part-time farming is a problem or resource in rural development.

Agriculture and the part-timer

1) The production from part-time farms is insignificant as far as feeding the world and yet of sufficient size to affect price of all farm commodities in the domestic market. Many commercial farmers say that part-timers should not be allowed to produce and yet the same land in the hands of the commercial farmers would result in some economies of scale, but the increased production could mean even less total revenue coming back to the farmers considering the inelastic demand for food. In other words the part-time farmer is usually less efficient than the commercial operator.

2) Many full-time farmers have been allowed to escape from agriculture because of the demand from part-time farmers for their farms at prices that allow them to quit. This reduces total production, assuming the part-timer is not going "all out", and the commercial farmer should benefit.

3) Feedlot operators have openly acknowledged that the part-time cow-calf operators in Ontario have allowed them to be less dependent on the West for replacements.

4) Many hobby farmers have the resources to purchase and develop superior breeding stock which filters down to the commercial operator. The development of the so-called exotic beef industry in Canada is financed extensively by those not dependent on farming and yet our total livestock industry and the consumer will be the ultimate beneficiaries.

The Community and the Part-Time Farmer

It doesn't take a computerized survey to see what has happened to many communities with the influx of part-time farmers. From an economic standpoint everyone from carpenters, to storekeepers to antique dealers have benefited from the buying power of the new farmer. Many of our rural communities were literally dying with older farmers only. Today some of these same communities are alive and well with an excellent balance of young and old, not always because everyone new is part-time farming but it is a combination of people returning to live in the rural areas as well as the novice farmers.

161

Whereas at one time doctors and teachers were flocking to the large metropolitan areas because of the so-called social and vocational amenities, we now see a number of them reversing the trend in order that they may do their "thing", namely to farm. Although in terms of totals in any given profession they may not represent a significant percentage, just one good teacher or young dentist entering practice in the smaller communities is an asset.

The Part-Time Farmer

From a selfish standpoint as well as society's standpoint, many families are much better off economically and aesthetically living in the rural areas whether or not the farm actually contributes to the standard of living. Many labourers, particularly, can provide a better setting in the country to bring up their families than they could afford under urban conditions. They themselves are also much more content if they have a longing for country life.

There have been some devastating experiences in part-time farming. Some people have lost everything; others have witnessed such a humiliating and frustrating financial bath it has ruined them psychologically if not financially. Spouses have parted company over hobby farming. An educational program will never reach every novice farmer, but even if we influence the few we do reach at least the individuals involved should be better able to cope with a whole new ball game.

QUESTION PERIOD

P. Hannan (Ontario Federation of Agriculture)

To what extent do you think government programs are encouraging hobby farms? High house prices in an urban setting, the low farm returns so that farmers are eager to sell their land, lower assessment for anyone who keeps a cow on 10 acres or more, tax rebated, all this making it very attractive (much cheaper) for city people to live in the country.

G. Hutchinson (Continuing Education, Guelph)

There is no way you do any farming to take advantage of government programs or to beat the government. The same with the income tax, you get a maximum reduction of only $5,000, off your taxable income, if you have losses of at least $7,500. Unlike many taxable assets (like a summer cottage) you cannot close down a farm especially those with livestock. The farm is your master.

M. Troughton (Geography, Western)

I sense that it is not the specific programs, but the reverse, the lack of direction and consistent land-use policies, failure to control land prices and speculation. It encouraged the buying of land as a hedge against inflation for speculative purposes. Punter (York) recognises this as one of the elements in the Toronto exurbia.

L. Reeds (Geography, McMaster)

Do the agricultural representatives have time to deal with the part-time people? In my experience they are so busy advising the full-time commercial farmer.

G. Hutchison (Continuing Education, Guelph)

We have an unofficial agreement with the Extension Branch of the Ontario Ministry of Agriculture and Food that we will start these people off and then they would take over. However, in the Niagara area, where there are probably 60% to 70% part-time farmers, the extension people are inevitably involved with them. The problem is that neither extension people nor university faculty are trained to teach the part-timer farmer.

L. Reeds (Geography, McMaster)

In the past extension workers have been reluctant to deal with these people and have considered them odd-balls!

G. Hutchison (Continuing Education, Guelph)

This is a problem. I think by teaching the fundamentals of farming to a class of 60, the extension worker is saved from working at different levels with 60 individual people.

G. Stock (Alberta, Agriculture)

Perhaps we are forgetting that many government programs explicitly exclude the part-time farmer. In addition, the hobby farmer works off-farm exactly the same office hours as the extension worker, so they can rarely meet.

G. Hutchison (Continuing Education, Guelph)

I feel professional people who are also hobby farmers can often take time off during office hours!

R. Edwards (Tennessee State University)

I am aware of an extension program run in Indiana for part-time farmers. It was done as a lunch-time seminar at a local plant, planned by the extension agent and plant personnel. Thirty to fifty people would be interested out of several thousand employees.

J. Poirier (Environment Canada)

As a part-time farmer myself, I would like to ask to what degree do you think part-time farmers specialize or generalize their operation?

G. Hutchison (Continuing Education, Guelph)

In my experience there are examples of both; from country squatters with one cow and a goat to highly specialized operations near the city.

A. Fuller (Geography, Guelph)

One way of answering J. Poirier's question would be to record the enterprises operated by people attending the part-time farming course. This depends upon what proportion have a farm when they join the course.

G. Hutchison (Continuing Education, Guelph)

Fifty percent of the people we handle have never been on a farm.

J. Poirier (Environment Canada)

Do you encourage specialization?

G. Hutchison (Continuing Education, Guelph)

I advocate a sufficient level of specialization to make it worthwhile going out to do the chores, but some diversification as a hedge against markets and to spread the work load. We try to avoid a farmer having five different crops on fifty acres as there are no economies of scale and a custom operator is less likely to come onto a farm to work ten acres.

J. Poirier (Environment Canada)

Is there any one field of specialization that you recommend as more suitable to begin part-time farming?

G. Hutchison (Continuing Education, Guelph)

Up to the last year everyone has been getting into beef. In many ways a cow-calf operation fits well into the running of a part-time farm. With prices the way they are it is not a popular choice today. There are some city people and retired farmers beef farming in Eastern Ontario and there are some cash croppers in the South West. Part-time farmers are often more interested in trees than they are in soil — which has its advantages as they improve the land they occupy.

J. Mage (Geography, Guelph)

We do have information on the question of specialization versus diversity. It appears, with the exception of dairying and high cost cash cropping such as tobacco, that part-time farmers specialize rather than diversity. The maps in the display on enterprise combinations show the areas in which one or two enterprises dominate the part-time farm operation. Addressing a question to M. Troughton. How much land is actually held by hobby farmers in the study area? Secondly, how many of these people are not producing anything, that is, are they farmers to begin with?

M. Troughton (Geography, Western)

I cannot answer those questions in a precise way. In terms of farm size, hobby farmers have less land, and therefore have less potential impact on production. Hobby farm areas are most costly near the city and tend to occupy more scenically attractive landscape such that there are blocks of hobby farms which effectively push out commercial operations. In answer to your second question, many hobby farmers who do not produce anything themselves do have income from land rentals, implying the land is being used by a local farmer.

A. Lerner (Agricultural Economics, Guelph)

Would not that situation be equivalent to a census farm, being on rented land, by the man who is doing the farming?

M. Troughton (Geography, Western)

Yes, this is counted as part of a census farm. We have been trying to identify the full-time, part-time, and hobby farm in order to obtain the rental linkages and respective acreages in order to know what constitutes a full-time farm. Land available for rental supports the notion that hobby farming is not necessarily detrimental. On the other hand we have evidence that many properties are not being used for any commercial production. They may be used for horses or recreation, where the emphasis is on amenity uses.

A. Lerner (Agricultural Economics, Guelph)

Should these people be classed as farmers? Surely a hobby farmer must produce something?

165

M. Troughton (Geography, Western)

Yes, the term hobby farmer is a difficult one to work with. I would be in favour of differentiating between the large operator of an estate who is looking for prestige and who farms in a conventional or recreational sense and the small operator who may be using the land for residence or farming it in some way as a small part-time farmer. I tend to think of the hobby farmer as one who has no need of a farm income.

A. Fuller (Geography, Guelph)

On the assumption that hobby farming might underutilise available agricultural resources, alienate land from public access and increase land prices, do you think, from society's point of view, that the University of Guelph should mount a program that might encourage hobby farming?

M. Troughton (Geography, Western)

I assume from G. Hutchison's paper that those who successfully complete the part-time farming program might engage in some commercial production, although they might not operate at a fully intensive level. There might be, however, those who are only interested in learning about government subsidies, landscaping or acquiring knowledge for recreational purposes.

G. Hutchison (Continuing Education, Guelph)

We have everybody, including the ones who only want to have a country estate. Of course there are others who aspire to be commercial producers.

P. Hale (Natural Resources)

Throughout the day there appears to have been the assumption that professional people are the hobby farmers. In the study referred to tonight (the London area), where only properties of over ten acres were considered, it was found that over 50% of the owners were in fact blue collar workers, with only 30% with managerial and professional occupations. It did turn out, however, that the largest farms were owned by professional people. We should get away from the stereotype of the hobby farmer as the rich professional with his country estate.

P. Brasher (Tiny Tay Planning Board)

As a hobby farmer myself I would like to ask about the aspect of "persistence" in part-time farming, which seems to have been defined as anything over six years. Has anyone any information on the persistence of part-time farming into the second generation. To my mind this may be a valid motive, just as much as a hedge against inflation. Do you, for example, get second generation students in your courses at Guelph?

166

G. Hutchison (Continuing Education, Guelph)

There are some families who come to the classes, but generally speaking I do not think that they are a significant number of the 3,000 that are enrolled. To my mind the blue collar workers are the significant ones as they are the sons and daughters of the former owners who could not make a living from farming and who work in a factory in town. This is excellent and we should concentrate on these people and make sure we do not exclude them from entering farming as full-time operators.

R. Sinclair (Geography, Wayne State)

Is there any cleavage in attitudes between the hobby farmer and the full-time farmer, particularly as it effects local politics? For example, the hobby farmer is more likely to resist the things that the full-time farmer would like to have, such as paved roads, utility extension and regulation of his ability to speculate on his land?

M. Troughton (Geography, Western)

The full-time farmer and the hobby farmer might have more in common than the part-time farmer especially as the latter may be looking to realise the speculative gain on his land. The full-time farmer who wants to stay in the urban fringe will be looking for protection via zoning by-laws and protection against expropriation. The hobby farmer who has invested considerable amounts in that land will similarly want to protect his position. The part-time farmer on the other hand may have a more traditional viewpoint and will want to realize the capital gains from selling his land. However, there are also some hobby farmers who are purely speculators.

R. Edwards (Tennessee State University)

The hobby farmer who is there for aesthetic reasons, is he treated for income tax purposes like any farmer or is there a distinction made?

M. Troughton (Geography, Western)

He is treated as any other farmer providing he fills the minimum production requirements. This has recently been changed to a minimum of $2,000 of farm sales.

R. Bollman (Geography, Toronto)

I would like to make two comments. First, there is the question of identification and motive of why there are part-time farmers. It has been acknowledged that the return for one hour of off-farm work is likely to be higher than for one hour of farm work. In which case, why are not all farmers part-time farmers? Second, with reference to A. Fuller's analysis of part-time farming in different areas, it will be useful for prospective graduate students to know that longitudinal studies of part-time farming development can be made from the 1966 and 1971 Census of Canada, Agriculture and Population linkage and that this will probably be matched in 1976.

P. Hannan (Ontario Federation of Agriculture)

I would not necessarily agree with R. Bolman's first comment because, when a full-time farmer takes on additional work the marginal returns for extra work is where his profit lies. When costs have been covered then extra units of production (cows or acres) represent the farmer's profit.

SESSION III

**PROBLEMS ASSOCIATED WITH PART-TIME FARMING
— PROBLEM OR RESOURCE**

CHAIRMAN: R. IRVING (Geography, Waterloo, Canada)

PAPER: J.A. MAGE (Geography, Guelph, Canada)
"Comparative Analysis of Part-Time Farming and Full-Time
Farming in Ontario — Some Selected Aspects"

A COMPARATIVE ANALYSIS OF PART-TIME FARMING AND FULL-TIME FARMING IN ONTARIO — SOME SELECTED ASPECTS

Julius A. Mage

INTRODUCTION

In Ontario an ever increasing proportion of farm operators is engaging in work off the farm in addition to farming. In the past, it has been argued that such a phenomenon bridges the income gap between farming and non-farm employment and serves two purposes: "it supplements the income of farm families, and it provides some of them with the essential first step towards full-time non-farm employment."[1] It has also been stated that researchers often view farm adjustment processes in terms of absolutes by emphasizing the inefficiency of small scale farming and offering solutions based on "upward mobility to a viable state for a few and withdrawal for the rest. It is becoming increasingly clear, however that life is producing a third solution: part-time farming."[2] The latter notion suggests that part-time farming could be a distinctive end result in itself rather than only a transition stage or adjustment process into or out of full-time farming. Undoubtedly both possibilities exist.[3]

The problem of generally defining part-time farming has been discussed in Session I of the Symposium and the suggestion has been made that the phenomenon consists of a number of types which can be identified along a rural continuum, the extremes of which represent rural non-farm situations and full-time farming situations. Inherent in this system is the idea that in the "farming" element of the continuum maximum differences for a range of attributes will occur between the small scale hobby situation and the full-time farming situation.[4] Furthermore, one can hypothesize that at some point along the continuum the operator's main focus of activity turns from farming to non-farm work and results in a "true" part-time farming situation. Recall, however that we initially consider part-time farming to involve off-farm work (in any amount) by the farm operator. Hence in studies wherein specific types of part-time farming have not been determined on an *a priori* basis, it has been customary to analyze the part-time farming group as a more or less homogeneous entity. Implicit also is the notion that part-time farmers as a group differ from full-time farmers not only on the basis of the presence or absence of off-farm work by the operator but also on the basis of other criteria. The norm in each instance is set by the full-time element or group and one expects deviations from this norm by the part-time group.

It is the purpose of this paper to:

1) compare part-time and full-time farming in Ontario at the macro level on the basis of land area operated and gross dollar returns from farming.

170

2) to assess relative threshold levels at which increasing off-farm work commitment of the operator affects average farm size and average gross farm incomes

3) to apply these threshold levels regionally in attempting to answer the symposium question, "part-time farming — problem or resource?"

Macro Scale Comparison

In Ontario, during the past 2 decades, the incidence of part-time farming (as reflected by the number of farmers reporting work off the farm) has tended to increase in spite of the absolute decrease in the total number of census farms. Note (Table 1) that during the period 1951 to 1971 the number of census farms has been reduced by over 55,000 yet the number of farms with operators reporting off-farm work has remained at about 40,000 and has increased in the relative sense from 26.5 per cent to 42.8 per cent of all farms. Operators with off-farm work controlled over 6 million acres (about 38 per cent) of Ontario's farmland in 1971 and sold over $340 million worth of agricultural produce (or about 25 per cent of the value of Ontario's total output). The phenomenon, therefore, is well entrenched in Ontario's agricultural economy (Table 2).

Table 1

Number of Census Farms and Number of
Farm Operators Reporting Off-Farm Work
Ontario 1951 - 1971

	1951	1961	1971
Total Census Farms	149,920	121,333	94,722
Farms with Off-Farm Work by Operator	39,772	42,584	40,499
Percentage with Off-Farm Work	26.5	35.0	42.8

Comparisons Based on Gross Farm Output

Special cross-tabulated census data were acquired from Statistics Canada for each county of Ontario.[5] The variety of socio-economic variables are cross-referenced in most instances by 10 categories of days of off-farm work by the farm operator.[6] The researcher can thus establish the part-time farming population along very liberal or very specific constraints of off-farm work commitment. Similarly, the initial full-time farming population base can be established by including farms for which the operator has reported zero days of off-farm work.

171

In a commercial agricultural economy, such as in Canada, the gross dollar value of agricultural products sold is a good indicator of the size of the farm enterprise and, in the absence of specific data for net returns from farming, an acceptable surrogate reflecting the degree of commitment to, and the degree of success in, farming.

Table 2

General Characteristics of Full-Time and "Part-Time" Farm Operations, Ontario, 1971*

		Part Time as % of Ontario Total
Number of Part-Time Operators	40,499	42.8
Number of Full-Time Operators	54,233	
Total Operators	94,722	
Farm Area Operated by Part-Time Operators (acres)	6,027,038	37.8
Total Farm Area (acres)	15,963,056	
Acres Improved Land Operated by Part-Time Operators	3,890,106	35.8
Total Improved Land (acres)	10,864,601	
Acres of Cropland Reported by Part-Time Operators	2,872,729	35.9
Total Acres of Cropland	7,855,890	
Value of Agricultural Products Sold by Part-Time Operators	$342,373,860	24.8
Total Value of Agricultural Products Sold	$1,376,567,090	

*The term "part-time" here reflects all farm operators reporting off-farm work during the census year.

Source: Statistics Canada, Census of Agriculture 1971, Special Tabulations

In 1971, for Ontario as a whole, over 40 per cent of all part-time situations involved gross farm sales of $2,500 or less and only about one-quarter of all part-time farms generated $10,000 or more gross sales. In the full-time group over 20 per cent of all operators grossed $2,500 or less but nearly one-half exceeded the $10,000 sales level. More complete sales profiles exist in Table 3. Note that the part-time

172

Table 3

**Value of Agricultural Products
in $1,000's Ontario 1971**

	>$50	$35-49.9	$25-34.9	$15-24.9	$10-14.9	$7.5-9.9	$5-7.49	$3.75-4.9	$2.5-3.74	<$2.5
Total Farms	4,603	4,041	5,698	11,532	9,950	7,111	9,416	5,898	7,418	28,971
No. Part-Time Farms	914	871	1,372	3,178	3,285	2,764	4,051	2,935	4,086	17,037
No. Full-Time Farms	3,689	3,170	4,326	8,354	6,665	4,347	5,365	2,963	3,332	11,934
% of Part-Time Farms	2.3	2.2	3.4	7.8	8.1	6.8	10.0	7.2	10.1	42.1
% of Full-Time Farms	6.9	5.9	8.0	15.4	12.3	8.0	9.9	5.5	6.1	22.0
Average No. Days O.F.W./ Farm Reporting O.F.W.	94.2	86.9	93.5	99.6	123.4	140.6	162.6	177.7	187.3	213.3

173

element occurs in every sales category in spite of its concentration in the low income class and that over one-third of all full-time farmers reported gross farm incomes of less than $5,000.

One can hypothesize that, unless direct substitution for operator farm labour losses occurs, there will be an inverse relationship between the intensity of off-farm work and the level of gross farm sales. The more effort a farmer puts into his non-farm job the less time he can devote to farming and consequently farm output decreases. Such an inverse relationship exists, (Table 3), with part-time farmers in the lowest sales category devoting the average of over 200 days per year to off-farm work and those reporting sales in excess of $50,000 devoting an average of about 90 days to off-farm occupations.

Notwithstanding the above interpretation of the relationship between days of off-farm work and farm income, it is difficult at the macro scale, to determine whether generally lower farm income is a function of extra off-farm work by the operator, or whether low farm income determines off-farm work by the operator. In any event, for Ontario as a whole, low farm income part-time operators appear to be in a better position financially than their low farm income full-time operator counterparts. This apparent truism takes on added significance when we consider the fact that fully one-third of all full-time operations generate less than $5,000 of sales per year. If we further consider only those part-time operators in the "non-commercial" sales class (ie. less than $2,500 sales) and multiply their average number of days devoted to off-farm work (ie. 213.3, 8 hour days) by the minimum hourly wage rate ($2.50 per hour in 1971), then the average small scale part-time farmer realizes nearly as much from non-farm earnings as the gross amounts accruing from farm sales on about one-third of Ontario's "full-time farms".[7] It would appear that, in terms of income criteria, potential problems in the rural farm sector of Ontario emanate from full-time farming situations.

There is a need to examine the regional variations of average farm sales of the part-time and full-time groups. For each of the fifty-four counties and districts of Ontario the average per farm sales was computed for all full-time operations, all part-time operations, and all farms for which the operator reported more than 229 days of off-farm work.[8] For Ontario these average ratios exceed $19,000 per full-time farm, $8,400 per part-time farm and $4,700 per farms with operators reporting more than 229 days of off-farm work (Table 4). Figures 2, 3 and 4 present the spatial variation of each ratio. The general distribution of farm income in Ontario has been well documented before but has usually been presented for the total farming population.[9] Note, Figure 2, that the highest per farm sales (exceeding $30,000) for full-time operators occur in the agricultural heartland of central South-Western Ontario and that average gross returns are less than a third of this amount in the Shield counties of the Province. Similar distributional patterns of sales obtain for the two classes of part-time operators but at a reduced intensity of actual gross sales. There is however, a clear concentration of relatively high per farm sales for those part-time operators reporting more than 229 days of off-farm work in the Waterloo-Perth-Oxford

Table 4

Average Farm Sales, Ontario 1971

	Full-Time	All Part-Time	Part-Time with >229 Days O.F.W.
$ Value Total Sales	$1,034,193,230	$342,373,860	$81,781,816
No. Operators	54,223	40,499	17,239
Proportion of Total Operators	57.2%	42.8%	18.2%
$ Sales per Farm	$19,069	$8,453	$4,744
Proportion of Full-Time per Farm	100.0%	44.3%	24.9%
Contribution to Total Ontario Sales	75.1%	24.9%	7.9%

heartland (Figure 4). Here, average gross sales on part-time farms (with operators working the equivalent of a full-time off-farm year) actually exceed average sales on full-time farms in portions of Eastern and Northern Ontario. (Table 5 lists the average sales for each county.)

The above comparison of absolute sales ratios should be qualified by the type of agricultural enterprise existing in each region. That is, a cash crop farm in South-Western Ontario probably has to produce higher gross sales than a beef farm in central Ontario in order to offer similar net returns to the farmer.[10] In the absence of specific net income data, we can assume that the average sales per full-time farm in any county represent the evolved norm or general farming potential of that county. By comparing the returns from part-time farmer against the full-time ratios the relative degree of "farming success" of part-time operators can be established for each county. A correlation coefficient of .720 between average part-time and average full-time farm sales indicates that sales levels of both groups vary positively spatially. In the majority of counties then, average sales for the whole part-time group reflect average sales for the full-time group but are about 55 per cent lower.

To this point the discussion has concentrated on the comparison of broadly established groups of part-time and full-time farmers. Let us pursue the relationship between time devoted to off-farm work and levels of farm sales in more detail. For each county the average gross sales for part-time farmers were calculated cumulatively by the ten "days of off-farm work" categories and the results compared to the average full-time sales.[11] In this manner, using full-time sales as the "norm", one can establish a critical threshold of days devoted

175

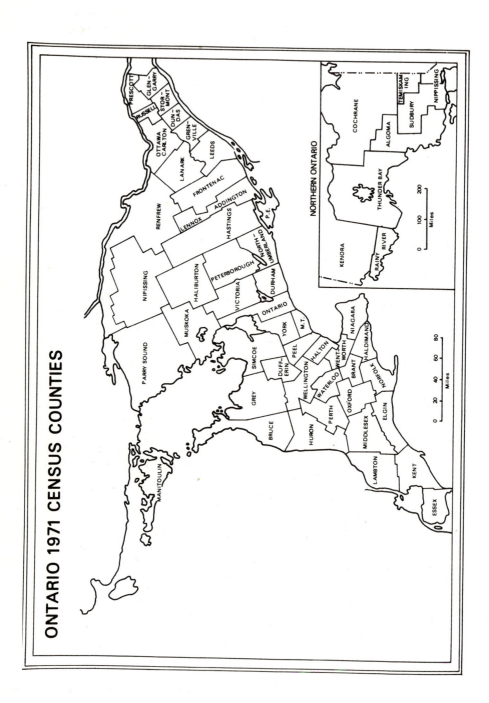

ONTARIO 1971 CENSUS COUNTIES

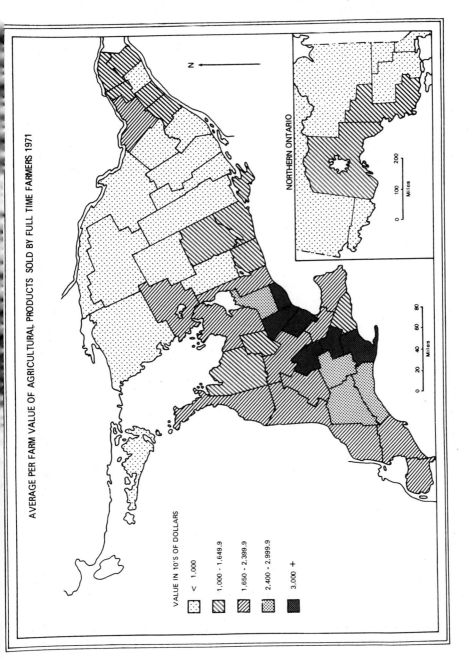

AVERAGE PER FARM VALUE OF AGRICULTURAL PRODUCTS SOLD BY FULL TIME FARMERS 1971

NORTHERN ONTARIO

VALUE IN 10'S OF DOLLARS

< 1,000

1,000 - 1,649.9

1,650 - 2,399.9

2,400 - 2,999.9

3,000 +

Figure 2

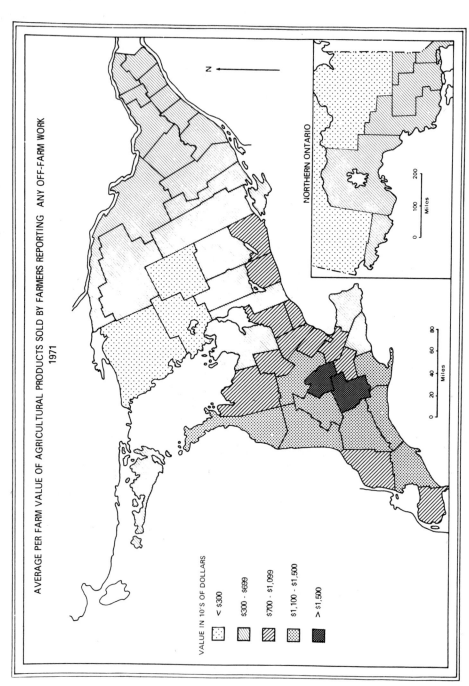

AVERAGE PER FARM VALUE OF AGRICULTURAL PRODUCTS SOLD BY FARMERS REPORTING ANY OFF-FARM WORK
1971

VALUE IN 10'S OF DOLLARS

< $300

$300 - $699

$700 - $1,099

$1,100 - $1,500

> $1,500

NORTHERN ONTARIO

Figure 3

178

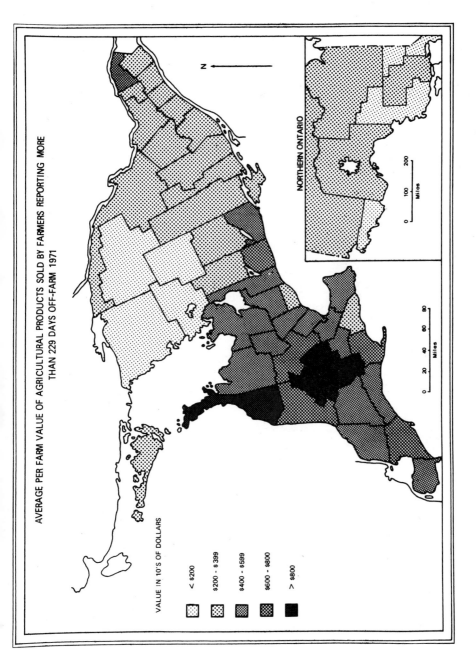

AVERAGE PER FARM VALUE OF AGRICULTURAL PRODUCTS SOLD BY FARMERS REPORTING MORE
THAN 229 DAYS OFF-FARM 1971

NORTHERN ONTARIO

VALUE IN 10'S OF DOLLARS

< $200
$200 - $399
$400 - $599
$600 - $800
> $800

Figure 4

Table 5

Comparison of Average Per Farm Sales — Ontario Counties 1971

County	Full-Time	All Part-Time	>229 Days O.F.W.	County	Full-Time	All Part-Time	>229 Days O.F.W.
Algoma	$10,256	$3,015	$1,232	Niagara	$21,779	$6,131	$4,322
Brant	32,515	10,296	5,961	Nippissing	8,654	3,799	1,908
Bruce	19,028	12,433	8,563	Norfolk	33,592	14,354	6,643
Cochrane	8,108	2,532	2,058	Northumberland	13,803	7,030	4,070
Dufferin	15,930	8,711	4,372	Ontario	17,678	6,432	4,157
Dundas	11,370	6,602	3,666	Ottawa Carelton	18,220	5,448	2,545
Durham	15,873	7,716	6,160	Oxford	27,141	15,016	9,006
Elgin	28,517	13,007	4,831	Parry Sound	6,204	2,470	1,378
Essex	17,014	9,054	5,445	Peel	31,669	7,268	4,179
Frontenac	8,198	3,728	2,192	Perth	22,107	14,863	9,325
Glengary	12,099	6,326	3,044	Peterborough	10,368	5,013	3,233
Grenville	12,420	3,918	2,055	Prescott	12,221	6,573	4,541
Grey	11,114	7,065	4,275	Prince Edward	13,906	6,080	2,113
Haldimand	13,692	6,422	3,347	Rainy River	7,349	3,426	1,944
Haliburton	2,610	1,874	722	Renfrew	7,078	4,516	2,470
Halton	31,676	7,331	5,542	Russell	11,378	6,387	3,415
Hastings	9,212	4,087	2,115	Simcoe	19,739	6,776	4,030
Huron	20,741	13,685	6,758	Stormont	9,973	5,331	3,047
Kenora	9,491	2,938	2,802	Sudbury	8,075	3,129	3,128
Kent	22,844	13,020	6,848	Thunder Bay	14,843	4,642	3,340
Lambton	18,593	9,097	5,350	Timiskaming	9,541	4,097	1,721
Lanark	8,786	4,953	3,053	Metro Toronto	39,037	7,221	2,466
Leeds	9,761	4,109	2,488	Victoria	8,879	5,103	3,456
Lennox & Addington	9,445	3,622	2,536	Waterloo	30,282	16,862	9,343
Manitoulin	6,485	4,864	3,768	Wellington	22,087	11,022	6,553
Middlesex	25,022	12,040	5,861	Wentworth	21,589	7,543	4,903
Muskoka	19,070	2,763	1,602	York	24,255	7,169	4,872

to off-farm work beyond which sales drop in relation to the expected full-time norm. These threshold levels were mapped. Figure 5 presents the upper limit in days of off-farm work at which average part-time sales are equal to (or exceed) average full-time sales in each county. In 21 of the 54 counties and districts even nominal amounts of off-farm work are related to average sales which are lower than full-time farm means. Note that in southern Ontario these areas are centred on the "Golden Horseshoe" and axes emenating north to the Muskokas and west to the London area in Middlesex county. On the other hand in very few areas can a farmer devote more than 72 days to off-farm employment and maintain gross returns equal to the full-time farmer (for example Stormont county in eastern Ontario, at 126 days, represents the highest threshold possible).

Because a threshold level based on gross farm returns equal to full-time farming operations is a very stringent measure, a second threshold map reflecting part-time ratios of 85 per cent or more of full-time scales was constructed. Figure 6 depicts that the basic core centered on the urbanized western end of Lake Ontario still exists. With the exception of Wentworth and Middlesex Counties (where the average part-time operator can devote up to forty-eight days per year to off-farm work) even a small amount of off-farm time appears to prevent farmers from attaining sales values 85 per cent of that of full-time situations.[12] Of more interest to us here is the fact that in the traditionally "best" agricultural areas of Southern Ontario (for example Waterloo, Wellington, Perth, Oxford and Huron Counties) some farmers can devote the equivalent to half a working year (126 days) to off-farm pursuits and still operate farms returning 85 per cent or more of full-time mean sales. These operators appear to be making substantial contributions to both the agricultural and non-agricultural sectors of Ontario's economy.

Comparison Based on Area of Land Operated

The second consideration, isolated for specific comparison in this paper, is the amount of land effectively controlled by farm operators with off-farm work. In this instance the census category reflecting "farm area operated" is used. Recall (Table 2) that in Ontario farmers reporting off-farm work operate nearly 38 per cent of the total farm area — a figure approaching their relative numerical importance (42 per cent). Indeed the distributional profiles, by size of farm categories, indicate that part-time farms are not overwhelmingly small holdings (Table 6). As expected, there is an inverse relationship between size of farm and days of off-farm work with part-time operators of very small farms (less than 10 acres) devoting an average of 221 days to non-farm jobs and those operating farms in excess of 400 acres reporting an average of only 112 days. In isolation, the proportion of part-time farmers with more than 229 days of off-farm work decreases very rapidly when farm size exceeds 400 acres (Figure 7).

Average farm sizes were computed for the full-time group and the two part-time categories for each county and mapped. Figures 8, 9 and 10 indicate that we must again compare part-time and full-time farming on a regional basis within a spatial context as the overall Ontario averages (Table 7) are subject to wide variation in diverse geographic areas and reflect, undoubtedly, the types of agriculture that have evolved over time.[13] A simple correlation analysis re-

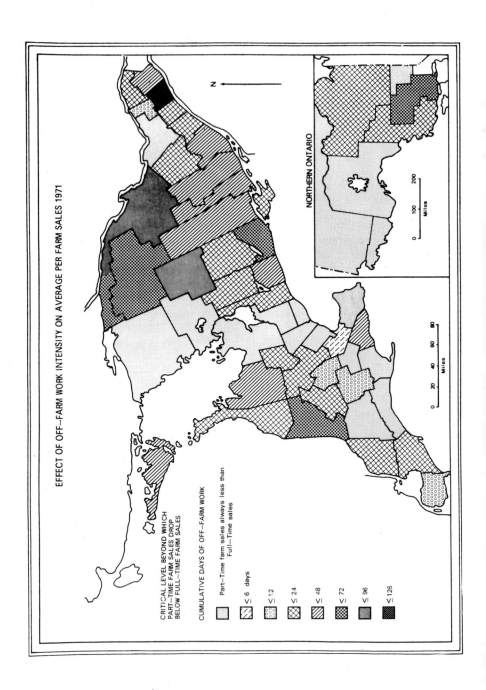

EFFECT OF OFF-FARM WORK INTENSITY ON AVERAGE PER FARM SALES 1971

NORTHERN ONTARIO

CRITICAL LEVEL BEYOND WHICH
PART-TIME FARM SALES DROP
BELOW FULL-TIME FARM SALES

CUMULATIVE DAYS OF OFF-FARM WORK

Part-Time farm sales always less than
Full-Time sales

≤ 6 days
≤ 12
≤ 24
≤ 48
≤ 72
≤ 96
≤ 126

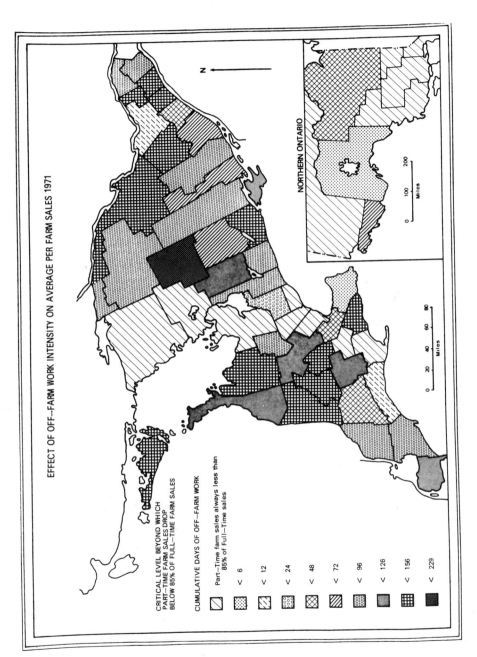

EFFECT OF OFF–FARM WORK INTENSITY ON AVERAGE PER FARM SALES 1971

NORTHERN ONTARIO

Miles
0   100   200

Miles
0   20   40   60   80

CRITICAL LEVEL BEYOND WHICH
PART–TIME FARM SALES DROP
BELOW 85% OF FULL–TIME FARM SALES

CUMULATIVE DAYS OF OFF–FARM WORK

Part–Time farm sales always less than
85% of Full–Time sales

< 6

< 12

< 24

< 48

< 72

< 96

< 126

< 156

< 229

Figure 6

Table 6

Size of Farm Area Operated
Size Categories in Acres

	<10	10-69	70-129	130-179	180-239	240-399	>400
Total No. of Farms	5,148	16,763	26,278	13,440	13,051	13,315	6,718
No. Part-Time Farms	2,782	9,158	11,738	5,140	4,632	4,646	2,403
No. Full-Time Farms	2,366	7,605	14,540	8,300	8,419	8,669	4,315
% of Part-Time	6.9	22.6	28.9	12.8	11.4	11.5	5.9
% of Full-Time	4.5	14.0	26.9	15.3	15.5	15.9	7.9
Average No. Days of O.F.W./Farm Reporting O.F.W.	221.4	210.8	181.7	154.2	142.8	124.4	112.5

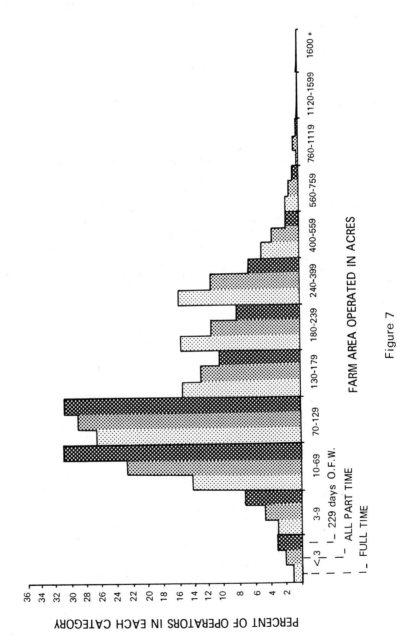

FARM AREA OPERATED BY FULL-TIME, ALL PART-TIME AND > 229 DAYS OF OFF-FARM WORK

ONTARIO 1971

PERCENT OF OPERATORS IN EACH CATEGORY

FARM AREA OPERATED IN ACRES

229 days O.F.W.

ALL PART TIME

FULL TIME

Figure 7

185

Table 7

Average Farm Size, Ontario Counties 1971

	Full-Time	All Part-Time	Part-Time with >229 Days O.F.W.
No. Operators	54,223	40,499	17,239
Area Operated (acres)	9,936,018	6,027,038	1,861,812
Average Acres/ Farm	181.4	148.8	108.9

vealed a high degree of spatial covariation between average farm sizes of full-time, all part-time and all operators with more than 229 days of off-farm work.[14] Hence, knowing the average size of a full-time farm in an area, it is possible to predict, with about a 77 per cent accuracy, the average size of holdings for the total part-time farming group and for those part-time farmers effectively engaged in full-time off-farm work. In the majority of cases the average full-time farm is about 22 per cent larger than the average (all) part-time farm and 67 per cent larger than the average farm operated by farmers with full-time off-farm work.

The critical threshold level, in days of off-farm work, at which the average per farm acreage of part-time farms drops below the norm established by full-time farms was also calculated and mapped (Figure 11). For Ontario as a whole, farmers who reported up to 156 days of off-farm work operated an average farm acreage equal to, or greater than, the average full-time acreage. At the county level, very few low threshold levels appear (Norfolk and the Ottawa-Carleton Region being the two exceptions in Southern Ontario). Note (Figure 11) that in the agricultural heartland of South Western Ontario farmers devoting an average of half a man year to off-farm work still maintain farm sizes equalling their full-time farmer counterparts.

By comparing the results of the gross sales and the area operated threshold analyses it is apparent that in certain portions of the Province (eg. the "Golden Horseshoe" area) farmers with off-farm work operate more land than the average rate of gross farm return would appear to justify. For example, in the Counties of York, Peel, Wentworth and the Niagara Region even nominal amounts of off-farm work are associated with lower average sales, yet some farmers whose focus of activity is clearly off the farm maintain farms equal in size to full-time units.[15] In good agricultural areas such a combination of phenomena reduces the potential agricultural output and may in fact suggest a "problem" to us here.

On the other hand should a fairly high degree of commitment to off-farm work not detract substantially from average gross sales (see Figure 6), one would expect a similar high threshold for "area

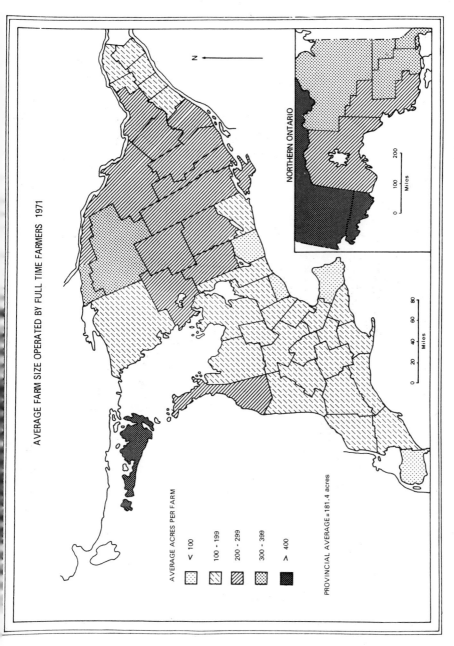

AVERAGE FARM SIZE OPERATED BY FULL TIME FARMERS 1971

NORTHERN ONTARIO

AVERAGE ACRES PER FARM

< 100

100 - 199

200 - 299

300 - 399

> 400

PROVINCIAL AVERAGE=181.4 acres

Figure 8

187

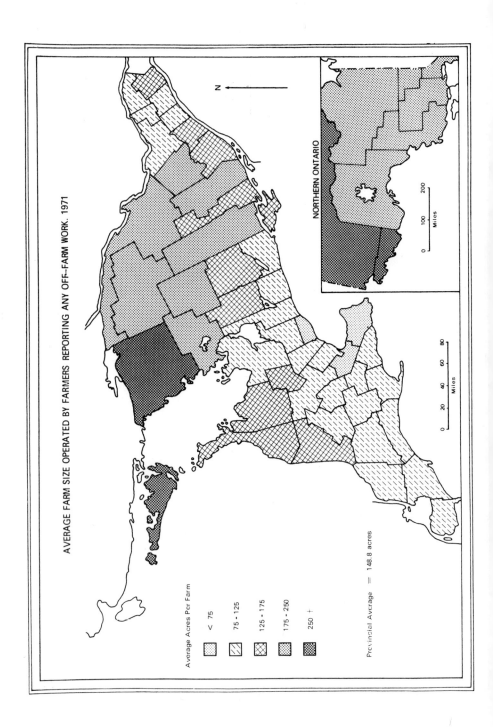

AVERAGE FARM SIZE OPERATED BY FARMERS REPORTING ANY OFF-FARM WORK. 1971

N

NORTHERN ONTARIO

0   100   200
Miles

0   20   40   60   80
Miles

Average Acres Per Farm

☐   < 75

▨   75 - 125

▧   125 - 175

▦   175 - 250

▩   250 +

Provincial Average = 148.8 acres

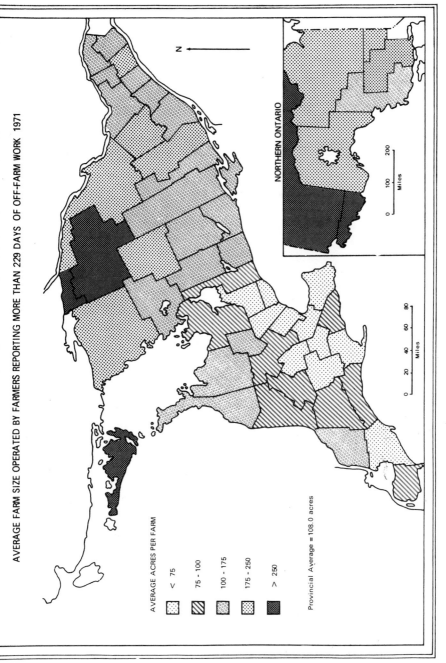

AVERAGE FARM SIZE OPERATED BY FARMERS REPORTING MORE THAN 229 DAYS OF OFF-FARM WORK 1971

NORTHERN ONTARIO

AVERAGE ACRES PER FARM

< 75

75 - 100

100 - 175

175 - 250

> 250

Provincial Average = 108.0 acres

N

Figure 10

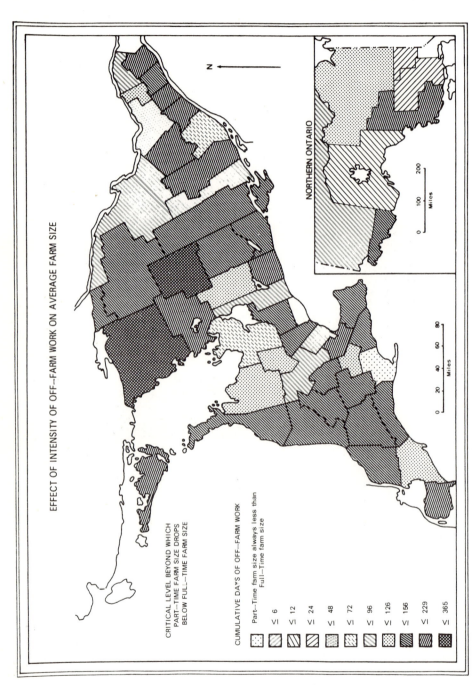

EFFECT OF INTENSITY OF OFF—FARM WORK ON AVERAGE FARM SIZE

NORTHERN ONTARIO

0   100   200
Miles

0 20 40 60 80
Miles

CRITICAL LEVEL BEYOND WHICH
PART—TIME FARM SIZE DROPS
BELOW FULL—TIME FARM SIZE

CUMULATIVE DAYS OF OFF—FARM WORK

Part—Time farm size always less than
Full—Time farm size

VI 6
VI 12
VI 24
VI 48
VI 72
VI 96
VI 126
VI 156
VI 229
VI 365

Figure 11

190

operated". This combination occurs in Bruce, Essex, Huron, Oxford, Perth and Waterloo Counties and Lanark, Dundas and Stormont Counties in Eastern Ontario. In these areas farmers who work up to 156 days off the farm operate farms equalling the full-time average acreage and obtain gross farm returns averaging at least 85 per cent that of the full-time average. Part-time farmers, in this "time" category, do not appear as a "problem" to agriculture generally and through their off-farm labours contribute to other sectors of the economy and increase their total family income.[16] This latter point may be particularly significant in low farm income areas of Ontario. The introduction of a certain amount of off-farm work (in some areas up to one-half a man year) need not necessarily disrupt agricultural output and would have a positive effect on total farm family incomes.

CONCLUSION

The comparison presented here between part-time and full-time farming has emphasized the apparent effects that increasing amounts of off-farm work have on average farm sales and average farm size. A notable "lag" effect has emerged for most areas in that average sales (relative to full-time sales) decrease rapidly with the introduction of even nominal amounts of off-farm work by the operator, while average farm size can withstand a higher critical threshold. By mapping these threshold levels it is possible to ascertain, generally, the relative "farming success" of operators reporting off-farm work and also the relative amounts of land effectively controlled by part-time operators. There is a need to expand these analyses to include categories of different land use types and thus determine in what way part-time operators are using their land. Furthermore the resultant patterns should be qualified by the types of off-farm jobs and farming types reported by part-time farmers.[17]

Of direct practical importance, the approaches offered here should aid policy makers who are currently struggling with the question of whether part-time farming should be viewed positively or negatively or simply ignored. Based on only two criteria pursued here — land and sales, it appears that **part-time** work off the farm by operators could be encouraged — but only up to a point and only in certain areas if some kind of "maximization" of the use of land and resultant returns are the objectives. In other areas it appears that "whole" farms are being operated by part-time farmers at sub-par levels. Here the practice should be questioned, especially in prime soil capability areas. Finally, we should consider that at least one-third of Ontario's full-time operators are very low farm income farmers. We need to identify the regional concentrations of these folk as they probably present a greater problem to agriculture than do individuals who have additional incomes from off-farm work. Finally any assessment of "problem" or "resource" must be done on a regional basis. Policies formulated for Ontario as a whole must be flexible enough to accommodate the range of possibilities and situations which are inherent in geographical diversity.

NOTES AND REFERENCES

1 **The Challenge of Abundance,** Special Committee on Farm Income in Ontario, Ontario Department of Agriculture and Food, January 1969, p. 129.

2 **Proceedings of the Canadian Agricultural Congress 1969,** Ottawa: Queen's Printer, 1969, p. 407.

3 The idea of part-time farming as a permanent feature of the agricultural landscape has been supported in other symposium papers by Benson, Fuller and Mage.

4 Terms as used in J.A. Mage "A Typology of Part-Time Farming", Part-Time Farming Symposium, Guelph, 1975. Session I.

5 Those data were purchased with funds from O.M.A.F. made available to the Geography Department under Program 33 at the University of Guelph.

6 These categories are as follows; 1-6 days; 7-12 days; 13-24 days; 25-48 days; 49-72 days; 73-96 days; 97-126 days; 127-156 days; 157-228 days and; 229-365 days.

7 This hypothetical, and very nominal sum, works out to about $4,300 per part-time farmer. We cannot at the present, at this scale of analysis, determine total off-farm incomes by farm operators or the farm family. Some preliminary results for the whole of Canada have been published by Bollman who used the 1972 Agricultural Enumerative Survey of approximately 6,000 census farms. See R.D. Bollman, "Off-Farm Work by Operators of Canadian Census Farms — 1971," **Canadian Farm Economics** Vol. 8, No. 6, 1973, pp. 1-5.

8 Recall this is the highest category of off-farm work and probably reflects full-time off-farm employment by the operator.

9 See, **Planning for Agriculture in Southern Ontario.** A.R.D.A. Report No. 7, Centre for Resources Development, University of Guelph, 1972.

10 Farm enterprise combinations are analyzed in J.A. Mage, **Part-Time Farming in Ontario — A Macro Scale Overview.** Centre for Resources Development, University of Guelph, forthcoming summer 1975.

11 Average sales were computed for farmers reporting: 1-6 days, 1-12 days, 1-24 days and so on.

12 Recall that the premise here is that off-farm work will affect farm sales. These individuals could of course be attempting to increase their total income via off-farm employment.

13 For example, average full-time farm size varied from a low of 74 acres in the Niagara Region to a high of 471 acres in the Kenora District.

14 The correlation coefficient between average full-time farm acres and; average total part-time acres was .883 and; average farm size for operators with more than 229 days of off-farm work was .874.

15 Muskoka, Parry Sound and Middlesex are other such examples.

16 In this sense these individuals should be effectively removed from the "part-time" category.

17 Some of these aspects have been analyzed in J.A. Mage, **Part-Time Farming in Ontario — A Macro Scale Overview,** Centre for Resources Development, University of Guelph, forthcoming summer 1975.

QUESTION PERIOD

A. Lerner (Agricultural Economics, Guelph)

When considering the amount of land and the amount of sales on part-time farms did you also take into account the amount of hired labour? What if an individual can hire someone to work the farm for less than that individual can earn off the farm, so that really it is a full-time operation only the farmer instead of working himself pays someone else to do the labour?

J. Mage (Geography, Guelph)

I started out on the assumption that there would be no direct labour substitution for the operator while he was at his off-farm job. We have to do this because we have no total labour figures for the farm at this scale of analysis.

A. Lerner (Agricultural Economics, Guelph)

But there is no indication of whether any of the sales come from his (the operator's) labour or not.

J. Mage (Geography, Guelph)

We do not have figures for the amount of labour hired by farmers. I am simply comparing part-time farms versus full-time farm as dictated by the constraints of off-farm work by the farm operator. The results that emerge here should be qualified by the nature of the off-farm job as well as the nature of the farm enterprise. It appears that in cash cropping mixed livestock areas it is possible for a man to work more than half a year off the farm and still maintain operations comparable to full-time units. That is as far as we can take the comparison at this time.

M. Troughton (Geography, Western)

The one county that emerges on your map as "part-time farm size always less than full-time farm size" is Norfolk County. In your opinion is that directly related to the tobacco areas?

J. Mage (Geography, Guelph)

I would think so. We have not had a chance to put a survey team in that area but I strongly suspect that that is the case.

M. Troughton (Geography, Western)

This would highlight the fact that the county unit is a bit too gross a mesh in the sense that the tobacco area could be defined in terms of adjacent townships and some of the surrounding towns.

J. Mage (Geography, Guelph)

That leads to a very interesting point. This scale of analysis, using counties, is probably better for the Canada wide picture. For the Ontario situation we do have some township information. Unfortunately in townships where there are fewer than about 60 part-time farmers, cross-referencing 12 income categories by 10 off-farm work categories results in data confidentiality problems. Therefore cross tabulated information does not seem to work below the county average. We have to work with the census people to try to overcome that problem and obviously if you are interested only in Norfolk county the current information will tell you how it fits in with the scheme of things in Ontario generally.

R. Crown (Agriculture Canada)

On the assumption that your proxy variable, namely the operator off-farm labour, is some indicator of the total labour available on the farm, would you be prepared to say that your threshold level measures the degree of labour redundance in agriculture?

J. Mage (Geography, Guelph)

Yes, I think I was hinting at that. I do not want to label full-time farmers inefficient but it appears that there are key areas (these areas being in the good agricultural zones) where farmers, if they wanted to, could obtain higher incomes by some off farm work. The assumption here is that the opportunity to the full-time farmers is the same as to the part-time farmers to obtain job in the first place.

With reference to your first point. We have completed a number of surveys to pursue the labour question. I refer you specifically to the hand out of some work which I have done in Huron County. There the majority of part-time farmers do not have direct substitution for their labour on the farm while they are at their off-farm work. Furthermore, the ratio of family labour, that is the wife and children, to the total labour input on a farm unit is very similar for full-time and part-time farms. This means that, in a relative sense, full-time farm families are contributing about as much as part-time farm families to the total labour on the farm. In some instances there are of course high amounts of hired labour. The statistics used in this morning's paper were generated from about 2,200 farmers per county and one would assume that there is some kind of balancing effect.

G. Hutchison (Continuing Education, Guelph)

It appears geographers are falling into the same trap that the agricultural economists have been in for several years by basing everything on gross income. A man can be in full-time farming and grossing $30,000 a year from dairying. He can then work off the farm for 250 days a year and still gross $35,000 a year because he switches enterprises. I do not know how you resolve this problem because statistics are not likely that complete, but unless you go to enterprises I do not really think you can make some of the statements you are making that people are underemployed. In my case I spend 250 days off the farm and I gross $30,000. If I reduce my off-farm work down to 150 days I would also reduce my gross sales because I would switch to a sow-weaner operation which would tie up my labour a lot more but net me more because of the higher return on my labour. We must consider this fact.

J. Mage (Geography, Guelph)

I agree that the matter of enterprise types is very important. We did in fact generate a series of enterprise combinations. However, one must realize that data pertaining to enterprise type are available only for farms with more than $2,500 sales. Given the fact that 60 percent of the part-time farms are below that category could you tell me how we can measure what the operators of these farms do? Generally, from survey work, we found that the part-time farmer does what the full-time farmers do around him — with a couple of exceptions. Part-time farmers stay out of dairying, for obvious reasons, they stay out of highly capitalised cash cropping operations and they do not have a range of enterprises on their farms. In other words, they specialise. A full-time farmer may have beef and hogs whereas a part-time farmer will probably have one or the other but not both. If we had income figures based on net farm sales then we could make these comparisons at a much more sophisticated level. Furthermore in this analysis it does not matter what the net ratios are. If a farmer obtains only $10,000 gross sales from a full-time farm in Eastern Ontario the net income will not be very much. If he can supplement this low farm income with off farm income then in fact he has increased his level of living.

G. Stock (Alberta, Agriculture)

There seems to be another possible explanation for off-farm work by the "full-time farmer". Quite often it depends on how much debt the farmer has. We have noticed this repeatedly in Alberta. I think it is probably the biggest explanation for having to go off his farm, not necessarily because of low net returns but because of his ability to carry the debt load.

196

SESSION IV

**WHAT SHOULD BE DONE ABOUT PART-TIME
FARMING — IMPLICATIONS FOR POLICY**

CHAIRMAN: A.M. FULLER (Geography, Guelph, Canada)

PAPER: R. CROWN (Head, Rural Affairs Unit, Canada Department
                                  of Agriculture, Ottawa, Canada)
           "What Should Be Done About Part-Time Farming —
           Implications for Policy"

PAPER: R. WIETFELDT (Research Director, Ontario Federation
                                  of Agriculture, Toronto, Canada)
           "Attitudes of Farmer's Unions Towards Part-Time Farming"

PAPER: P. HACKMAN (Agricultural Economics, Helsinki, Finland)
           "Attitudes of the Farmer's Union to Multiple Jobholders
           in Finland"

WHAT SHOULD BE DONE ABOUT PART-TIME FARMING — IMPLICATIONS FOR POLICY

Robert W. Crown

We can certainly conclude from the evidence presented at this Symposium so far, that there are three main paths along which part-time farming and part-time farmers progress. Some farmers are working their way into farming through enterprises that do not fully occupy them, some are working their way out of farming by cutting back their farming operations, and a significant number are permanently in that state of combining farm and non-farm employment in an attempt to derive the livelihood that they feel uses their resources best. It seems to me that it is also useful to begin thinking about the possible strategies that public policy could embody with respect to part-time farming and farmers in a parallel set of paths. There appears to be a policy problem related to the recruiting of a "next generation" of farmers, another related to the ease with which farmers can retire from farming, and a third relating to the treatment of that significant segment of persistent farmers, who, like it or not, will be part of the general structure of the agricultural industry regardless of public interest in their well-being.

The comments that follow will consider what policy or strategies might be open and the consequences of selecting one or another of these options as I see them.[1] Although my comments are related to the Canadian scene, I hope that the participants from other countries generalize from them to their own situations. I will try to be as concerned with principle as possible rather than with Canadian policy problems *per se*.

PART-TIME FARMING AND ENTRY INTO AGRICULTURE

To become concerned that a public strategy with respect to part-time farming as a means of recruiting the next generation of farmers is desired, we have to be convinced that under the situation that now exists and under the trends that we now see evolving, there will be an inappropriate number of farmers in the future, given the kind of society we want to have. In other words, before we decide that part-time farming is a feature we should encourage as a means of increasing the number of new entrants into agriculture, we should be certain that the number that have already selected this means of entry, without the benefit of an overt policy to encourage them, is too small (given the rate of exit) to give the number of farms that we think is needed. We would also want to be sure that the part-time farming path into agriculture was one of the more desirable means of generating the farmers we need.

One estimate for Canada shows that we might expect a net decline in operator numbers of about 14 per cent between 1971 and the census count in 1976, and a further decline of 12 per cent by the end of this decade. Looking at Table 1, it is evident that the decline is expected to be very rapid in Canada's Atlantic provinces, although Quebec and Ontario also can be expected to lose farms rapidly. Of course, the loss

Table 1.
Number of Census Farm Operators by Province— 1951 to 1981 Inclusive

	1951	1956	1961	1966	1971	1976*	1981*
ATLANTIC	59,969	55,010	31,639	24,684	16,036	10,983	8,456
period change					(-32%)	(-23%)	
QUEBEC	134,073	122,617	95,777	80,294	61,257	46,261	36,584
period change					(-25%)	(-21%)	
ONTARIO	149,573	140,602	121,333	109,887	94,722	83,513	73,195
period change					(-12%)	(-22%)	
PRAIRIES	247,764	232,016	210,442	194,344	174,643	155,629	138,884
period change					(-11%)	(-11%)	
B.C.	26,343	24,748	19,934	19,085	18,400	18,142	17,831
period change					(-1%)	(-2%)	
CANADA	617,722	575,015	479,125	428,794	365,068	314,528	274,950
period change					(-14%)	(-12%)	

Excludes Newfoundland

*Projected on the basis of 1951 to 1971 changes in age cohorts over time.

Source: Statistics Canada — Census figures
(for Census purposes a farm is defined as an agricultural holding of one acre or more with greater than $50 in sales)

of farm operators does not mean necessarily that farm production will decline, or that land and other resources will be withdrawn from agriculture. It signals, however, an agriculture where farms are more land extensive, and capital intensive, each with a larger market share.

But it is not the fact that we can expect to see about 275,000 farms in Canada that would concern most people. I cannot see most persons feeling particularly insecure or threatened by the thoughts of cartel action by "so few" businesses. But there might be a concern that this reduction in farm numbers (and so, farm population) would make goals related to an optimal distribution of the population more difficult to achieve (considering that the reduction of farm numbers for want of entrants tends to be more of a regional issue in Canada that directly effects the ability of certain regions to hold population relative to others). Further, interpreting recent evidence on the relation between structure of agriculture and the viability of rural communities, published by Heady and Sonka[2] at Iowa State University, one could be very skeptical of the ability of fewer larger farms, even with larger per farm incomes on average, to support a rural economy to the same extent as more smaller farms, each with lower average incomes. One might also be concerned that the inter-generational transfer of assets is becoming more difficult as a result of a general rise in asset values, or that fragmentation of farms into non-economic units could result without some assistance to new entrants.

The need to overcome the financial constraints on entering farming in an age where land prices have risen dramatically, where large stocks of machinery are required to employ the most efficient technologies that are available today, and where the structure of demand and costs is such that very high volumes of production per man are required to yield a satisfactory level of income from farming, has been effective in changing some minds about the role of part-time farming as a means of entry into agriculture. Recently, the Canadian Parliament has approved amendments to the regulations governing the operations of the Farm Credit Corporation (a Federal agency in Canada that is a significant source of capital for the agricultural industry) to allow it to extend loans to individuals who will still hold off-farm jobs for a period of up to five years as they develop their agricultural enterprises. So, there is an implicit recognition now in Canada that whatever one feels about part-time farming as a permanent feature of agriculture, or as a way out of agriculture, it is an acceptable state as far as entry is concerned.

But there are other questions that need to be answered before it is decided that the encouragement of new entry via the part-time farming route is an acceptable general strategy, whatever the need for new farm entrants, and the desirability of having more farms in the future that currently appear to be forthcoming as a result of "natural forces". In the first place, we agree, I think, that one of the main obstacles in establishing a farm today is the high cost of land (even land that is **not** under the influence of immediate urban pressure or speculation). By encouraging and enabling individuals to pay more of the asking price for land and other assets by allowing him to combine public capital and his private capital earned through off-farm employment, are we doing anything more than institutionalizing

200

the high asset price into the future; that is, removing elements of "buyer resistence" to the high price? Further, having assisted the individual to establish himself in a part-time situation, are we really **going** to have the political or moral will to force him to go to a full-time situation (which may be sub-optimal for the family) or get out when his "trial period" terminates? Or, having encouraged the individual to establish himself on a part-time basis, are we going to be prepared to guarantee him the returns that are sufficient to cover costs, living expenses **and** leave enough for capital accumulation sufficient to get into farming full-time, and overcome all other constraints that make a full-time situation better for him than a persistent part-time situation? One shudders at the real costs of doing this.

What frightens me more is that by taking a perspective that is too short, allowing ourselves to be pressed towards programs that will do nothing more than ensure that we become locked into the program itself, we can miss the goal that we originally sought.

I think that a scenario outlined for me by a very astute farmer in Saskatchewan, in response to a concern I had expressed that we might soon have too few farmers, contains a tenable hypothesis (even if its practicality rests on several assumptions). Suppose that we now have a farm that contains a considerable acreage and other assets, whose owner is now considering retirement. Probably no single individual has the capital to purchase it all as a going concern, so the farm may well become fragmented again. Assuming that under present technology it is still possible to earn a reasonable living on a fragment of the original holding in a family farming situation, it may well be desirable **not** to have a program to allow a single individual to evolve himself into a position where he assumes control of the entire original holding. Or it may be desirable to invest public funds in development of technology that favour smaller holdings rather than investing in a single transfer of high priced assets from one person to another, while preserving the old technology. Therefore, whatever the appeal of encouraging part-time farming as a means of entering agriculture, one needs to ask whether we are prepared to live with the side effects of the action, and whether there are other strategies that might also be effective in encouraging entry directly into a full-time situation.

PART-TIME FARMING AND EXIT FROM AGRICULTURE

Individuals who are winding down their farming operations by managing fewer enterprises on smaller scales over time present a special sort of policy problem. In many cases it is the relatively poorer individuals, and older individuals, who are involved. The feelings motivating our concern are partially economic and partially humanitarian. We feel that individuals should have a right to a graceful retirement, taking with them the full value of their accumulated assets that were hard won over a lifetime of work and relatively lower levels of consumption. At the same time there is a feeling that the resources tied up in the hands of an operator who is winding down might better be used by a farmer who feels the constraints of resource scarcity as he tries to expand or enter farming. Quite apart from concerns we might have that there may be too few farmers from a rural development viewpoint, we are at least concerned that the farms that do exist are viable and using resources well.

So it would appear that programs dealing with part-time farmers who are already trying to leave agriculture on their own volition may have a positive sum outcome. But problems would arise rapidly if it were perceived that a public program was available that was a "market of last resort" for resources that were not essentially wanted by the private sector at the price that the part-time farmer thought he should get for them, or if it became apparent that there was a program that provided a "fail safe" out for individuals who had erred in commiting resources to agricultural enterprises that were not viable. A more serious problem would arise if it were perceived that the public program was being used too aggressively in trying to reduce the incidence of part-time farming leading some individuals into sub-optimal long-term situations with respect to their family resources by making the immediate liquidation prospects overly attractive.

However, it appears plausible that an appropriate screening of prospective participants in a public program, and the provision of administrative directives that permitted public holding of assets in trust until suitable "next users" were found could overcome most of the problems associated with retiring part-time farms and farmers. Some fundamental questions would remain, such as whether or not we are really satisfied that the rate of resource transfer from retiring farmers to next users is proceeding too slowly; or whether the capital realized by farmers releasing their assets is too low relative to what the resources are really worth; or whether the resources held by part-time but retiring farmers are being essentially misused because the enterprises they operate are somehow inefficient (in say, the economic sense that the use of the resource in the part-time enterprise contributes marginally less than it could contribute to overall well-being by being used in someone else's enterprises). What is really at stake, then, is not the question of whether we can agree on a set of circumstances which we equate with failure of an asset market to give the outcome we find socially acceptable, and whether in fact these sets of circumstances are materializing with regularity.

PERSISTENT PART-TIME FARMING

The central issue as it appears to me, however, is to decide what strategy should be adopted with respect to persons who have found that engaging in part-time farming is an optimal way for them to use their family resources in the long term. What is most sobering to me is the fact that a significant number of these farmers appear to exist even in the face of being excluded from many of the current programs now operating in support of farmers and the agricultural industry.

For reasons that must have seemed reasonable at the time, programs that have been developed for agriculture in Canada have adopted several criteria for eligibility. Most currently embody the idea of what a *bona fide* farmer must be: a person whose principal occupation is farming; a person deriving more than 50 per cent of his income from farming; a person whose **family** derives more than 50 per cent of its income from farming; a person "known in his district as a farmer"; a rural resident utilizing a calculated 120 man days per year in farming or a farmland owner utilizing a calculated 400 man days per year of hired labour; a person who reports to a surveyer that he is a farmer[3], to mention a few.

In a paper that will be published in the near future[4], Professor Lerner demonstrates how completely arbitrary the "part-time" definition is and shows how individuals performing exactly the same agricultural functions can be considered *bona fide* farmers or not, depending on product prices, their family compositions, and how they combine their own labour with family and hired labour. Professor Lerner also points out that there are several sets of situational factors relating to the circumstances that constrain an individual, as well as personal factors that relate to the individual himself, that combine to create visible part-time farming. He also shows that there are full-time farms that would really only warrant the part-time attention of the operator, if there were opportunities for non-farm work. What we are really led to appreciate in such work is that an individual finds the situation for himself that satisfies him, given the limitations that he has and that society has placed on him. The problem for public policy is to decide whether it is beneficial for the individual and society to remove any of the constraints on him.

Traditionally, agricultural policies have tried to create an environment in which farming would be efficient (with large pay-offs of this for the non-farm sector), and have farmers rewarded equitably, both in terms of the incomes accruing to them in the sector as a whole and incomes accruing to farm families within the sector. How policy approaches part-time farming would be largely conditioned by how well proposals seem to have positive pay-offs in terms of equity and efficiency, for the part-time farmers themselves and for others involved in agriculture and in the rural areas. So immediately, it seems to me that the most severe attitude that public policy could adopt at this point is to retain the approach as it now is, that is, continue to define by appropriate eligibility criteria, a set of intended clients who are *bona fide* farmers. Whatever the gains to others that harsher treatment might yield, it would be difficult to demonstrate that these gains would warrant moving individual part-time farmers to positions that they would find to be sub-optimal relative to their present situations.

I do not see, for example, the validity in an argument that would claim that part-time operations necessarily harm the full-time operator's position in commodity markets. The price in a competitive market is determined by the marginal unit of product being offered against the marginal unit of demand. But whether the market for any given agricultural product is controlled or not, it is by no means clear whether the last marginal unit is really that offered by the part-time farm or the full-time farm. The apparent persistence of the activity certainly is evidence that enterprises that are seen on a part-time basis do not just appear when prices are good, nor do they necessarily expand more rapidly or less rapidly than full-time farming operations when prices warrant.

The persistent nature of part-time farming would also be evidence that a certain efficiency did exist with respect to resource use, since if we grant the operator some business sense, using one's own resources when opportunities are available to let someone else use them shows that they are working in an acceptable manner for their owner. In a short term, we might suspect that speculative or other motives would lead an individual to use his resources in a way that would appear inefficient; but I would be more skeptical of the claim that part-time farming was inefficient if it persisted.

Yet it is not immediately clear that positive measures need to be taken to encourage enough part-time farming so that society benefits, even though there are probably social benefits to be had from part-time farming if the only other alternative for resource use was to have fewer but larger farms. The fact that some people have found part-time farming an acceptable situation for themselves when they could have chosen not to acquire part-time enterprises, indicates that they feel better off having done so. But would the life style that they have found acceptable be the style chosen by others if they had the chance? Further, many persons who are now in part-time farming in one way or another are anything but needy, either in monetary terms or in terms of production and management advice.

An analysis of the income tax returns of approximately 366,000 individuals who reported any farm income in 1971, soon to be published by the Economics Branch of Agriculture Canada[5], shows that there is a positive correlation between the levels of net farm income and levels of non-farm income for classes of individuals with net incomes from zero up to $20,000 from all sources. In other words, when no distinction is made between the type of farm or farmer, and emphasis is placed simply on the fact that the individual earns income in agriculture, groups of people who earn higher incomes from non-farm activities also seem to earn higher incomes from the farming activities, on average. Of course, the average clouds the fact that within any income class, there will be a distribution of incomes by source as well, and whether or not this distribution leads to a different conclusion about the tendency indicated by the class-wide averages is still to be seen. The point is that there seems to be an ability that some persons have to earn from any source, while others simply do not have this ability. Part of this ability would also be the ability to organize and manage one's personal resources well (in addition to actually having the human and non-human resources to manage). So if public policy is concerned with the fact that some individuals appear to have less than their fair share of income, it is reasonable to expect remedial programs to focus on the individual and his circumstances rather than on regulating and encouraging various potential sources of income.

WHAT SHOULD BE DONE ABOUT PART-TIME FARMING?

What public strategy with respect to part-time farming would accommodate the trade-offs that are involved with this feature of the agricultural industry? If we keep in mind the fact that part-time

204

farming was a choice that a family made, I think that part of the strategy becomes clear, since we cannot have a public strategy that will **make** people happier. We can only have one that allows them to be happier if they wish to choose it. If we keep in mind that part-time farming is a feature of the agricultural industry that does use resources, and will continue to (since I do not think the public would accept the implications of forcing part-time farming out of existence), public strategy should make sure that the resources are used as well as possible within the constraints that ownership and private decision-making establish.

I conclude therefore, that the best strategy with respect to part-time farming is one of "benign neglect". This concept was put forth by President Johnson's assistant Pat Moynihan to describe an appropriate way of "dealing" with Blacks in the United States. What I mean by using it here is that public policy should be completely indifferent to the existence of the phenomenon; taking action neither for it nor against it — (almost as if to say that once we cease thinking of part-time farming as an "issue", what we identify now as problems with it will, in fact, simply go away). The real problem seems to me to be how to get attitudes changed, in effect "liberalized" to the point where there is the genuine benign neglect.

How might this view be implemented? One readily administered scheme would be to simply remove all eligibility criteria which make reference to *bona fide* farmers from programs for agriculture. The resulting attitude would be that anyone who had an agricultural enterprise, singly or in combination with others, would be eligible for assistance to make that enterprise productive. We would not assume that it was the production of full-time farms alone that was of value in consumer markets, only that the production was important. We would not be declaring as we now do in effect, that you have to farm full time to be efficient, but rather, that anyone with the motivation to use resources he commands in the agricultural enterprise should be encouraged to have them used efficiently (which may, incidentally, lead one to advise the resource owner for his own sake to lease out the resource he owns to an other user).

What interests me more from a rural development viewpoint, is that by becoming indifferent to whether or not people have enterprises that do not warrant their full attention, we permit ourselves to really do something about equity and rural revitalization. It seems to me that forcing an individual to declare himself as a full-time non-industrial worker as a pre-condition for further action limits the chances of retaining families in rural areas and adds to the cost and the scale of the non-farm production projects that have any hope of being successful when located in rural areas. I can imagine an individual who is, as Professor Lerner describes, a full-time farmer on a part-time farm, becoming considerably better off by actually moving to a genuine part-time position with respect to his labour resource, and marketing the rest of his labour in a smaller or seasonally varied non-farm endeavour. But if we continue to be very interested in the feature of organization and structure of agricultural enterprises to the exclusion of interest in the human consequences of the structure, we will continue to limit possibilities that could pay off well.

However, for some of the reasons that I described relating to the demand for assets and their prices, I would not go so far as to establish a program to encourage part-time farming overtly (although I must confess that I do not see anything to be lost by developing technologies that make smaller scale collections of resources productive when used in agricultural enterprise). Even if the programs were there, I am not sure they would be used.

Well intentioned individuals often press for public interventions to encourage situations that they view as desirable. I would be generally sympathetic to this process. In the case of part-time farming, however, it seems completely adequate (a) to jettison the assumption that its persistence creates any real issue, and (b) to make public policy neutral with respect to it.

NOTES AND REFERENCES

1 The comments made in the paper are in no way to be taken as reflecting the views of policies of Agriculture Canada, or the Federal Government of Canada. The author is gratful for the comments of Professor Lerner, University of Guelph, which were helpful in preparing this paper.

2 Heady, E.O., and Sonka, S.T., **Farm-Size Structure and Off-Farm Income and Employment Generation in the North Central Region.** North Central Regional Center for Rural Development, Ames, Feb. 1975.

3 This is not a program eligibility criterion, but the effective definition of a farmer used in Canada's Labour Force Survey statistics.

4 Lerner, Arthur, "Classifying Part-Time Farmers for Agricultural Policy Purposes", **Canadian Farm Economics,** Forthcoming.

5 Darcovich, W., Davey, B., Gellner, J. and Piracha, Z., **An Income Profile of Farm Taxfilers, Canada and Provinces, 1971.** Economics Branch, Agriculture Canada, Ottawa. 1975. I have not taken individuals with declared negative income into account here, considering that these negative returns probably reflect some contrived situations which are not likely to persist over time.

ATTITUDES TOWARDS PART-TIME FARMING BY FARMERS' UNIONS

Richard Wietfeldt

"Many, if not most, farmers in Canada are part timers!" With this recent exclamation Professor George Winter implied that this should be a surprise to us. I would suggest that the ancient art of farming has **usually** been a part-time affair. I will attempt here to outline a few changes in the history of agriculture and farm structure. This should help us to understand why modern agriculturalists find it a surprise and sometimes an offense that farmers are so often part-timers. It will also help us to understand the inability of farm organizations to find a consensus on how to approach the question of part-time farming.

When I speak of multiple jobholding or part-time farming I am referring to work done off the operator's farm, or at least, outside of the operator's farm enterprise. Off-farm work would include work on a neighboring farm (unless this labor is returned on a communal or partnership basis), custom machinery work, and any selling or distributing or small industry the farmer carries on, as well as work in factory, forest, or office. But as soon as we have defined the area in this way, we have made ourselves a great puzzle. It is easy to conceptualize agricultural activity — the work of growing crops and rearing livestock — and to separate it from other work. It is very difficult to find actual persons or communities that do just agriculture.

Of course there are areas that one could only describe broadly as farming areas. My point here is that there is a conceptual difficulty about the "part-timer farmer", for while we can abstractly conceive farming as a separate and distinct activity, farmers as actual people usually do several things besides grow their own crops and livestock. The farmer as a concrete person who just farms has not often existed.

Only a little reflection on the long story of agriculture shows that this conceptual point is borne out historically. It was perhaps 6,500 years before Christ, in the Middle East, that men first learned to leave some seeds scattered on the ground to improve the next year's crop, and to domesticate the animals. This change, from being a predator to being a shaper of plants and animals, was a fundamental revolution for mankind. It meant, among other things, that the seasons became much more significant than before. Now intensive periods with the hoe, the plow, or the harvesting blade were interspersed with periods of new-found leisure. Accordingly men developed in association with agriculture the arts of brewing, weaving, the manufacture of pottery (to cook their cereals) and the making of polished stone tools. As there was likely little specialization in these crafts, it would appear that farming was a part-time activity from the first. So long as farming is a subsistence activity, with the produce being for consumption by the farm household rather than for sale, the cultivators spend a good deal of their year making clothing, tools, etc. Under subsistence agriculture part-time farming remains the rule.

The necessary condition of civilization is the ability of sustained surplus production of food. When first achieved, in ancient Mesopotamia about four thousand years before Christ, there began what has been common in most civilizations where money has played a relatively small role; that is, the ruling urban order extracted from the farming classes this surplus, either in the form of labour services or as a share of the agricultural produce. In either case the peasant labours a substantial amount of time for ends other than farming for his own profit. However, more of his time is now spent at agricultural activity. The society has become specialized to some extent. While in early Sumer trade between the peasants and the specialized craftsmen was very limited, the descendents of these peasants three thousand years later were able to trade some surplus grain for iron tools that their ancestors had had to make for themselves from stone or wood. Increasing urbanization and trade made it possible for the peasant class, too, to specialize more fully in agriculture. Examples could be added and aspects multiplied, but this general point seems to hold.

Turning now to our own situation, our North American forefathers were far more self-sufficient than the farmer today. In mid-19th century Ontario the following activities, in addition to husbandry directly occupied farmers: cutting and clearing forest land, the logging connected with this land improvement, making pails or tubs for the house, repairing tools or making new ones, dressing the flax for spinning, making linen for bags as well as for the house, making boots, mittens, and harness from the hides they had tanned on shares, splitting and making shingles for the roof, making home furniture, melting pewter and making spoons with moulds, shoeing horses, leaching ashes and boiling lye to make potash for sale, labouring on public roads as required by statute, slaughtering meat for the household, transporting products to market and hauling in all building supplies, splitting rail for fences, and digging the well. Some farmers still do some of these, and those of us over thirty-nine years old remember our grandfathers doing many more. But the mere listing of them reminds us of the degree of specialization in modern farming — a sharp change over a mere century and a half.

A separate but related factor is that farmers have specialized in fewer commodities per farm. This has often increased the seasonality of their labour requirements, releasing more labour at other than seasonal peaks. My point is that modern mechanized and specialized farming has lower labour requirements. Some of this labour has not found off-farm opportunities, leading to the controversial underemployment in agriculture. Much of this surplus labour has moved from the farms into urban residence and employment. And some surplus farm labour has shifted into combined farm/non-farm employment; often this only represents a shift of production of goods and services from the traditional location on the farm to a specialized commercial establishment.

The increase in income per capita that has resulted from this recent industrialization has come to farmers as well, though less abundantly than to society generally. More profitable alternatives have presented themselves for their labour and skills than agriculture could provide. This has reflected badly on the occupation of farming. It creates pressure on those who continue to farm —

pressure to justify their own continuation as farmers, pressure to defend farming as a way of making a living that is integral and respectable.

Certainly an element in such integrity is that a man should earn a level of income that enables him to offer his labour. To the extent that part-time farming has been adjustment of farm manpower into more profitable employment, it shares in the implication that agriculture is not an occupation that is integral in the modern, affluent world.

The feeling that a man should be able to make a living from his farming alone is a strong one, certainly in the Ontario farm community. There is regularly a corresponding feeling of guilt or shame with the man who has to take a job off his farm. Some of the emotional impact of the family farm concept derives from this — the concept of a self-contained farm unit where the family labour is utilized fully and where family labour is largely sufficient.

The conflict, or perceived conflict, of urban and rural forces in our society is another element in the disfavour shown by many farmers of multiple jobholders. For farm-minded folk these have been times not only of advances in technology and freedom from hard, tedious physical labour, and long-sought opportunities in a new spirit. These have also been times that wiped out real, positive values that their grandparents and parents had fought for and won. These values include the stable rural community with its communal work patterns and neighborhood visiting and the local council, the respect for honesty in work and business, the ability of schools to teach arithmetic and reading and other exact skills, and the old-time religion based on the transcendent and guarding the bonds of family life. When they see their children leap into teenage marriages with, too often, a tragic result, when they see the waste, the abandonment to passion, the restlessness, when the blaring broadcasts and the glaring signs indicate a wide-spread insensitivity to beauty, then it is often a conceived urbanization that is blamed as the origin of these evils.

And if then the full-time farmer has a young neighbor who mentions that he now earns $7 per hour at his town job, that he would like to give it up but he cannot, that his eight hours leave him fresh and free for plenty of field work, the full-timer may wonder whether he should not have asked at the plant for work. But if that farmer's neighbor is, say, an accountant from the city who paid $2,000 per acre so he can raise his kids in the country and do a bit of farming, the resentment is bound to burn the full-timer a little. And if the accountant talks rapidly and often, and wins a seat on the municipal council and pushes for an expensive new school, and if his son and friends roar too fast on their motorbikes up and down the concession, then the local farmers' union may be urged to take action to protect the community against the intruders. The group may pass a resolution denying capital grants or tax revenues to those earning forty per cent or more of their income off their farm.

Farmers' organizations have not, by and large, found room in their ranks to support the part-time farmer. In Ontario, at least, and seemingly generally, few people that are perceived to be part-time farmers are active in farm organizations. The key is in what is acceptable to farm organization people as off-farm activity. Most acceptable seems to be farm business sidelines, such as selling fertilizer or seed. It may be that such activity keeps the part-timer close to farmers and farm attitudes. It may also be that being around the farm during the daylight hours is an important element toward qualifying as a farmer. Certainly one simply logistical factor in not representing part-time farmers is that union activities are not adjusted to their schedules. Union meetings are not held on weekends, for example, but most part-time farmers would be more able to attend on Saturday or Sunday afternoon than on weekday evenings.

The least acceptable part-time farmer probably is one who works a day-shift the year round, particularly if he exhibits urban styles. One element of urban style that inspires suspicion is apparent instability or impermanence. On the other hand an established farmer who spends a third or a half of his time on boards and in organizational work may retain farm manners and may be fully accepted as a full-time farmer.

A common attitude on membership drives is that part-time farmers will not join, so they are not worth the trouble to ask. Those who attend a meeting may well be ignored or made uncomfortable. The farm organization speaks not just for farm interests but for farmers — the particular farmers who form the active membership and leadership. They have organized to defend the rural and often this means defend in the face of the impinging urban. Precisely as organized, therefore, they are the more set to detect and parry urban influence. To the extent that in some areas under the urban shadow part-time farming does represent a stage in the retreat of agriculture, the union has accurately located an advance line of its real foe in part-time farming.

It should be added that negative attitudes toward part-time farmers seem to be softening in recent years. Seemingly, too, negative attitudes were less prevalent on the Prairies, where the seasonality in the large grain operations is more pronounced.

Others at this conference will have given evidence that, at least in some areas, part-time farming seems to be a permanent, not only a transitional, feature of modern agriculture. I believe that this is so, and most farm organizations are taking some steps toward recognizing this as well. In view of the policy-making function of farmers' unions, then, I have one recommendation to make. It is simple but, I believe, sufficient to facilitate realistic policy formulation.

The recommendation is that the approach toward part-time farmers be formulated with respect to the particular end or objective of the policy in question.

1) If the policy objective is increased quantity of food production, then evaluate part-time farmers just as one does full-time farmers — on how their production per acre measures up — and design measures to prohibit the low production.

2) If the policy objective is soil conservation, or quality of food, or community weed or pest control, or other quality factors with social implications, then examine part-time farmers' — and full-time farmers' — husbandry practices and abilities, and upgrade or discourage the incompetent.

3) If the aim of a policy is low-cost production, then test the efficiency of the part-time operators — and of full-time farmers.

4) If there is a policy objective of stabilizing or increasing rural population in order to better rural community life, then the organization might adopt measures supporting rural employment opportunities of all sorts, farm and non-farm, might encourage small land holdings for all rural residents to enjoy farming, and might generally foster part-time farming as well as full-time.

5) If the objective is to raise the incomes of those who rely solely on farm income, and this is a measure of welfare assistance to a disadvantaged but desirable portion of the society, then perhaps exclude from the program those who earn less than a stated percentage of their family's living from their farm operation.

This procedure of distinguishing the ends of any policy would solve all the problems I am aware of regarding farm organizations and their policy toward part-time farmers. We cannot possibly expect to ferret out and approach constructively the manifold aspects of part-time farming unless we clearly differentiate the yardsticks by which we are measuring this phenomenon. Once these criteria are articulated, then the different kinds of part-time farming will easily be distinguished and evaluated separately. Only an implicit beginning toward discriminating policy aims is evident in the answers from the farm organizations I have polled on this issue.

I have made some broad sweeps in this short paper but the summation can be brief.

1) Most farmers have been part-time, for they have lived in subsistence economies where they did not exchange much surplus food for services and other goods. They must provide these other services and goods for themselves, but this is non-farm activity.

2) Our surprise at the prevalence of part-time farming is because we have forgotten how recently farmers have left a more subsistence type of farming and have begun to purchase goods and services, notably manufactured farm inputs which only recently they provided for themselves. As farmers have come increasingly to exchange surplus produce for factors of production, we should only have expected that much of their labour released thereby would have found its way into non-farm occupation.

3) All the same, there is some good reason for individual farmers and even more for farmer organizations, to fear and oppose part-time farming. I have not tried to justify their attitudes, only to explain them as part of their reaction to urbanization and some of its ill effects.

4) If farmers became more able to articulate the objectives of their policy and to distinguish one policy aim for another, they would find part-time farming less perplexing. My own experience is that schools and universities are, alas, becoming less inclined and less able to teach the skills of clear reasoning and clear expression that could bring that potentiality to being in farmers' unions in the future.

NOTES AND REFERENCES

Black, John D., **The Rural Economy of New England: A Regional Study,** Cambridge, Mass. Harvard University Press, 1950.

Bloch, Marc, **The Feudal Society,** Vol. I, Chicago: University of Chicago Press, 1964.

Census of Canada, **Agriculture, Canada and Provinces,** Ottawa: Statistics Canada, 1971.

Clark, Colin, **The Conditions of Economic Progress,** 3rd ed., London: Macmillan, 1955.

Clark, Colin and Haswell, Margaret, **The Economics of Subsistence Agriculture,** 4th ed., London: Macmillan, 1970.

Haight, Canniff, **Country Life in Canada,** reproduced Belleville, Ont.: Mika Silk Screening, 1971 (1885).

Lerner, Arthur, "Progress Report on Classification of Part-Time Farmers." Unpublished paper.

MacDougall, John, **Rural Life in Canada,** Toronto, Westminster Co., 1913.

McNeill, William H., **The Rise of the West: A History of the Human Community,** New York: Mentor, 1963.

Mage, Julius, "Economic Factors Associated with Part-Time Farming in Southern Ontario and Waterloo County." Published in **Geographical Inter-University Resource Management Seminars,** Vol. 3 (1972-73), Department of Geography, University of Waterloo.

Perkins, Brian, **Multiple Jobholding Among Farm Operators,** Guelph, 1972.

Schultz, Theodore, **Transforming Traditional Agriculture,** New Haven: Yale University Press, 1964.

Uppal, I.S., **Disguised Unemployment in an Underdeveloped Economy,** Bombay, New York: Asia Publ. House, 1973.

ATTITUDES OF THE FARMER'S UNION
TO MULTIPLE JOBHOLDERS IN FINLAND

Patrick Hackman

INTRODUCTION

In the parts of Finland where field cropping is practiced the growing season is fairly short. In the far North it begins about the 10th of May and ends about the 25th of September, that is, about 140 days. In the South the growing period begins at about the 1st of May and ends about the 20th of October, thus being about 180 days. Because of the climatic influence of the Atlantic Ocean and the long light-period of summer days, field cropping in Finland can be rather productive.

Considering these conditions it is natural that, during the time when field cropping has been practiced, farmers have tried to find income creating activities which could match the heavy seasonal labour demand of crop production. As this has not been possible within traditional agriculture complementary activities were found in fishing, hunting and crafts of different kinds. In the recent past, however, seasonal surplus farm labour was largely used for cutting and hauling wood for fuel, for local building construction, and for industrial raw material. The cutting and hauling was almost totally performed in the winter. The small farm with only a little adjacent forest was apt to send labour to forest working sites even far away from the farm for several months at a time.

In the last decades field cropping has changed markedly, and similar to the harvesting technology in the forests, it has tended to become more and more mechanized. But while forest harvesting now is increasingly performed around the year, the need for labour in field cropping is still subject to severe seasonality. Given the seasonal underemployment of a great number of farmers, in a time of rising aspirations regarding living standards and the decreasing role of subsistence economy of farms, we are presented with the problems of the rationality of the part-time farms both on the level of business economy and that of the human society.

Marketing of agricultural produce in Finland is dominated by large co-operatives founded some fifty years ago by the farmers themselves. These co-operative enterprises have, during the past three decades, besides reaching their present strong position within the agricultural sector, forcefully expanded into sectors more or less separate from it. Consequently, as the co-operative enterprises become very large and structurally more complicated, the possibility of farmers controlling the activities of the co-operative enterprises has rapidly diminished. Market prices of the main agricultural products — milk, meat and cereals — have for some time already been maneuvered by the government in accordance with the almost annual income deals made in co-operation with the trade unions.

Most Finnish farms also produce wood for industrial use, but in this sector the farmers' co-operative enterprises have not decisively influenced the market situation. Neither have any price deals regarding roundwood been very successful.

The market situation of agricultural products in Finland today is for the Farmer's Union a difficult one. There is constantly a surplus production, especially of animal fat and eggs. Even cereals, especially wheat, have been produced above the level of national consumption. Either there is a surplus production, or there is a generally noticed surplus production capacity — this will naturally influence the market price situation. Even if there is no actual play of free market forces, a surplus will seriously influence the negotiation positions of the Farmer's Union. For the time being the Farmer's Union people apparently feel the surplus capacity of Finnish agriculture detrimental considering the possibilities of carrying through a strategic price policy for agricultural products.

CHANGING CONDITIONS

Off-farm work has been a familiar phenomenon ever since the times of subsistence economy. The character of the off-farm employment, however, changed to become more of a salaried occupation during the phase of semi-industrial development which in Finland began about three or four generations ago. Then, the woodworking industry started employing lumbermen, haulers, timber floaters, forest supervisors, and so on. In the beginning of this century much of the building and industrial activity was still taking place in rural conditions, and cutting and transporting wood was, up to the fifties, the major source of off-farm employment. During the last two decades, however, the trend has been towards decreasing labour inputs in the forest harvesting activities by heavy mechanization. This has meant taking more and more of the cutting and driving operations into the hands of the corporations which buy and use the wood as a raw material. In this way much of the initiative, and thereby also an increasing part of the market power, has passed into the hands of the woodworking industry.

By the use of heavier mechanical equipment, and by the use of efficient labour planning, the need for labour in forest harvesting has diminished drastically. However, it still remains to be seen whether the reforestation and the maintenance of young, densely stocked forest stands can be rationally taken care of if the number of people working in the woods continues to diminish. If significantly new technological solutions are not soon brought about, forestry is once again apt to offer some economic employment to those farmers who wish to choose multiple jobholding for a living.

In the past, women were much less frequently than men performing work away from their homesteads. Traditionally, women, especially the wives of the farmers, took care of the home and the animals. Due to the fact that economically active females of statuses other than farmers' wives usually no longer stay on the farms, female farm labour on the whole has lately diminished. On the other hand, the increasing mechanization of the animal production on the farms, the increasing occupational ability among young farmers' wives, and the urbanization of the home maintenance and family life might suggest an increase of off-farm labour among farmers' wives, provided that there is employment at hand within commuting distances from the farms.

Multiple jobholding among farmers is more and more apt to be concentrated in the urban fringe areas of the southern parts of Finland where industrialization already has reached a certain level. However, the service sector that seems to continue expanding might offer some off-farm employment to both farmers and farmers' spouses also in the rural regions.

ATTITUDES TOWARDS PART-TIME FARMING

Up to now there have been no actual conflicts between full-time farmers and part-time farmers. However, some contemporary literature written on rural life in general, and also some later social studies reveal some distrust between those farmers who lived from farming alone, and those who took up off-farm employment. The opinion that it was disgraceful for a farmer to work away from the farm has been observed by the Finnish sociologist Antti Eskola, according to his publication on rural and urban people edited in 1963.[1] The money income from a source not very well known, and the labour conditions in the working sites often situated far away from the farmsteads naturally caused disturbances to the prior structure of life. Part-time farms were then said to be less well maintained than the full-time farms. Moreover, the agricultural oriented farmers' extension service organizations seem to have striven against multiple jobholding among farmers referring to its economic inferiority. In the twenties, it is said, there was even a rhyme saying: Logging in winter will make your fields grow only flowers in summer.

Forest economists, on the other hand, found the multiple jobholding very practical also from the viewpoint of the farm business, as it provided economic use of both labour, horses and equipment during winter.[2]

In the farmers' organizations the farmer representatives have been the most concerned not to have too many multiple jobholders in the farm sector. Generally, it seems, the closer the representatives were to the grassroot level, the tougher their opposition. Only very recently, in the wake of the specially difficult income negotiations of 1969 and 1974 between the government and the separate trade unions, there was some serious criticism coming from the level of local Farmer's Union leaders against treating part-time farmers on an equal basis as the full-time farmers. They stressed the point that part-time farmers during hard times do not sufficiently support the farm sector in the battle to ensure the appropriate farm product prices, which naturally is of crucial interest for the full-time farmers.

On the grassroot level it is generally considered that multiple jobholding farmers are less interested in taking part in the actions of the Farmer's Union. The situation of a farmer, who works at a workshop or an industrial plant with workers who belong to the labour union of that particular sector, often becomes somewhat schitzophrenic. Especially if his job is of a continuous kind the pressure to join the labour union may be severe. The loyalty towards fellow farmers may then be poor, as traditionally other farmers may appear as competitors in many ways. In spite of this, the statistics seem to show that there is about the same proportion of part-time farmers among the Farmer's Union members as among farmers in general.

Some Statistics on Finnish Farmers[3]

1) Number of farmers according to registration in 1972, somewhat over 215,000;

2) Number of part-time farmers according to the same register as above, denoting the farmers who consider themselves as permanently working away from the farm, 17,885;

3) Number of farmers belonging to the Farmer's Union in 1972, somewhat over 164,000 for the Finnish speaking organization and 11,000 for the Swedish speaking organization.[4]

Because of the increased rate of change regarding social conditions, and also because of the complexity of today's society, the Farmer's Union apparently could not act properly without the aid of salaried officials. The group of Union officials, thanks to the good possibilities of being well informed, in fact forms an influential outpost considering agricultural policy matters. The opinions of the Union officials regarding the part-time farmers are thus of great importance. Naturally, the elected farmer representatives influence the lines of action of the Union administration, but in fact they decide who is chosen to be a Union official. They will apparently make their choice among people who have strong connections with the farm population. Thus, many of the Farmer's Union officials are sons of farmers. Furthermore, many of them have received their professional education within the sphere of agriculture. Some of them have even inherited a family farm, and are part-time farmers themselves. The Union administration is, perhaps because of these conditions, not ready to start any great anti-part-time farming action without a careful analysis of the impact of part-time farming on the whole farm sector.

For the time being, according to the Farmer's Union administration, the Union takes a positive attitude towards all kinds of subsidiary income activities performed by farmers.[5] On the other hand, the Union takes a strictly negative attitude towards any kind of part-time farming that might hide land speculation, escaping income and property tax, and agribusiness. These principles have been applied when preparing recent laws and other policy measures taken to, among other things, diminish the total output of agricultural products.

The actual part-time farmers, whose farm organizations (i.e. production patterns) are influenced by jobs performed away from the farms, however, have been left "afloat" without an explicit legitimization, although the Farmer's Union itself in its attempts to industrialize rural parts of the country evidently has created new possibilities of part-time farming.

The influential farmers' co-operative firms have not applied any segregative measures separating full-time farmers from part-time farmers. Neither has the ideological instance of the producer-oriented co-operative movement yet made any explicit distinction between the two categories.

The agricultural extension service, recently reorganized better to meet the ends of the government — however, still highly influenced by the Farmer's Union — has not yet taken up any kind of information work that would be specially designed to suit the part-time farmers. A survey made in September 1972 by the author proved that in only two of the eighteen extension districts there had been some occupational training designed for multiple jobholding farmers during the past year. Among the extension workers there was nobody who in any way had specialized in part-time farming problems, or was specially appointed to take care of counselling part-time farmers. Eight of the eighteen district managing directors stressed that plans had been made to increase, or start to produce, means of information specially designed for part-time farmers. The budgets for this kind of activity, however, were reported to be insignificant.

A generally shared view among the extension district managing directors was that part-time farmers should not be detached from the fellowship of farmers.

Table 1 shows the opinions of different instances within the Farmer's Union in Finland regarding what would be the consequences of a significant increase of part-time farming.

Table 1

Opinions of individual farmers, farmer representatives, and officials of the Finnish Farmer's Union regarding some possible consequences of a significant increase of part-time farming according to discussions, interviews and statements in writing as observed by the author during the period 1964 – 1975.[*] (Opinion stressed x, opinion mentioned o.)

Negative consequences	Individual farmers	Farmer[*] representatives	Union officials
Retards land consolidation	x	o	o
Increases misuse of land		x	o
Increases misuse of farm capital resources		x	
Increases surplus production in agriculture		x	o
Weakens the cohesion and loyalty among farmers		x	
Increases heterogenity among farmers regarding goals and means of the Union			x
Positive consequences			
Improves the living standard on the small farms	x		o
Increases the possibilities of having a feasible service standard in purely rural districts			o
Eases the understanding of farm problems among people of other economic sectors			o
Increases the farmer's knowledge of income standards in other sectors of the economy			o

[*]Farmer's Union local society meeting discussions, an interview study made by the author among farmers in 1967, an interview with Union officials in 1975, and daily papers and agricultural magazines 1964 – 1975.

[*]Farmers who represent their colleagues in the bodies of the Farmer's Union.

NOTES AND REFERENCES

1 Eskola, Antti, **Maalaiset ja kaupunkilaiset.** Helsinki. 1963.

2 Helander, A.B., "Metsatalouden tarjoamasta ansiotyosta," I Kruunun-metsat vv. 1911-1913. Acta Forstalia Fennica 26. Helsinki, 1923.

3 Monthly Review of Agricultural Statistics No. 12. Helsinki, 1974.

4 The Finnish speaking Farmer's Union Maataloustuottajain Keskusliitto was founded in 1917. The Swedish speaking equivalent Svenska Lantbruksproducenternas Centralforbund was founded in 1945. Both organizations claim to consider the interests of the farmers of all sizes of farms, however, the membership figures are the highest for the size categories between 10 and 50 hectares of arable land per farm. The two organizations work in close cooperation.

5 Annual reports of the Farmer's Union Organizations M.T.K. & S.L.C. Helsinki, 1972.

INTERNATIONAL PANEL

Four international speakers were invited to address the symposium briefly on the status of part-time farming in their respective countries. Each was specifically requested to comment on the theme of the session by noting the recognition given to part-time farming by government and by farmer's organizations.

Members of the Panel:

V. SAFVESTAD: Part-Time Farming in Sweden

A. CAVAZZANI: The Problem in Italy

G.V. FUGUITT: Implications for Policy

G.E. JONES: Part-Time Farming in Britain

At the conclusion of the panel session questions were invited from the floor pertaining to the whole of Session IV.

INTERNATIONAL PANEL DISCUSSION ONE:
PART-TIME FARMING IN SWEDEN

Vikar Safvestad

Introduction

Referring to Tables 1 to 4, there are 43,000 farms in Sweden and in my district (Jonkopings) there are just about 8,000 between 0 and 125 acres in size. Income from outside the farm (1973 Census) was 54% for all Sweden — which is high and is increasing every year. Twenty-six per cent of all our farmers spend one month or more outside the farm (Figures 1 and 2).

A Case Study

I would like to tell you about some research that has just been started in Jonkopings community where part-time farming is a significant factor. We are going into 4 small communities within the province, 2 of them good farmland and 2 with poor farm land. We will have cross-tabulations with two communities near the city, where there are good job opportunities, and two of them far away. We hope to have the results a year from now. Our researchers are going out to every farmer, about 400 in total, with approximately 100 farms in each small community. We will try first to develop a map of what is going on in respect to part-time farming in these four districts. For example, time distribution between farm and off-farm work, in costs of hired labour, travel distances and the volume of production from full-time and part-time farmers. With this map to start with we can look at the future and consider alternatives, of what can be done by the Government and by the farmers union considering the economic consequences of any possible action.

Policy Questions

It is very interesting to notice that the discussion around Part-Time Farming is quite new. Of course, now and then there has been some discussion in the early sixties. In 1964 I published a study of a community on the Swedish west coast and since then some other studies have come. However, the more intense discussions have started in Sweden only a couple of years ago. There has been up to now no final standpoint given concerning these questions either from the government or from the farmers associations.

a) Government

Before 1967, part-time farmers as a rule were not excluded from support by the governmental loan and grant system for farmers. However, afterwards it seems that they very seldom got any essential support. From 1967 it is stated by law that support to part-time farming is not allowed. A part-time farmer is in that respect a farmer who takes the main part of his income from sources outside his own farms. There is one limitation: if you need at least one man year on the farm you are not a part-time farmer even if you derive the greatest part of your income from off farm sources. Usually we do not count

SWEDEN

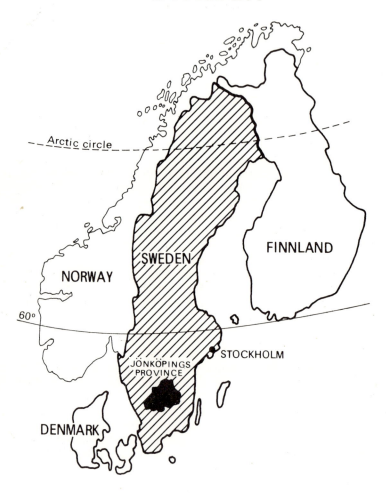

Figure 1

ECONOMIC IMPORTANCE OF AGRICULTURE
FOR DIFFERENT CATEGORIES OF FARMERS
(Forest areas of Gotaland   Gsk   1972)

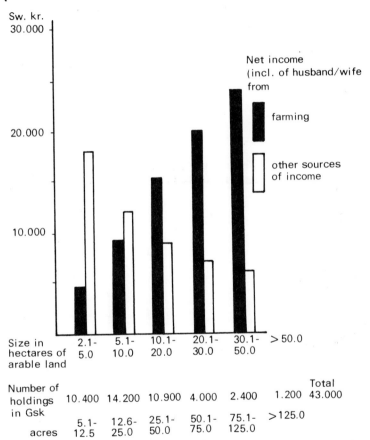

Figure 2

Table 1. Number of Holdings

	I 1961	II 1971
Full-time farms	169.000	92.000
Part-time farms[1]	64.000	58.000
	233.000	150.000

Table 2. Net Income From Sources Outside Agriculture
Percentage of Income

Year	South and Middle Sweden		Northern Sweden	Whole Country
	Plain areas	Forest areas		
1966	27	39	54	37
1973	44	54	69	53

Table 3. Percentage of Farmers with 1 Month
Activity Outside Own Farm[1]

1971	24	26	34	27

1. Work in other person's forest not included.

Table 4

Farmers' work outside own holding in
1961, 1966 and 1971

Whole of Sweden

Year	Number of farmers	Number of day's works. Percentage distribution				Tota
		0	1-50	51-150	150	
1971	149.100	52	15	10	22	100
1966	178.500	66	6	13	15	100
1961	224.100	68	7	12	13	100

Data Source· Statistical Yearbook of Agriculture 1974

the combined agri-business, the combined forestry and farming, as a part-time farm. The law concerning loans and grants to the combined farm is in one respect like that one for part-time farming. This means that the agricultural part has to be a full-time business besides that one of forestry to qualify for governmental support. I have an investigation going in my province where I have as a goal to legalize marriage between forestry and agriculture. It is **not** now!

There is now only one exception from what I have told you. That concerns milk production. Since 1971 we can give support to owners of small farms with at least a production of 50,000 kg milk a year. It may be looked upon as a support to milk production and also as a temporary support to a farmer above 40 years of age until he leaves his farm. In this situation we have some part-time farmers who have received support.

b) Farmers Union (LRF)

Dec. 1974: "The increasing importance and number of part-time farmers also has consequences for the Farmers Union. A growing part of the members are part-time farmers. For that reason we need to know more about part-time farming. We need to analyze its impact on the number of farmers, production and income. Built on such an analysis we have to make an LRF-policy concerning part-time farming for the future." In its directions for the investigation group LRF has stated that the part-time farm has come to stay and that its importance probably will be greater in the future.

1. An analysis:

What has happened in the past concerning the number of part-time farmers? What is the reason for increasing numbers? What will happen in the future?

Points to look upon:

(a) Increasing mobility in the labour market as a whole

(b) Shorter work time per week and longer holidays

(c) Better communications

(d) Technical changes in farming resulting in less demand for labour

(e) Impact of tax laws

2. This analysis will be the basis for the judgement about the consequences for LRF as a union and as a cooperative movement. This analysis will also provide material for discussions around agriculture as a whole for the future.

The analysis will be used as an instrument to highlight the private economy, regional and country economy and the social-political effects of the development of part-time farming. Finally it will be used to form the part-time farming policy of the organization LRF.

I would like to take up another question which we discussed yesterday afternoon and stress it again. Yesterday we discussed the studies that had been done earlier by agricultural economists and my friend on my left side stated that those studies are too close to the agricultural farm and that they are particularly biased in the research. I have to admit that you are right. Now, geographers and sociologists are very interested in part-time farming, but there is the danger that they will make the same mistakes that we have done. So I have a prayer and I have a wish that you think of team work in the future. I think that part-time farming is such an important question that we need to have team effort to avoid the past mistakes of the economists. If you do so we will probably be able to answer the question, "Is part-time farming a resource or a problem in rural development?"

NOTES AND REFERENCES

1) Isaksson, N.I. & Johansson, J.E., 1972:

Importance, Character and Significance of Part-time Farming. Reports of the Royal Agricultural College of Sweden, No. A163 Uppsala

2) Safvestad, V., 1964:

Part-time Farming — It's Problems and Possibilities. Reports from the Agricultural Economics Research Institute, No. 2 — 1964 Stockholm.

INTERNATIONAL PANEL DISCUSSION TWO:
THE PROBLEM IN ITALY
Ada Cavazzani

I think that what Professor Safvestad says at the end of his talk has to be explained in a certain sense. When I say that part-time farming cannot be explained only by agricultural students, I simply refer to the situation we have in Italy.

In Italy, agriculture is not only an economic activity, it is not only an economic branch of the economy, but, it is mainly also what we call a social sector of society, or a political sector of society. I therefore think I should explain the main functions of the agricultural sector in Italy from this point of view. On one side of course it has the function of producing food and breeding livestock, but on the other side it has had, historically, the function of being a sort of place to keep labour when the other systems of production were not able to offer enough job opportunities. So we had a history of agriculture that, going back especially to the Fascist period, increased very much the number of small farms because of this special need of providing a way of life for families in a country which was not yet industrialized. This tendency of having a large proportion of small farms continued after World War II, and is just in the last 5 years being arrested by a new policy, which is coming not so much from the national government but mainly from the European Economic Community. So now, to understand the problems of agrarian policy in Italy we cannot refer to national policy, but we must consider mainly the European community policy which is giving the main framework for what the other governments should do. So, as you probably know, the tendency now is that of discouraging small farm activity and encouraging the larger size of farm and the better level of economic activity in agriculture. Also in Italy this tendency is in sharp contrast with the other function that agriculture has, that is, the social function. Therefore I think that when we see part-time farming spreading all over the country, this reflects a typical way of solving the small farm problem. This is because the state is no longer willing to help small farms mainly because of the European policy. This policy has not yet gone through the country because it takes a very long time to change years of a policy which has been in the other direction; in the direction of keeping people on the land. But still, part-time farming can be seen as a sort of a contrary tendency to the general tendency coming from the outside, and not only from the outside — from the European community — but also from a specific sector of agriculture. That is, the sector of the better-off farms that we call the capitalist farms. These two forces are mainly against part-time farming. In fact, the Mansholt directives say that people not working mainly in agricultural activity cannot be allowed to farm or receive any help from the state. Now these directives have finally been applied in Italy with a special note which provides that the small farms will disappear from the agricultural scene in the long run. These are the forces trying to eliminate part-time farming. In a realistic sense however, part-time farming is increasing and the small farms are not at all disappearing as one imagines when we read the official

227

statements. So our agrarian policy is mainly ambivalent. On the official level they say that part-time farming must be discouraged, or at best, neglected, as also we heard this morning, but in practice the government and the regional government in particular are indifferent to the situation and are not happy to attack the problem. This is the dilemma in Italy.

INTERNATIONAL PANEL DISCUSSION THREE: IMPLICATIONS FOR POLICY

Glenn V. Fuguitt

These have been very stimulating papers and comments. I was particularly struck by Dr. Crown's provocative statement that part-time farming is a "non-issue". Although I would not go that far, I do believe a basic difficulty in formulating part-time farming policy is that concern about the practice is most appropriately represented as part of several other major issues of rural society. This may be related back to our interest in typologies, for different types of part-time farmers fit into different policy concerns. Three examples follow:

(1)   Under actions to alleviate rural poverty, job assistance programs could include, as part of their activities, assistance to the part-time farmer. For some people, movement out of subsistence agriculture might well be encouraged, but for others the most effective route out of poverty might be the combination of farming and a non-farm job.

(2)   Concern about the problems of population decentralization has intensified as more and more former urbanites are moving into rural areas well beyond compact suburban developments. As a part of coping with this phenomenon, more attention will need to be given to the hobby farmers, with programs such as the one described by Dr. Hutchison last night.

(3)   The future scale of commercial agriculture is an issue which has attracted considerable attention lately. Will the trend toward greater capital investment and enlarged farm size threaten the future of the family farm? We have found that a number of young part-time farmers aspire to farming full time when they can build up enough capital. Thus, programs having as a goal the encouragement of the moderate sized commercial family farm might well include efforts to assist some young part-time farmers to make the shift to full-time farming.

So much for how part-time farming might fit into policy and action programs. I have been asked to say something about U.S. policy as it relates to part-time farming. Over the past twenty years there has been a considerable increase in interest in the problems of rural and nonmetropolitan America, but with this has come little mention of the part-time farmer. I will review this period briefly, and speculate as to why part-time farming has not been a major concern.

A massive movement of people out of farming began about 1940 in the United States. Most of the writings during the period assumed that the movement was a good thing. Enlargement and mechanization of agriculture, with declining work force requirements was thought to lead to an equalization of farm—non-farm income differences, and it was assumed that the people moving out of rural areas would improve their lot. There was a belated recognition that the non-farm job opportunities might not be sufficient, and that the former farm workers might not be prepared to take advantage of them. Particularly following the urban riots in the 1960s there was increased demand for a policy that would slow down population concentration brought about by movement to metropolitan areas. (I might add parenthetically that there are two ironies here. One is that by that time the rural-urban migration had almost run its course. The other is that subsequent research has not shown that urban poverty and its attendant problems are directly attributable to rural-urban migration.)

About this time (1967) the President's Commission on Rural Poverty issued its report, which included this basic statement of belief:

> Every citizen of the United States should have equal access
> to economic and social advancement without discrimination
> with regard to race, relion, national origin, or place of resi-
> dence. (p. xii)

The last phrase, of course, implied that the government has an obligation to make opportunities available to people where they choose to live, rather than to encourage redistribution of people to match them with existing opportunities. The Commission recommended manpower services to assist rural people including vocational counciling and guidance, and had this to say about the combination of farm and nonfarm work:

> We believe a viable commercial farm economy has major
> national benefits and farms should be sufficiently large to
> sustain incomes above poverty level with minimum public
> assistance to those in full-time farming.

> However, those farmers unable to attain or maintain viable
> farm units, and without non-farm income to bring them
> above poverty level, need assistance either in gaining
> access to non-farm sources of income, or increases in farm
> income or both. (p. 142).

A Commission Report does not automatically become official U.S. policy. A number of state and federal programs have been established to assist the development of rural America, however, and in 1972 a Rural Development Act was passed by Congress and signed into law. The bulk of these programs provide loans and grants to encourage industry and upgrade community facilities. Also, there has been some related job training and relocation activity in rural areas. Where these activities have been effective they must have made part-time farming opportunities available. But except for the report of the Poverty Commission, I could find virtually no reference to part-time farming in rural development literature.

From the standpoint of changing overall population trends, it is generally agreed that up to now the investment in rural development programs has been too small to have much impact. Nevertheless, there has been a turnaround in population trends in the United States. Since 1970, for the first time, nonmetropolitan areas are growing more rapidly than metropolitan areas, and we know that this is not merely metropolitan spillover (Beale and Fuguitt, 1975). With this population turnaround, concern about a national population distribution policy will probably wane, but undoubtedly there still are problems at the local community level that can be related to rapid population growth or rapid decline, or to too high or too low a population density.

Why was part-time farming not high on the rural development policy agenda? Here I can only speculate, but I suggest four possibilities:

(1)   The migration out of agriculture is about over in most areas. Generally, influencing this mobility (which might involve part-time farming) has not been a direct concern in rural development efforts.

(2)   Part-time farmers, although now a high proportion of all farmers, are a low proportion of nonmetropolitan residents in most areas.

(3)   There continues to be confusion between part-time farmers and low-income farmers. The agricultural establishment has been criticized for ignoring low-income farmers, or rural people in poverty. New programs are being developed for this group, but to my knowledge few special ones for any type of part-time farmers.

(4)   There is ambiguity about how to view part-time farming from a value perspective. The value basis was discussed very well by Wietfeldt in his paper. Almost everyone would agree that farming is good, and should be encouraged, but what about part-time farming? Here we have the problem of the general disdain for the amateur or the dilettante, in contrast to the "professional", which cuts across all endeavours. Extension people who may not want to "waste time" on part-time farmers are really no different from professors who would rather teach graduate students than freshmen. As Dr. Crown says, part-time farming is here to stay, but there is not likely to be much pressure either to promote or discourage this practice.

INTERNATIONAL PANEL DISCUSSION FOUR:
PART-TIME FARMING IN BRITAIN

G.E. Jones

I have learned a very great deal about the farming of Ontario, particularly from maps, and was left with an impression of quite a lot of similarities with the U.K. However, there certainly are some quite crucial differences and it would be the same comparing any two countries, of course. These arise from differences in basic culture ritual, certainly in British institutions, particularly the legal institutions, and, underlying it all, the structure of British society. Right now we are down to slightly over 2 per cent of our population in agriculture, but about 30 per cent of our population is rural. The number of farm holdings in the U.K. is somewhere around 325,000 and still decreasing; common market policies, which others have referred to, are still encouraging this and probably we have also reached somewhere near the bottom in terms of the movements, certainly of farmers and farm workers, out of farming. There is some evidence that this, what is thought of as an increasing non-agricultural rural population, is, of course, getting involved with this business of part-time farming.

We know very little about our part-time farmers. It is a matter of some concern, it is an issue which people are interested in here and there, but it is certainly not that anybody has done any detailed work on it and the government does not seem to be very interested in it, and we have no data about it, certainly since 1941. But we know that we have a wide variety of them; they range from true peasants almost in the Franklin sense of the term to the rich urban professionals who, in the rural society, range from the people who are rather slummy, small part-time farmers to those who make beautiful little mini-estates out of their holdings. Most of them, I think, simply merge into the rural and agricultural landscape and are very difficult to distinguish. What does happen though is that these small scale farmers who are usually part-time do often express a variety of values. They differ among themselves, but most of them tend also to be in conflict with the commercial farming population. This conflict is something which so far has been ignored by the farmers unions, but they are beginning to take some interest in it.

I think as far as our part-time farming policy is concerned, it is either non-existent, vague, ambiguous, and certainly ambivalant and it has varied over time. If one takes as the beginning of a very conscious agricultural policy for Britain after the repeal of the corn laws in 1846, then we certainly had a growth of small farms and part-time farms coming in at the end of the 19th Century. Having got away from the prosperous high farming of the 1860s and 1870s into the depressed era at the end of the century, many of our bits of legislation regarding part-time farming were taken from that time. Again, after the First World War, there was a kind of "settle the heroes back on the land" movement. Due to both of these factors, part-time farming is certainly in this generation an accepted norm within the agrarian structure; it is there, it has a history, it has a tradition, but nobody really does anything about it. Of course, the part-time farmers benefit from any agricultural policies concerning economic policies just as much as anybody else, but there have been very few policies which are specifically for them, not that they are discriminated against particularly, with one exception, until very recently the advisory services or extension services more or less very consciously had nothing to do with them. There are one or two exceptions to this and the notable one was a small farmer scheme we had in the late 1950s and 1960s which had a kind of viability test for people to be eligible, but that did lead to some part-time farmers, through government aid, becoming full-time farmers, and what little evaluation that has been done with that would suggest that it was a very temporary thing, and they slipped back again to being part-time farmers. Right now I think, as Ada Cavazzani has said, our policies are very much more being influenced by planning processes. They certainly are beginning to provide the broad framework of thinking and the main talk you usually pick up in the literature about the Mansholt Plan, back in the late 1960s, deals with farm development, farm improvement, farm amalgamation, structural change, pensions for elderly farmers to leave farming, and with training for farmers and farm workers. It also deals with social economic advice and counselling. This trio of directives (159, 160, 161 of the Mansholt Plan) forms the basis of policy from Brussels. But they are apparently contradictory, because on the one hand they are there to stimulate the phasing-out of small farmers and the amalgamation of farms, and yet, through things like the training facilities available and the social economic advisory facilities, part-time farmers could well be encouraged to stay. Now I say apparently contradictory because I do not think it is really a contradiction. It links up with what Mr. Hutchison was talking about last night to some respect, that if you can provide an input of education, training, a backup of an intellectual kind, to people who may be marginal, but economically and socially can cross over into a state where they can be viable in their own sense, maybe both economically and certainly in the social sense, then one has a kind of reconciliation to the total policy.

There is just one final point. Another aspect which concerns the long-term future where policies are unclear, except in a democratic society where one likes to believe that the future is determined by the people themselves, is that there are certain images of the future which are **not** of the kind of high efficiency economics, which we have learned to live with in the last twenty years, coming out. These concern notions of the quality of life, and so on. Some people are going to get the kind of quality of life they wish, I think, out of part-time farming. It may give them relaxation, recreation, as well as some part of their work. Presumably, as Dr. Crown was mentioning earlier, there is a place therefore in the overall policy for this.

QUESTION PERIOD

J. Girt (Geography, Guelph)

This question has been stimulated by Dr. Crown's paper, so I will direct one question to him and maybe certain questions to other people on the panel. I would be interested to know what his image of part-time farming was, and from other people, what should policy makers' image of part-time farming be? The thing that bothers me about his paper and about much of the conference is that we've been looking at part-time farming in relation to the agricultural production system. We have looked at problems in relation to this but we have not considered other problems associated with part-time farming. We really have not looked at part-time farming as a function of the system that creates it. What trends in part-time farming are a result of reasonable social processes and which ones are not? Is the migration of people from rural to urban areas socially beneficial or not? Are the effects of these part-time farmers, for instance on the inflation of land prices, necessarily socially beneficial?

Earlier (this is a commentary about this paper) we were considering part-time farmers; we seem to be considering policies related to part-time farmers when the part-time farms themselves may be having impact on the system which has to be adjusted. I am thinking in terms of the increase road cost that is going to be incurred by part-time farming. To conclude, talking about urban part-time farming, mainly to focus things a little bit, we could perhaps consider the part-time farmer as an indicator of a problem with an inequitable solution. That is, we have some people who are perhaps avoiding stress in urban areas by moving out and gaining access to a limited available resource, at the same time inflating it for their own benefit. Furthermore, the tax system that we have at present may be unfair because of the fact that these people do not necessarily pay any more taxes for these privileges. All these questions are, in fact, interfaces between systems and government at the present time. All the equity problems that we seem to be facing in relation to this problem, or many others, are the concern of the Canada Department of Agriculture and the concern of urban Canada; they are all at the intersection of these ministries. What should be the image that government has of part-time farming for reasonable policy making?

R. Crown (Canada Department of Agriculture)

The image that I would have, and this is by no means representative of a government, quite clearly, is best expressed by Mrs. Cavazzani, in that it is an aspect of our social economic life. This is my picture of it. It is a choice which individuals have made for their own good reasons. We have, in effect, penalized it in the past by singling it out for specific sort of exclusion from a collection of programs that have been instituted for whatever good reason. We have also implicitly worked to the detriment of all small-scale enterprises. All of them are effected, be they agricultural pursuits of people who call themselves small-scale farmers, or people who you want to call part-time farmers who have only one enterprise. We have failed, I think to provide the choice of technologies that an individual can select if we grant him the ownership of a resource and he wishes to use it effectively in one way or another.

The image that I hold is one of liberalising an attitude, or removing the distinction against, part-time farming. I would think that one could support the liberalisation, but not the open advocation, of forming new part-time units.

Rules against part-time farming imply that it is an integral part of the agricultural production and income distribution systems, or whatever. What I am saying is, why do you not just shrug your shoulders and let life go ahead.

M. Troughton (Geography, Western)

Just a comment. I was very impressed by the approach that Mr. Wietfeldt took about suggesting that one should look at part-time farming from, in his case, an agricultural union point of view in relation to compartmentalizing the problem. I felt worried about Mr. Crown's willingness to let the problem go in the sense that he is in a position where he should be, although not treating it as a central issue, thinking about part-time farming in terms of some of the major policy issues of the Canada Department of Agriculture. For example, how does part-time farming relate to the national food policy, a national land use policy, regulation or non-regulation of the urban fringe, the current migration or immigration policies and the social aspects of these interesting issues. It seems to me that he should be concerned, as Mr. Wietfeldt was concerned, to view part-time farming in each of those concepts however separate they might be, rather than to ignore it as a problem.

A. Lerner (Agricultural Economics, Guelph)

I think Wietfeldt and Crown are both right, because Wietfeldt was talking about attitudes of other farmers towards the part-time farmers, and how these might be affected by how government programs behave. Now, I am fully in agreement with him here that the way in which part-time farmers should be treated, or whether part-time farmers should be excluded or not from a particular program, should depend on the objectives of the particular program. If a program has something to do with encouraging the production of a particular thing, then anybody who is producing that thing should be included, whether he is full-time or part-time is not really relevant. On the other hand, if the program is devoted to a particular person, his own economic situation, say, some kind of income maintenance or welfare program, then this should be directed to the income or welfare situation of the individual concerned, whether it is a farmer or anybody else. In that sense, R. Crown's attitude of "Benign neglect", I am taking to mean: we should neglect the fact that the part-time farmer **is** a part-time farmer and, if there is a program that protects somebody that does farming, then it should be directed to whoever does farming, whether he is part-time or not. For example, to go outside the sphere of agriculture, if the government makes a program for encouraging the establishment of industry in a particular area of low employment and is willing to give a subsidy to a firm to set up, for example, a chemical works, then the question of the manager's full-time or part-time work commitment to the production of chemicals is irrelevant.

M. Muszynski (Institute of Rural Development, Poland)

In agriculture, there must be something that people want to have. I mean, maybe it is a way of living and working with the land, and maybe it is what they are getting from the earth. So, in the past, when the work on a full-time farm was a necessity for life, people started to escape from the land and came to big cities in the developed countries, like England or some others where less than 10 percent of people working in agriculture produced enough for all the others. But, if in a modern society we found that production and being on the land, owning and working the land is a good way of living, some other people found it a means of giving pleasure. I think that it will be a right way to let them do it because this is a way of life and if so many people find this way desirable it does not matter if it is called pleasure farming or part-time farming, or like it is in my country. Anyway, I think some of us yearn for the countryside and if we are able to supply it, then let us do it.

CONFERENCE RÉSUMÉ

Immediately following the closing luncheon Dr. D. Christodoulou was invited to address the symposium by giving a résumé of the proceedings and by offering his conclusions on the future research priorities on part-time farming.

D. CHRISTODOULOU: "Symposium Résumé and Future Research Priorities"

Following the résumé and a note of thanks to the many people involved, the First Rural Geography Symposium at Guelph closed at 3:30 p.m.

SYMPOSIUM RÉSUMÉ AND
FUTURE RESEARCH PRIORITIES
D. Christodoulou

INTRODUCTION

Proposing a résumé of so richly packed three days of discussion and intricate argument would overawe even a much better man than the present speaker, but I meekly submitted to doing the task given me because others have volunteered to do similar "instant" jobs at this Symposium. I have made my task easier by deciding that (a) the last thing you want is a mere listing of main points and issues thrashed out here, and certainly I am not in a position to apportion praise, or disposed to level criticism; and (b) perhaps you may not be averse to my using my international experience, such as it is, especially in connection with research and action programmes in a variety of situations, to bring to bear on our work here at the Symposium some sort of overall view and some extra dimensions of the problem area and the state of knowledge.

To do this latter job I have tried to stand back a bit and view the Symposium's work and other efforts in this field and reflect on my impressions in a sort of thinking aloud process. I have been concerned also to discover some way through which some tangible international action may emerge from here to make this Symposium more of a landmark than it already is. Naturally all the credit for this landmark goes to our hosts who have shown vision, dedication and capacity for initiative as well as professional competence and organizational ability.

Why then, do I propose to bring into this already creditable achievement some extra dimensions? It is not, of course, that there are deficiencies. The reason is more basic: Our hosts' efforts, combined with other initiatives in the past, have generated a maturation process which enables us all now to go forth building on the success of our hosts and that of their forerunners. We are in effect proposing to put to good use all this accumulated capital, largely our hosts' contribution.

THE SYMPOSIUM: A SUMMING UP

This Symposium can be looked at as made up of an inner core and a rather loosely formed outer shell. The core is the work of our hosts : the facts and the empirical knowledge gathered and the understanding enhanced through observation, analysis, evaluation and reflection, the extremely useful theoretical and methodological tools evolved and displayed here are the analysis of experience gained from testing them.

Our hosts have naturally used their immediate environment as their primary laboratory, but not as the only one. Their internationalism has not been absent as the nature and coverage of this Symposium testifies. But their true strength, like that of mythological Anteus, is derived from planting their feet firmly on mother earth. All the same, like any good farmer, they have also learnt from looking over the fence at their neighbour's crops. Hence, their contacts with the rest of Canada, the U.S.A. and a good part of Europe. What we have had presented here by our hosts so effectively constitutes in my view our main patrimony and a most valuable capital for future dividends..

238

The outer shell is a later evolution in this maturation process. It is still loosely formed because of the nature of things. We can all agree that we are dealing with a most complex phenomenon — part-time farming — which has deep local roots and strong and multiple linkages, deeply embedded as it is in the socio-economic political system, and therefore isolated contributions from across local and national boundaries cannot amount overnight to a firm and fully formed outer shell of experience. But I am convinced that at this Symposium these shafts of light from outside have illuminated the local sky and have provided insights into both the local and the distant situations, throwing into relief some similarities and some sharp contrasts. They have brought home sharply, to the unwary at least, the vast extra space to be explored and the new dimensions of the problem area.

From a secure home base and the few drawbridges to the outside world, this Symposium has ushered in an international phase and a process of great potential.

THE PROBLEM AREA

It is proposed here that some well-known premises and familiar landmarks should first be rapidly and briefly surveyed with some pertinent comments thrown in here and there and in passing. I make six points:

1)   Part-time farming has rarely achieved a status other than as a cinderella in research, policy-making and concern. Some interest is shown, mostly ancillary to tackling such themes or issues as agricultural population, employment, low-income, small-farm problems, commuting or migration, and agrarian structure and its reform. Surveying some of the more easily accessible literature, one is struck also by periodic ups and downs in interest in this subject, as observed at this Symposium already: there was some interest in the depression pre-war years; more recently a marked interest was noticeable in the mid-sixties with an ample output of studies and publications; there has been a relative lull until recently when interest has been again revived — is it the depression again responsible, one wonders. We must be entering now a period of literature boom because it is symptomatic that the Food and Agricultural Organization (FAO) has taken it up specifically for the first time in connection with the World Census of Agriculture — that of 1980 which is now under preparation. What is contemplated by FAO at this stage is concentration on key items which are essential in the planning of special surveys aimed at collecting detailed information regarding this phenomenon. One can, therefore, envisage a rising interest, this time perhaps on a world scale.

2)   These recent developments — and this Symposium spent considerable time on this — have once again raised the question of whether there is a general, let alone world-wide, concensus as to what part-time farming is, in the sense of what constitutes its middle-ground at least, if not where the lines of demarcation of its whole territory are to be drawn. Plainly there is no such consensus and, one might add, for good reasons.

(a) Part-time farming is a most complex phenomenon (or set of phenomena) characterized by varying parameters and intricate interactions and it would be unrealistic to believe it

239

easy (or even possible) to identify it and delimit it with precision on a more than relatively local scale. In fact, very wisely in my view, most studies in depth refer to no more than local situations. We have no comprehensive knowledge of the problem area, in sufficient detail or depth to generalize from, with adequate validity. This comprehensive knowledge and understanding will eventually be built up, like a mosaic, from the little bright stones of local situations; but the guiding hand is also needed of a craftsman (or a co-operative of craftsmen) who know(s) what to aim at in this mosaic building. In less metaphorical language we need a **working typology** of a very comprehensive nature but with scope for dividing and sub-dividing within types and sub-types. More of this below.

(b) Connected with the above is the fact that part-time farming — at least under that name — has been presumed to be a problem of fairly developed, industrialized or urbanized societies. The very few studies carried out in developing countries[1] refer to situations close to urban areas. But the problem cannot be easily resolved that way. There are situations which are of a mixed nature either geographically or historically speaking.

One can cite the case of under-developed areas within an overall developed country, for example, Italy and its South as highlighted by Professor Cavazzani in her stimulating paper, or for that matter, Southern Europe in close proximity with industrialized Central and North Europe. Then there is the case of a fast industrializing (or industrialized) country with rapid transition from "part-time farming" of a distinct kind (perhaps an illegitimate one) to "part-time farming" of another kind, perhaps the legitimate one.[2]

(c) The most distinctive feature that characterizes situations prevailing in poor, predominantly agrarian, countries and sets them apart from developed or industrialized countries pertains to the nature and extent of non-agricultural employment with a tendency in the latter (developed) countries for employment to be both diversified and on more specialized and differentiated lines. It is interesting perhaps to recount my own family's experience. My father was a small farmer, at first full-time on a part-time farm (i.e. he had no other job), until he got a job and became a part-time farmer on a part-time farm. Later he ceased to be a farmer because his land was taken by the village usurer in the 1930s when the debt could not be serviced even from his other jobs' earnings! Similar experiences, legions of them, are found in Asian countries, ironically at times engendered by the "Green Revolution".

Significantly, the fuss we make about part-time farming, as distinct from dual or multiple job-holding of any **other** kind, is essentially a carry-over or relic from days when agriculture was the only, or the original, or the primary, or at least the residual, occupation. This is the case in all

240

developing countries today. Therefore, we cannot shut the problems posed by poor countries out of our considerations, even though it can be readily conceded that those problems are qualitatively and quantitatively far more difficult to study, let alone tackle.

One final observation on this score, already made by Wietfeldt, very pertinent to our enquiries concerns the recognition that non-specialized farm management is a multiple occupation, with seasonal characteristics, to the extent that one cannot easily draw the line between the "farming" and "non-farming" activities of a farm operator or his household.

(d) Finally, many definitions, delimitations and treatments of the subject were related to government action or policy, or to specific investigations likely to lead to policy and/or action. Thus inclusion in a population and agriculture census was motivated by policy objectives aimed perhaps at discovering the facts about problem groups. Similarly, legislation to help such groups has to spell out the coverage of the legislative provisions, that is, identify the beneficiaries or designated groups.

So much about delimitation; now something about actors;

3)   The problem area has often been seen as having at least three main facets: the part-time farm operator, the part-time farm household, and the part-time farm. This has generated investigations in various directions and has enlarged understanding of problems and issues; integration has, however, remained weak. Curiously, as already observed by some participants at this Symposium, little has been said here about the part-time farm household, a key actor in the whole affair. This is especially true when "feminization" of agriculture is often observed in such studies.

4)   Reference has already been made to the employment aspect of the problem. Income has, however, been an equally, if not more, vital consideration, especially in the minds of policy makers or policy oriented researchers. In evaluating the merits or defects of the phenomenon of part-time farming, a great number of criteria have been used, additional to employment and income, such as the efficiency of such farmers (sometimes linked also to the part-time farmer's efficiency in non-agricultural jobs), the efficiency and effectiveness of such economic activity from the regional or national point of view, the non-material satisfactions it offers to part-time farmers and others or the community at large, and the opportunity costs of the resources involved.

5)   Finally, a historical view has often been taken of the phenomenon and related trends, and even some deterministic conclusions have been drawn. In this context some empirical work has been done, pioneered by Professor Fuguitt whom we have the pleasure to have with us, relating the waxing and waning of the phenomenon to the life history of a household. Furthermore, and in a wider context, linkages were sought with stages of economic development and especially urban, industrial or service sector growth.

6)   A postscript can be added here and it refers to value judgment introduced into the relevant considerations. Even our Symposium asks the question "A Problem or Resource in Rural Development?". Usually, of course, it is both — a problem for some or for all and a resource for someone or other. No conclusive statement can be made except on the basis of thorough analysis as to accruing benefits and losses and to whom. Other value judgements are introduced concerning attitudes of part-time farmers to the whole problem area, and attitudes of others towards part-time farmers or farming.

THE TASKS AHEAD

Simply stated, the tasks ahead comprise (a) more in-depth research and (b) a more thorough working out of the complex inter-relationships and linkages involved in order to achieve a sounder and more satisfactory understanding of the problem area. This will help both learning and policy making, leading to effective action. In more detail the tasks include the following:

1. Conceptual Issues

Much has been written before on this and discussed at this Symposium. Most of the controversy has been useful. No generally accepted conceptual frame is as yet in sight nor, in my view, is to be expected soon, nor — one may venture to say — could as yet be of great operational utility, other than as a guide for investigation. More urgently needed at this stage are: additional empirical research, more discovery and analysis of inter-connections and interactions of phenomena, and geographically and situationally more varied and wide-spread coverage. When experience is enriched enough, then a successful conceptual synthesis and classification can take place. Then and only then an effective tool would have been forged. Meanwhile, a researcher can identify his own concepts and problem coverage and get on with the specific job in hand, namely of studying specific problems in the field or specific phenomena and their inter-relationships.

Hopefully the FAO efforts towards a world coverage through the 1980 World Census of Agriculture will provide the first data on a considerable, if not world, scale collected almost contemporaneously, and therefore, the first comprehensive raw material for a broad view of the problem area and for the first steps towards more promising, synthesizing and conceptualizing efforts. The twin approach of specific in depth studies and data gathering on a world scale and their analysis should prove a complementary effort with great promise for a real grasp of realities and concepts.

2. Specific Studies and Action

In practice, studies are carried out when and where opportunity offers, but a set of theoretical priorities can serve as a useful guide. The suggestions made below are not meant to impose any limits on the search for knowledge but are an attempt to make knowledge more pertinent and certainly more useful to those who are in need of help or can be in a position to help.

242

(i)   In this context, the first consideration is problem-solving research in the sense that an important problem — usually of a socio-economic political nature — exists and chances seem to exist also that action towards its solution may be taken. Such research is intended to aid policy and action and should be aimed at existing and emerging problems. Thus, in **developed** countries, low-income rural groups, unemployment or underemployment among the farm population, returning emigrant workers, commuting worker/farmer issues, the plight of the old farm people, the "feminization" of farm operation, the undercapitalization and low efficiency and productivity in farming, and the escape into the rural areas by people who find urban life intolerable, are some aspects of part-time farming that spring readily to mind which merit priority in research. Other specific issues deserve attention for **negative** reasons, namely, to prevent hasty conclusions and policies derived from uncritical study of imperfect statistics and data, thus resulting, for instance, not in helping really poor part-time farmers but lining the pockets of rich tax-dodgers or wealthy hobby or amateur farmers.

(ii)   The problems facing the developing countries or the depressed areas within relatively developed countries (their "Third World" as Professor Ada Cavazzani styled them) merit urgent study and on a high priority basis. It will be argued, and perhaps validly so, that their problems are not basically a part-time farming issue, but a much wider and far more acute complex of structural problems. They are essentially one of gainful employment often reduced to a desperate search for means to eke some existence. The role of part-time farming properly evaluated can be of considerable help in action programmes such as agrarian reform, land settlement, rural development and employment promotion.

The line between situations in developed and under-developed countries (or regions) often turns out to be drawn arbitrarily in time or space in what is in reality a continuum. In any case the problem area has intrinsic importance in under-developed areas and deserves careful attention. This Symposium and those to follow can become truly international when their interest becomes more widespread. And developed countries should know of conditions in developing countries and the repercussions of their policies at home on poor countries abroad.

(iii) There are some very interesting developments in co-operative farming and group action related to the problems of part-time farming which, as suggested by Dr. Perkins the other evening, deserve attention. An interesting study by FAO in Spain has brought out some interesting features and lessons very pertinent to the Symposium's work. For instance, non-farming landowning persons enter into co-operative or group agreements with relatives or other people and they form farming groups of, say, ten to twenty members, of whom only three to five are farm operators of the pooled land and other resources, the others bearing full financial liability and retaining some decision-making while they work in other occupations away in towns. This is part-time farming of a special nature, and very much conducive to better farming and larger scale operation including new advanced lines and vertical integration.

(iv) It is a matter of regret that the problems to be found in social-ist agrarian structural systems have not been considered at this Sympoisum, owing to inevitable last minute changes in the programme. The admissibility or otherwise of part-time farming within socialist agriculture and country variations within the overall system have been discussed from time to time elsewhere, and only fleetingly touched upon here, but the subject is of tremendous importance and universality and re-search requires that the matter be fully and appropriately explored.

3. A Comprehensive Typology

The problems of developing countries and of socialist agri-culture (in developed and developing socialist countries) touched upon above, raise the issue of a comprehensive typology. Such a typology should aim at satisfying as harmoniously as possible certain re-quirements. Thus it should: (i) be as all-embracing as it can meaning-fully be, taking in, that is, as many situations as it can without straining the system unduly or causing it to lose cohesion; (ii) provide ample opportunities for strategic distinctions to be sharply drawn; (iii) allow plenty of scope for further development of specific types capable of refinement and increased precision; and (iv) be flexible and adjustable without undue distortion.

This is not the place to discuss typology in any satisfactory manner, especially since it is a long-term affair in any case, but some considerations can be hinted at. The present writer often likes to have recourse to an old formula, much used in morphological studies: namely, to study types from three aspects: structure, stage, process. If this formula is adopted it will involve:

(i) Analyses of situations bringing out all the relevant impor-tant characteristics of part-time farming. This is a task use-ful in itself in any case. But a great number of studies, especially if carried out on a relatively comparable basis, will contribute to a comprehensive picture and overall view of the problem area.

(ii) The problem is not static. The trajectory already traversed and the further evolution of the situation constitute fundamental insights which, properly identified and evalu-ated, illuminate the problem area and bring to the typology much needed realism.

(iii) The forces at work and how they affect the issues and problems and how they interact need to be clearly seen as fully as information and professional skill permit because they are the motive power and the controlling agents of evolving situations.

Some further considerations concerning typology aimed especially at showing the matrix within which the subject should be viewed are given at the end of this paper.

4. Coordinated International Action

Much work has been done both as regards studies of actual situations and as theoretical or methodological contributions — the latter, more often than not, of local or regional validity. The overall picture, therefore, has been to-date, one of a range of brave individual efforts or of initiatives of certain research bodies. Our hosts are now at the forefront of such efforts and this Symposium is evidence both of their success locally and also of their growing international influence. FAO has made some contribution on a regional scale through its Working Party on Rural Sociological Problems in Europe some years ago. The 1980 World Census of Agriculture will provide an opportunity for data to be collected in a great number of countries, if not actually on a world scale. The time may have come when some more determined and well co-ordinated effort may be made to deal with part-time farming on a more comprehensive, international plane. Two concrete moves are here proposed for consideration:

(i) The setting up of an International Centre for Monitoring and Co-ordinating Studies in Part-Time Farming and Related Structural Phenomena. Such a Centre will do promotional work in research in any way it can but its main contribution from the beginning will consist of providing a focal point for exchange of information and ideas through correspondence, or receiving visitors, or hosting seminars and symposia. Our present hosts have a very good claim to such an honour and responsibility if they have the inclination and the opportunity to respond. Since I arrived here I have canvassed the idea and our hosts seem ready to serve in such a cause. I suggest, therefore, that the Symposium should agree to recommend that the University of Guelph should consider accepting and acting upon this idea. This Centre will not be a substitute for, but an aid to, efforts by other institutions by being the locus for international action, the clearing house for research and action, and generally the home for a good cause.

(ii) The bridging of another gap between the developed and developing countries, this time concerning special promotional work towards filling the great void, namely the total neglect of the nature and extent and ramifications of part-time farming in developing countries. Guelph is considering the promotion of training in rural development on an international scale, mainly for the needs of participants from developing countries. Can this again be a way of making a beginning from Guelph on the road towards learning something of the problems of millions of really poor and disadvantaged who have a far greater claim to the fruits of the rarest of many rare gifts that we, the privileged minorities have been endowed with, namely capacity to acquire knowledge and use it? Could not this Symposium agree also to recommend that Guelph consider this aspect also in its efforts at rural development in the poor countries?

245

This exhausts my modest contribution this afternoon. It is not my task to express the appreciation of all of us to our hosts for this splendid opportunity to meet, discuss and make a fresh start in a great cause. Yet I do this with pleasure and wish to conclude by expressing FAO's appreciation for a truly great contribution to rural welfare and social advance.

SOME CONSIDERATIONS REGARDING ELEMENTS OF A COMPREHENSIVE TYPOLOGY OF PART-TIME FARMING

1) A typology of part-time farming must give due consideration to the three main actors: the farm operator, the operator's household and others employed on the operational unit, and the farm operational unit.

2) Part-time farming should be assessed as to whether it is voluntary or involuntary.

3) Population and employment structural features: farm population (ratio to rest of population, composition, trends, migratory movements, including commuting, etc.), man/land ratios, employment data (agricultural and non-agricultural), employment trends and composition of labour force.

4) Land structural features: physical and institutional limits to farm size expansion, land market, land taxation, land tenure data, size of operational units, vertical and horizontal integration, prevailing production structures, specialized production, degree of mechanization.

5) Detailed features of part-time farming: its prevalence as measured by labour force, land area covered, marketable or subsistence production, and income derived (all quantities in absolute figures and in ratios to rest); secular and long-term trends (secular trends related to such developments as economic cyclical fluctuations and intra-family changes).

6) Detailed, and even sophisticated, analyses of selected situations using criteria or measurements related to: time committed in, net income derived from, capital committed in, investment made in, management share, and productivity achieved within his own farm by the operator and his household as compared with what happens in his other occupations.

7) Identification of occupational structure and trends in a given area and discovery of linkages of part-time farming and other occupations.

8) Attitudes observed among part-time farmers and other farmers or other occupational groups or leisured or retired people vis a vis each other and in relation to part-time farming and for living (at least partly) in the rural areas.

9) Official policy and action with regard to part-time farming. Evaluation of special measures in support thereof.

10) Official definitions.

NOTES AND REFERENCES

1. For example, Adegboye, O. and A. Abidogun, "Contribution of Part-Time Farming to Rural Development in Ibadan Areas, Western Nigeria," in Ofori, I.M. (ed) **Factors of Agricultural Growth in West Africa,** University of Ghana, Legon, 1973.

2. Takeo Misawa illustrates this in his article "Characteristic Features of Part-Time Farming in Japan," **International Journal of Agrarian Affairs,** Vol. V, No. 4, July 1968, pp. 311-324. To some extent Patrick Hackman, in his paper submitted at this Symposium entitled "Attitudes of the Farmers' Union to Multiple Jobholders in Finland," illustrates the same historic transition.

PAPERS IN ABSENTIA

A number of invited contributors were unable to personally present their papers. These papers were distributed to the symposium participants. M. Muszynski read a synthesis and summary (Special Session) of the Galaj and Muszynski papers.

M.F. BUNCE: "The Contribution of the Part-Time Farmer to the Rural Economy"

D. GALAJ: "Part-time Farmers in Poland"

M. MUSZYNSKI: "The Economic Costs of Transforming Dual Occupational People into Single Occupational"

G. SIVINI: "Some Remarks on the Development of Capitalism and Specific Forms of Part-Time Farming in Europe"

OTHER SYMPOSIUM PAPERS

The following material, in addition to the official symposium papers, was available to conference participants in handout form.

A.M. Fuller, "The Part-Time Problem — A Scheme for Geographers", C.A.G. Conference, Winnipeg, June 1970. Reprint.

A.M. Fuller, "Towards a Typology of Part-Time Farming: A Conceptual Framework and the Case of the Val Nure, Italy',, I.G.U. Typology Commission Meeting, Verona, September 1974. Reprint.

J.I. Galloway, "The 'Persistent' Part-Time Farmer", C.A.G. Conference, Ottawa, March 1975, Reprint.

J.A. Mage, "Economic Factors Associated with Part-Time Farming in Southern Ontario and Waterloo County", **Proceedings of G.I.R.M.S.,** Vol. 3, 1972-73. Reprint.

J.A. Mage, "A Survey of Part-Time Farming in Huron County", Huron County Project, University of Guelph, June 1974. Reprint.

J.A. Mage, "A Comparison of Selected References Concerning Part-Time Farming in North America", Department of Geography, University of Guelph, June 1975.

THE CONTRIBUTION OF THE PART-TIME FARMER TO THE RURAL ECONOMY

Michael Bunce

The part-time farmer has been frequently caricatured as a parasitic member of rural society, contributing less than his fair share to the rural economy because he does not maximize his labour and capital inputs on the land. Such an image has, of course, been refuted by a number of studies, and part-time farming has been proposed as a stabilizing influence in rural areas (A.R.D.A., 1972).[1] Yet the predominant concern of existing research is with the role of the part-time farmer in the agricultural economy in particular rather than in the wider context of the rural economy. This is largely the result of a pre-occupation with the problems which are created by combining farming with other occupations.

The part-time farmer, however, is more than a special type of agriculturalist. He is, as Hathaway and Waldo (1964)[2] have pointed out, a rural multiple jobholder. His role in the rural economy therefore cannot be fully understood without reference to the non- or off-farm as well as to the farm facets of his economic activity. Indeed, even his impact upon the agricultural economy will be affected by the nature of the non-farming occupations. This paper is concerned, therefore, with the contribution the part-time farmer makes to the rural economy as a multiple job-holder, emphasizing, in particular, the impact of the non-farm job.[3]

Involvement in non-farm occupations does, of course, take various forms, and the multiple jobholder's contribution to the rural economy will therefore occur in a number of ways. Basically, two kinds of contribution can be postulated: a direct one, in which through his non-farm job he performs tasks which are an integral part of the commercial structure of the local community; and an indirect one, in which he creates both income and employment multipliers. Within these two crude categories, however, there will be a wide range of contribution to the rural economy in terms of both type and amount.

Measurement of this contribution does, however, pose some serious problems. What constitutes the rural economy, and how accurately can the share provided by the multiple jobholder's non-farm jobs be calculated? To the first question there seems to be no generally acceptable answer. Certainly it is impossible to delimit the area of rurality in anything but an arbitrary way, and a quantitative measure of the rural economy would be difficult to achieve. The economic contribution of non-farm jobs would pose even more complex computational problems, and it is doubtful whether a proportionate measurement of impact could be established with any confidence of accuracy.

I do not therefore set out in this paper to measure the extent of the multiple jobholder's contribution to the rural economy in any vigorously quantitative sense. Rather, the aim is to examine the ways in which the contributions are made and to suggest the variable impact

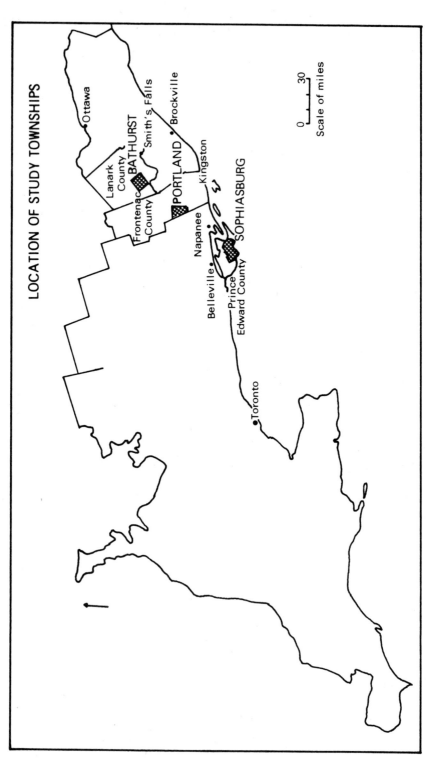

LOCATION OF STUDY TOWNSHIPS

Ottawa

Lanark County

BATHURST

Smith's Falls

Brockville

PORTLAND

Frontenac County

Kingston

SOPHIASBURG

Napanee

Belleville

Prince Edward County

Toronto

Scale of miles

0   30

Figure 1

created by different aspects of the non-farm occupations. The conclusions are based upon the results of a survey of multiple jobholding farmers in three rural townships of Eastern Ontario, carried out during the summer of 1973. Three hundred and forty-three farm operators were interviewed, of which 181 reported having some paid occupation in addition to operating his own farm. This figure excludes twenty-two self-professed hobby farmers, for the survey was concerned only with multiple jobholders who were committed to farming a productive unit.

The study concentrated upon the characteristics of the non-farm work of part-time farmers, and identified five parameters which most clearly indicated the variable nature of the contribution to the rural economy. These parameters were non-farm job type, regularity and duration of work, employment style, journey-to-work distance and non-farm income level.

Response to the questions posed on these particular aspects of the non-farm occupations of farmers suggests that the type of job has the most direct influence on the nature of the contribution to the rural economy. With 181 multiple jobholders reporting forty different types of non-farm jobs, there was clearly a wide-range of job experience. Thirteen broad categories of occupation can be identified from the full list, and these are shown in Table 1.

Table 1. Non-Farm Job Categories

Local Non-Farm Job Types		Urban Non-Farm Job Types	
Job Type	Number	Job Type	Number
Construction	3	Construction	14
Custom farm	13	Education	2
Local government	7	Factory work	49
Local industry	6	Institutional	12
Local services	39	Garage mechanic	7
Miscellaneous	5	Office work	7
		Retailing	7
		Truck driving	2
		Miscellaneous	8
Total	73	Total	108

However, in this table, the job categories are arranged into two groups, representing two fundamentally different classes of non-farm jobs. On the one hand, there are those jobs which involve employment within the multiple jobholders' local community. On the other hand are those jobs which are part of the urban economic structure, such as factory work and office employment.

251

The difference between multiple jobholding farmers on the basis of these two non-farm occupation groups, is emphasized by the information on journey to non-farm job and place of employment. A wide range of travel distances was reported, with some variation between the study townships being accounted for by the respective locations of nearest employment centres. Yet in the distribution of journey-to-work distances a high degree of positive skewness and a tendency to bi-modality reveals that multiple jobholders operated within two basically different spatial activity spheres (Figures 2 to 4). One was localized, involving non-farm work in the immediate area of the local community, generally within the township. The other was non-local due to participation in non-farm jobs away from the local community.[4]

There is, therefore, a strong relationship between the type of non-farm job and the place at which it is held, as Table 1 shows. There are, however, aspects of this dichotomy between local and non-local non-farm occupations which suggest the existence of two groups of multiple jobholding farmers with fundamentally different roles in the rural economy. Not only do job types differ between the groups, but so does style and regularity of employment as well as the level of income.

The majority of non-farm jobs held locally involved a large amount of self-employment by the individual. Hence over 70 per cent of local non-farm jobs were held on a self-employed or franchise basis, in which the multiple jobholder ran his own business. In contrast, all of the non-farm jobs of the group whose activity sphere extended beyond the confines of the local community involved the multiple jobholder as an employee.

The difference between local and non-local multiple jobholding was also evident in the regularity of non-farm work. As can be seen in Table 2, those who were involved locally tended not to do so on a full-time basis, the majority reporting year-round, part-time, or seasonal activity. Those with non-local non-farm employment were involved overwhelmingly on a full-time basis, that is, year-round with a five day week, eight hour day.

Table 2. Regularity of Non-Farm Employment

Regularity of Non-Farm Employment	Spatial Activity Spheres No. No. of Respondents			
	Local		Non-Local	
	No.	%	No.	%
Year-round full-time	23	31	87	81
Year-round part-time	18	25	7	6
Seasonal	25	34	12	11
Casual	7	10	2	2
Total	73	100	108	100

TRAVEL TO NON—FARM JOBS

Figure 2   PORTLAND

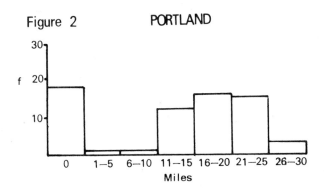

Figure 3   SOPHIASBURG

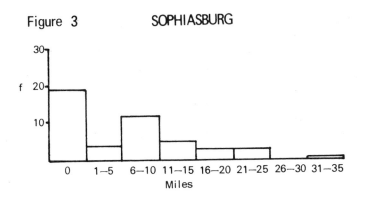

Figure 4   BATHURST

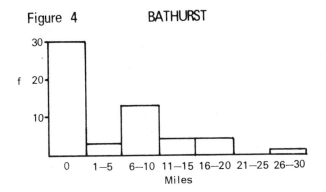

Income obtained from non-farm occupations varied considerably between the two groups of multiple jobholders. As can be seen in Table 3, those who commuted to urban non-farm jobs earned significantly more of their total income from non-farm occupations than did the local group.

Table 3. Income From Non-Farm Jobs

Non-Farm Income as % of Total Income	Spatial Activity Spheres			
	Local		Non-Local	
	No.	%	No.	%
20% and under	22	31.0	7	6.5
21-40	9	12.7	3	2.8
41-60	12	16.9	14	13.0
61-80	14	19.7	42	38.9
81 and over	14	19.7	42	38.9

CHI Square = 32.66 with 4 degrees of freedom

The non-farm job experience of multiple jobholding farmers in the study townships reveals, therefore, a clear dichotomy between local and non-local activity. This is likely to have an important influence upon the nature of the contribution to the rural economy. In particular, it suggests a distinction between direct involvement in the commercial life of the rural community and indirect impact made through various types of multipliers.

From the types of jobs reported, it is clear that the majority of farmers whose non-farm work occurred within the local community formed an integral element of the rural economy. The range of service occupations identified in the study was wide, as Table 4 shows. Thus, through the provision of artisanal, retail, transportation and various specialized services, the part-time farmer plays a broad and strategic role in the rural tertiary sector.

Table 4. Non-Farm Enterprises in Local Tertiary Sector

Building	Milk Trucking
Carpentry	Newspaper reporting
Farm equipment sales	House painting
Furniture repair	Odd jobbing
Garbage disposal	Road maintenance
Gas station operation	Snow ploughing
General labouring	School bus driving
Gravestone supply	Truck driving
Mail delivery	Well drilling

The direct contribution of these non-farm activities to the local economy appears to be achieved without a major shift in the occupational commitment of the farmer. As has been shown, the bulk of the service jobs neither occupied individuals on a full-time basis, nor did they bring in lucrative incomes. The fact, too, that like farm operation, the non-farm job involved self-employment suggests the establishment of enterprises which respond to the needs of the rural population. The farmer does not actively seek non-farm work, but rather, in line with the traditional non-specialization of labour in the rural economy, he absorbs the non-farm functions required by the community. Thus, the farmer, with no substantial change in his role as a farmer, becomes involved in other local enterprises without either a major time or income commitment.

Franklin (1969)[5] has emphasized the traditional role of the part-time farmer in parts of Europe where the maintenance of the commercial autonomy of the village has often depended upon farmers running non-farm businesses. The evidence of this study suggests a similar role in Ontario. Franklin also describes the participation of farmers in local government, and it is important to mention the small group of farmers in this study who were active, usually on a part-time basis, in employment with the local municipality. They were not self-employed as were the bulk of local multiple jobholders, but they are seen to perform again an important and direct role in the local tertiary sector.

The multiple jobholding farmer whose non-farm occupation involves urban employment in an extended spatial activity sphere clearly cannot contribute to the local economy in such a direct way. He is highly mobile and thus carries on his non-farm work away from the rural community. He works full-time in the non-farm job and has been assimilated as an employee into the time-work discipline structure of urban employment. What this means to his position as an inhabitant of and farmer in a rural community will probably vary from one individual to another. Yet one generalization can be accepted, that is, that the non-farm contribution to the rural economy will be an indirect one, involving no entrepreneurial participation in local commercial life beyond that of farming.

The impact of the non-local non-farm job upon the rural economy is likely to occur through a rather complex series of multipliers, the basis of which will be an income multiplier derived from urban employment. The study revealed that urban non-farm jobs yielded, for many, over 80 per cent of total income. Thus, this group takes back to their farm residence externally derived income, part of which will undoubtedly be spent within the rural economy. The main area of benefit would be the rural tertiary sector which should experience stimulated demand for essential services. A particularly intriguing aspect of this is that of one group of part-time farmers helping to maintain the non-farm enterprises of another! Indeed, one way in which urban income is spent is in the purchase of custom farm work from the local farming group. More generally, the income multiplier would help to provide a *raison d'être* for the persistence of local autonomy in retailing, artisanal services, transportation and local government, and could even encourage growth in this sector.

255

Of course, it must be recognized that the extended spatial activity spheres of those who engage in urban non-farm work present the possibility of a diminution of the role of these multiple jobholders in the rural economy. Non-farm income may be spent in the urban centre, in association with the place of work, or in consumer and recreational activities outside the region.

However, even with urban non-farm employment, multiple jobholders in Eastern Ontario maintained a commitment to farming. While non-farm income theoretically can increase capital formation propensity and thereby stimulate agricultural productivity, in the townships studied here the emphasis seems to have been more upon maintaining a certain, generally small level of income. In fact, stimulation of the agricultural economy is unlikely to have a major impact upon other sectors of the rural economy except in the unlikely event of large increases in farm income (Bunce, 1973).[6]

What is more significant for the rural economy is the maintenance of farming land in a productive state. Studies of the worker-peasant phenomenon in Europe (Mignon, 1971)[7] suggest that the commuting multiple jobholder, through increases in personal income and flexibility, can be a valuable element in the stabilization of rural economies. Substantial supplementary income permits the multiple jobholder to maintain operation of his farm and perhaps even build up sufficient capital to improve the efficiency of his operation. Land tenure is stabilized and the rate of farm abandonment diminished.

The potential contribution of part-time farming to the rural economy, then, falls into two categories. One involves direct participation in the commercial life of the rural community, with the resultant maintenance of the tertiary sector simultaneously with the preservation of agricultural activities. The other depends upon the stimulus of an income multiplier, derived from urban employment, and used in both the tertiary and agricultural sectors of the rural economy.

The extent of the part-time farmer's role in the rural economy is, of course, a complex issue. However, it is hoped that this paper illustrates some of the ways in which the contribution is made, and points to the relative significance of various non-farm job situations. The part-time farmer can be a valuable element of rural society. Just how valuable he is should be the concern of future research.

ACKNOWLEDGEMENTS

The author gratefully acknowledges the support of a grant from the Canada Council in the completion of the field work upon which this paper is based, and the invaluable assistance of Don Farquharson and John Menary in carrying out the field surveys.

256

NOTES AND REFERENCES

1. A.R.D.A. Directorate of Ontario (1972), **Planning for Agriculture in Southern Ontario,** Centre for Resources Development, University of Guelph, A.R.D.A. Report, No. 7, pp. 153-154.

2. Hathaway, D.E., and A.D. Waldo, (1964), **Multiple Jobholding by Farm Operators,** Michigan State University Agricultural Experiment Station Research Bulletin No. 5, East Lansing, Michigan.

3. By non-farm job is meant all remunerative occupations which are additional to the operation of the multiple jobholder's own farm.

4. For the purposes of statistical comparison, "local" involves a travel distance to non-farm work of no more than three miles. "Non-local" means any non-farm job held more than three miles from the farmstead.

5. Franklin, S.H. (1969), **The European Peasantry,** Methuen, London, pp. 52-53.

6. Bunce, M.F., (1973), "Farm Consolidation and Enlargement in Ontario and its Relevance to Rural Development," **AREA,** 5(1), pp. 13-16.

7. Mignon, C., (1971), "L'agriculture à temps partiel dans le Départment du Pûy-de-Dome," **Revue Auvergne,** 85, pp. 1-41.

PART-TIME FARMERS IN POLAND

Dyzma Galaj

Part-time farmers are an occupational and class group who have their origin in the rural areas during the period of rapid industrial development.[1] Their existence has also been stimulated by the condition of agrarian overpopulation and by the situation of securing manpower for the non-agricultural sectors of the economy without the simultaneous expenditures for apartment construction and social facilities in proportion to the increase in employment.

This group is a product of the increasing division of labour between the village and the city and, to a certain extent, within the village as well. The city creates an incentive which attracts the rural population (higher wages, a more attractive life style, etc.). But in agriculture, mechanisms are being created which displace this population (technical progress, industrial means of production, etc.). Dual occupation by the rural population in Poland is, above all, an income and social problem. As long as the peasant farm cannot assure a peasant family a sufficient living at a socially accepted level, the tendency to combine two occupations will be intensified. It is an objective truth that a significant portion of the small farms in Poland is not, and never will be, in a position to fulfill this condition, even with preferential government policy. For this reason, dual occupation is a structural problem which can only be definitively solved by the socio-economic reconstruction of agriculture or the liquidation of the disparities in income between village and city.

An equally important reason for the origin and growth of a numerous group of part-time farmers is the social situation in the rural areas. Although the peasants have obtained a number of social rights in the past few years, such as free medical care, significant reductions in the cost of medicines, and the opportunity to rent their farms, the access of the peasant population to channels — pre-schools, secondary schools, cultural facilities — is significantly more difficult than for the urban population. This situation is one of the chief reasons for taking a job off the farm because it gives the peasant greater social rights, such as a paid vacation and a pension.

THE EXTENT OF THE PART-TIME FARMER PHENOMENON

The Census of 1970 reveals that 35% of the actively employed members of peasant families and 30% (or approximately 1.2 million) of the heads of peasant families were permanently employed outside their farms. In 1960 the percentages had reached 28% and 22.6% respectively. According to estimated data, the income from non-agricultural jobs constitutes half of the income flowing from agricultural activity. Income outside agriculture is greater than the entire gross accumulation of the farm including social benefits.

Two quite distinct categories are contained in the notion "part-time farmers": The first is heads of peasant families, owners of farms, who have taken permanent employment outside the farm and

258

who, in their spare moments, work the farm. The second category is comprised of persons continually residing with the family in the village but working entirely outside the farm. They are, in the great majority, members of the peasant families. Table 1 presents the numbers and growth tendency of part-time farmers in the years 1960-1970.

The data of Table 1 point to the following conclusions:

1) the rapid growth of employment off the farm;

2) the increased number of persons working off the farm from families owning larger farms.

Lying behind the development process of the various groups of part-time farmers is migration from the village to the city. The portion of those employed in agriculture in Poland, in relation to total employment, fell from 61% in 1938 to 39% in 1960 to approximately 26% in 1973.

Up to this point in time, both general and particular factors have played a role in the creation of the dual occupational population. I have defined the general factor as the mechanism of the social division of labour. The specific factors have their origin in agricultural policies followed to the year 1970. One of the basic directives of this policy, and in force for some years, was to keep the incomes of the agricultural population on a static level. As a result, a disparity developed between the income of the agricultural population and that of the non-agricultural population, to the disadvantage of the farmers. The relatively low payments for agricultural products, the lack of sanguine expectations for the peasant economy, the declining attractiveness of the occupation of farmer, the unsolved social problems of the villages, particularly the lack of security in old age and the attractiveness of urban models of life; all these have spurred the development of the part-time farmer group.

It should be emphasized, however, that the main reason for the formation of such a numerous group of such people was the disadvantageous income situation for the peasants. A huge proportion of the small peasant farms were not in a position to assure peasant families the conditions of life at a socially acceptable level. In this situation the tendency to search for additional income, or a totally different source of income, was unavoidably strengthened. Thus, a mechanism was created which weakened the tendency toward permanent migration (due to the lack of apartments in the city, the low pay for unskilled workers) and intensified the tendency of commuting.

SOCIO-ECONOMIC DIFFERENTIATIONS WITHIN THE PART-TIME FARMERS

Part-time farmers do not constitute a monolithic group. It is possible to differentiate three main groups within this population:

1) **Peasant-Workers** — These are owners of farms of not usually less than 2 hectares. A majority of their income is derived from the farm.

259

Table 1

Part-Time Farmers in Poland in 1960-1970

Specification	Year	Total	0,1-50	0,5 and more	0, 5-2	2 - 5	5 - 10	10 and more
						Hectares		
Part-Time Farmers								
— total	1960	1829 919	380 634	1449 285	675 020	429 965	220 591	60 709
— total	1970	2620 125	474 152	2145 967	825 347	733 695	442 648	144 277
— rural portion		2078 932	224 874	1854 058	627 676	665 360	421 808	139 214
Index of Increase (1960 = 100)		143,2	124,6	148,1	122,3	148,8	200,7	237.7

260

2) **Worker-Peasants** — These are owners of farms usually with an area of .5-2 hectares. Although non-agricultural income provides a majority of their income, the farm continues to supply them with a considerable portion of their food.

3) **Workers with Gardens** — The basic support of these workers is derived from non-agricultural work and the income from tilling the land is of distinctly secondary importance. The area of the garden does not usually exceed .5 hectare.

With the passage of time, a large majority of the part-time farmers who take up non-agricultural work bind their existence in an ever-increasing degree to a non-agricultural occupation, and the farm is transformed into a garden plot. Certainly the transformation into the last of the above categories of part-time farmers is a lengthy process, usually lasting two generations. The final phase is a complete departure from agriculture, except for a garden plot and remaining in the village as a place of residence.

In all three groups the workers are predominantly unskilled, largely construction workers, although some are employed in factories, offices and institutions of education, culture, health, commerce and others. The lack of a skill occurs more frequently among the owners of farms and less frequently among other members of the peasant-worker families. In addition, the greater the area of the farm, the fewer are the persons who do not have industrial skills. From this, the conclusion can be drawn that peasant families with small farms export unskilled manpower. On the other hand, members of peasant families with larger farms take up non-agricultural work having first finished their education and having acquired an occupational skill.

Sometimes the motive for taking a non-agricultural job is the desire to acquire investment funds for the farm. In this case, non-agricultural work is a stage on the road to increased production on the farm. However, due to the dwarf character of peasant farms in Poland (the average size in 1970 was 5 hectares), especially those of part-time farmers, taking a non-agricultural job usually signifies a gradual departure from agriculture as the main source of income. Simultaneously, the prevalence of both tendencies (toward diminution and concentration of the land, with production at both poles) is reflected in changes in the agrarian structure, that is, the growth in numbers and percentage of both the smallest size farms (having the nature of a garden) and the larger size farms (over 10 hectares). At the same time the number of medium size farms has shrunk. It is necessary to add that despite the numerical increase of dwarf farms, the area occupied by them has decreased. This fact is an expression of the adaptation of the dimension of the farms to the needs and possibilities of the part-time farmer families and, also, of the ever more complete binding of their existence to employment in the socialized sectors of non-agricultural work.

This dynamic aspect has been characteristic of this phenomenon during the last ten years in Poland. In comparison with 1960, the number of persons occupationally active off the farm grew by 64.8%, which significantly altered the structure of this group. The proportion of farms with an area of less than .5 hectare fell 3 percentage points and that of farms with an area of .5-2 hectares fell 5.9 percentage points. On the other hand, farms larger than 2 hectares increased by 8.9%, which confirms the thesis that non-agricultural employment expands the proportion of families owning larger farms.

In Poland, both permanent migration and commuting have a considerable spatial differentiation. In areas with the greatest fragmentation of peasant farms and with large agrarian overpopulation (the south and southwest regions of Poland), peasant-workers constitute a higher percentage than in other parts of Poland. In 1970 part-time farmers constituted 31.9% of the total population, while in Katowice, Zielona Góra and Opole they accounted for 47.7%, 39.8% and 39%, respectively, of the population of these provinces. A significant fact is that in the last few decades, the large increments of part-time farmers have occurred in those regions which have concurrently declined in total population. This is the result of locating new industrial enterprises in areas with greater supplies of manpower. This policy is a characteristic trait of the development of a national economy under the conditions of manpower surpluses and simultaneous insufficiencies of investment funds. Until recently, this is exactly how the national economy developed in Poland. At present, however, a turning-point has been reached. The first signs of this are a manpower shortage and a relative sufficiency of investment funds. In conjunction with this, one can expect new tendencies to develop in the peasant-worker phenomenon.

The following indicates the income structure of the entire peasant population in 1970: 64% of the total consumption fund was derived from agricultural production (in 1960 — 76%) and 36% was earned off the farm, of which 28% was derived from wage work (in 1960 — 19%). One can perceive interesting transformations in this sphere among the various categories of farms. Families with farms of less than 2 hectares derived 71% of their general consumption fund outside agriculture (of this, 58% was wage work). In 1960 the analogous percentage had reached 59% (of which 52% was wage work). On farms with an area of 2-7 hectares, the portion of non-agricultural income grew by sixteen points (from 17-33%), and on farms larger than 7 hectares the percentage increased by five points (from 6-11%).

It is also necessary to point out that within the group of part-time farmers the proportion of younger age cohorts (18-30 years) and also that of middle cohorts (30-40 years) is growing. While both family heads and family members from small farms take non-agricultural jobs, on larger farms the share of family heads so employed is diminishing and wage work is primarily for young people.

Among peasant-workers men predominate (the ratio of women to men is 1:3), which, in turn, has created a new problem — the feminization of agriculture. The feminization problem has two basic aspects: economic and social. The former consists of the close dependence of farm productivity upon the sex structure of persons working in agriculture. As is known, the work of women on farms is less productive than that of men. Along this line, one can already observe on certain "feminized" farms disturbing symptoms of stagnation in certain spheres of agricultural production, as well as a weak response to the stimuli of agricultural policies and a slower rate of technical progress.

The social aspect, on the other hand, is a result of the weakening of the female's educational function in relation to the children and the family. In addition, the woman has increasingly less time for her own personality development. All these are factors which have weakened the social activity of the village in which there is a significant concentration of rural part-time farmers.

THE LEVEL OF PRODUCTION OF PEASANT-WORKER FARMS

For evaluating the effect of part-time farmers on production, the following criteria have been adopted:

1) productivity of the land;

2) costs and efficiency of increasing agricultural production;

3) the rate of accumulation and investment in agriculture.

In the group of peasant-worker farms of 2 hectares or less, the average level of production per hectare is higher than that of purely agricultural farms. In the group of medium size farms (2-5 hectares) one can say that the level of production on both types of farms is about equal. On larger farms (over 5 hectares) the productivity of the land of peasant-worker farms is lower than that of purely agricultural farms.

This situation is a result of many factors, some of which are the following. First, the farms of dual occupation families with small amounts of land possess a considerable supply of manpower. Taking non-agricultural jobs affects only the surplus of this manpower and has no important effect on the level of farm production. Second, the additional input of investment funds from non-agricultural work enables the farm to increase its purchases of commercial items (grain, fertilizer, seed) which, in turn, stimulates the development of agricultural production. Third, the development of numerous agricultural production services, chiefly those of Agricultural Circles, permit the farm to increase production without having to purchase its own durable means of production. With the money earned from non-agricultural jobs, part-time farmer families can easily afford these services. Fourth, a job in the city and the numerous contacts of a peasant-worker with the non-rural world expand his general knowledge. This, too, has a positive effect on the quality of farm management.

From the viewpoint of production costs, it should be pointed out that the scale of operation, as well as its goal (self-sufficiency in agricultural products) cause the average cost of production to be higher than that of purely agricultural farms. One should also be aware of the rather low level of investment in these farms and the expenditure of quite large parts of their income on non-productive, or only indirectly productive, investments, such as a house and its furnishings, means of transportation, education of the children, etc. This phenomenon constitutes the chief threat to the future growth of agricultural production on peasant-worker farms. This also demonstrates that the life goals of a significant majority of part-time farmers are oriented around permanent employment off the farm.

PART-TIME FARMING AND SOCIO-CULTURAL
TRANSFORMATIONS IN THE VILLAGE

The development of a peasant-worker group is conducive to the urbanization of the village. By urbanization is meant the increase in the number of rural population employed outside agriculture and also the aspiration to approximate the urban conditions of life and work in the village. Urbanization is also favourable to the new organization of rural space and the space between the village and the city.

Peasant-worker society occupies the peripheral areas of traditional peasant culture as well as those same areas of urban culture. The elements of both cultures, of both styles of work and life, form the personality of people comprising this group. However, with the passage of time, the bonds of the peasant-worker to his farm are loosened, bonds which define the very meaning of existence for the traditional peasant family.

Among the part-time farmers, the elements of urban culture gradually begin to predominate. This process is expressed not only in the altered manner of work, but also in taking advantage of technical services not yet widely diffused in the rural areas, in the manner of spending leisure time, in their diet, in the methods of child-rearing, etc. These people are an example to the purely agricultural families. If we compare the peasant-workers and the farmers in terms of their endowment with the good things of civilized life, we find that the former have far more. The ownership of such objects as radios, television sets, motorcycles, washing machines, is far greater among part-time farmer families. Only with families having farms larger than 10 hectares does an equalization occur in the ownership of such objects.

The following characteristics of the peasant-workers have a positive influence on the cultural development in the village: a higher average level of education and a lower average age in comparison to farmers. This causes the group of peasant-workers to be more susceptible to the influence of modern aspects of culture. The dual occupation population builds more modern homes, has a more rational diet, takes more frequent advantage of medical care, dresses better, gradually alters its language, etc. The traits of the peasant-workers, taken as a social group, are favourable to the introduction of urban and other aspects of culture into the village, aspects which are contradictory to the traditional and anachronistic aspects of peasant culture.

The dual occupation population plays a particular positive role in the area of transforming the relations between the family and the farm, the conditions of work, and the style of family life on the private peasant farms. The peasant farm, as is well known, defines the manner of work and life for the peasant family and creates the material conditions for knowledge of work on the farm and life in general, knowledge which is passed from generation to generation. The peasant farm is inward-looking, and even today it absorbs all of the thoughts of its owner and his family. This causes the isolation of the peasant family, the sense of immutability of fate, and the family's opinion that the farm is everything. To a significant degree, this fate is dependent upon weather conditions.

The peasant-worker's pattern of work and life differs from the traditional peasant life, and because of this, it becomes a stimulus of change in the arrangement of relations between the peasant family and the farm. In addition to the peasant worker's independence from natural conditions, his regularized work-day, vacation, pension, etc. are also attractive to peasant families.

It is necessary, however, to turn our attention to the negative effects of the peasant-worker phenomenon upon the social development of the village. The decay of ancient peasant culture, considerably hastened by the appearance of large numbers of part-time farmers, proceeds more rapidly than the village's acquisition of values created by urban society. This affects, first of all, non-material culture, chiefly moral norms, customary patterns of life and aesthetic preferences. The danger appears of submerging their form of culture because the least valuable elements of mass culture are easily accepted. Consumer attitudes spread, while, on the other hand, their creative abilities disappear. Among other things, this carries with it the dissipation of the value of folk culture upon which the elements of national culture, in various forms, should be based.

The loosening of social control, connected with the process of urbanization of the village, sometimes leads to phenomena bordering on social pathology, such as alcohol abuse, delinquency and disrespect for the property of others. A certain indifference to the social affairs of their local environment can also be observed. This is most likely caused by peasant-worker's lack of free time.

CONCLUSIONS

Part-time farmers constitute almost 30% of the total employment in the non-agricultural sectors of the national economy. In such sectors as transport, construction and agricultural services, their proportion is considerably greater. The labour potential actually represented by the peasant-workers in Poland is very large. Taking into consideration the somewhat lower average productivity of this population (due to the diverse occupational structure, lower skill levels, etc.), it can be estimated that the part-time farmers produce 25-28% of the national income. Many prognostications indicate that, even in the future, the role of this group, though relatively reduced, will still be very important in the development of the national economy. The permanence of such a significant role for the peasant-workers in the sphere of material production was, and is, possible in Poland for several reasons:

First, by calculating the approximate productivity of both part-time farmers and workers on the job and also the productivity of peasant-worker farms up to a certain size, it was demonstrated that a two-fold increase in employment of peasant-workers had a positive or neutral effect on productivity. Only after crossing the spatial threshold does the productivity of the peasant-worker fall, both on the job and on the farm. The same can be said about the length of the trip to the place of work: the shorter the trip, the more productive the work.

Second, the extremely high cost of obtaining labour very frequently enlarges the number of peasant-workers, because it is more advantageous to employ the manpower reserves from the rural areas than to create the conditions for their permanent migration from the village to the city.

Third, the dual occupation population is characterized by high mobility in both time and space.

Fourth, the objective and subjective difficulties of expanding apartment construction and the social infrastructure for the peasant-workers have played a basic role here. In the concrete situation of our country, which meant a reliance upon agrarian overpopulation, an abundance of manpower and a lack of investment funds, it was easier to offer employment to the part-time farmers and expand the means of transportation for them. The actual calculations indicate that the costs of transportation to average size cities in Poland from a 20 km. radius are lower than the costs of apartment construction, and this is the preferred area of residence by the peasant workers. However, the majority of peasant-workers commute from a greater distance, and thus, the cost analysis will have to be revised to take into account the future spatial structure of the hub city and the settlements of the peasant-workers.

Fifth, in the past, permanent migration and the uni-directional orientation of work were retarded or made quite impossible by the relatively slow growth of real wages.

In regard to the continued evolution of their employment and work, in regard to the necessity of their completion of education, one cannot give a uniformly positive evaluation of the various groups of part-time farmers. Even if their positive role in past concrete conditions in Poland did not evoke reservations, the practice of two primitive occupations cannot be recognized as desirable in the future. In this connection, a program is now being worked out in Poland for the gradual alleviation of this problem by the diminution of the numbers, the internal transformation, and also the displacement of this population to special settlements surrounding the cities which employ the part-time farmers.

NOTES AND REFERENCES

1 In Poland, two terms are currently applied to part-time farmers — peasant-workers and dual occupationalists. Unless specifically stipulated otherwise, all three terms will be used interchangeably in this paper.

THE ECONOMIC COSTS OF TRANSFORMING DUAL OCCUPATIONAL PEOPLE INTO SINGLE OCCUPATIONAL

Marek Muszynski

THE GOALS OF THE TRANSFORMATION

The transformation of dual occupational persons into single occupational is a common regularity as the social division of labour in the economy increases. As a result of this process, changes in the socio-occupational structure occur. The portion of the population working in industry and s, rvices increases, while the portion employed in agriculture declines. The transformation of the dual occupational population into single occupational, that is, the transformation of the peasant-worker into a worker employed in industry or highly industrialized agriculture, is a matter beyond discussion in the institutional conditions of Poland.

However, the transformation of an agricultural population, presently dual occupational, into single occupational is a complex socio-economic process of basic importance for the rate of economic development of a given country. On the other hand, the significance, scope and rapidity of this transformation depend on the level of economic development already attained. In this case, we have to deal with feedback appearing between economic development and the gradual shifting of agricultural population to non-agricultural employment.

This transformation is a process with momentous consequences for the entire economy, both agricultural and industrial sectors, for the entire society and particularly for the dual occupational population. In addition, the transformation is a process in which the current costs incurred by transforming the dual into single occupational people are converted in the long run into investment expenditures yielding interest in the form of increased effectiveness of management. The transformation also has a number of indirect consequences, which, based on the multiplier effect, are socially desirable in the final result. In agriculture, for example, it facilitates the turnover of land and the expansion of farms. Thus, it is conducive to specialization and concentration of production on farms, and it also hastens the initiation of scientific-technical progress and reduces its costs. In industry it permits better use of work-time by the dual occupational people and the growth of productivity, with the additional advantage of raising the occupational skills of the people encompassed in the process of transformation. The process also has enormous socio-cultural significance. All this complicates very much the calculation of costs and benefits in the transformation of a dual occupational population into single occupational.

TRANSFORMATION OF THE DUAL OCCUPATIONAL POPULATION INTO SINGLE OCCUPATIONAL IN THE LIGHT OF ECONOMIC CALCULATION

The Costs of Transformation

Preparing a cost-accounting of this transformation is a particularly difficult task. The difficulties consist not only of determining the types of costs which ought to be included in this calculation, but also in the manner of pricing the particular cost items. Various ways of approaching the division, classification and the pricing of the costs of this transformation are possible. We will consider the costs of the transformation from the point of view of the entire phenomenon's range of effect.

Possibly, the full costs of the transformation of the dual occupational population into single occupational ought then to include the costs borne by the particular sectors of the national economy, by agriculture, by industry, by education, and others. Fixing the price of the particular sector's share in the costs of transformation raises many difficulties. This is especially true wherever the costs of transformation are at the same time costs borne by society within the framework of achieving socio-economic and socio-cultural public policy. With these difficulties in mind, we propose a partial or incomplete calculation of the costs of transformation, one limited to estimating the profitability of selecting one of two forms of transformation with regard to the choice of the place of residence by the dual occupational population.

The Costs of Transformation: Permanent Migration vs Commuting

Analyzing the transformation as a process taking place over a long period of time and considering the phenomenon on the macro-scale, we shall accept the implied assumption that this is a uni-directional process. This means a gradual shifting of the dual occupational population to exclusively non-agricultural occupations. In this case, it is possible to look at the costs of transformation from the vantage point of costs borne by the population included in the process of transformation as a result of their choice of residence location. Such a formulation brings the calculation of transformation costs to a comparison of two elements: the costs of commuting and the costs of apartment construction in the cities. In the following discussion the subject of consideration is the simplified calculation of transformation costs taken exclusively from the viewpoint of the relative profitability of changing the site of residence versus the continued daily commuting of the rural population to the cities.

Elements of a Simplified Calculation of Transformational Costs

The goal of the calculation is to decide which of the two forms of migration — permanent or commuting — is more profitable from the viewpoint of the general public. The calculation, so understood, ought to give an answer to the extent to which economic considerations speak in favour of the transformation, of hastening the process and of broadening it.

268

In addition, we must examine the social costs borne by the dual occupational population commuting to work. By selecting this variant of migration, a price must be set for the time wasted in commuting. Precisely such a view of the costs of transformation permits us to speak about the social costs of the undertaking.

Assumptions of the Calculation

In making this calculation the assumption is accepted that the full freedom exists to select one of the migration variants. Considering the fact that the transformation is a process, it has been decided to make an input-output analysis of the costs of such a transformation. On the side of costs incurred under the title of commuting to work are:

1) the costs incurred by transportation enterprises connected with the depreciation of productive property and reckoned on the cost basis of one person-kilometer on passenger transport;

2) establishing a price for the time of travel to work and return, recognizing that commuting time to work constitutes an integral part of the work day only when it actually serves it. (Since this time is not productively useful, it can, in this case, be considered lost time.)

On the side of costs incurred under the title of apartment construction in the cities, which facilitates permanent migration, are:

1) the total cost of constructing an apartment in the city, less the average value of the residence left behind in the village. To the costs of the apartment in the city one must add the pro-rated expenditures incurred in building the social and technical infra-structure.

2) the freezing of fixed and circulating capital assigned to apartment construction.

Having considered the costs of the transformation from the point of view of the general public, we have introduced now the cost of the most quantitative form of transport, the average price of one hour of lost time and the cost of building an apartment on a mass scale. Comparison of the costs of transport to work on an annual basis with the enumerated flow of capital during the period of apartment construction decided which form of migration has an economic justification.

Results of the Simplified Cost-Accounting
of the Transformation in Poland

The simplified calculation of the costs of transformation was based on Polish realities of the 1970's in industrialized regions, and thus, in those areas where the process of transformation was particularly intense. In the calculation were included the costs of the dominant forms of mass transportation, that is, bus and rail transport, and the costs of apartments in co-operative construction of a dense, high-rise type.

From the calculation it appears that it is economically justifiable to commute to work if the distance does not exceed 15-20 km. With longer distances the costs of transportation are higher than the costs associated with permanent migration. Thus, after exhausting the possibilities of commuting within the given limits, it is necessary to support permanent migration. The permissible distance of travel to work, from an economic point of view, exhibits considerable regional differentiation and in each case depends on the degree of previous investment in the technical infra-structure, the form of transportation, and the costs of apartment construction.

The composition of the numbers of people commuting to work and the average distance of travel in particular regions made possible a determination of those regions where, taking into consideration the results of the cost analysis, the process of transformation ought to be accelerated. This also facilitated the estimate of material losses caused by the selection of a specific form of migration. The economic calculation of transformational costs presented above is a partial calculation, and its sole task is to assist socio-economic policy in determining the forms and rate of transforming the dual occupational population into single occupational.

FORMS AND METHODS OF TRANSFORMING THE DUAL OCCUPATIONAL POPULATION IN POLAND INTO SINGLE OCCUPATIONAL

The Significance of the Problem

The transformation of the dual occupational population into single occupational is a great socio-economic problem in Poland. Related to it are:

1) the previous rate of growth and the dimensions of the dual occupational phenomenon;

2) the requirements of the strategy for the intensive economic growth of the country;

3) the need for a more rapid adaptation of the agrarian structure to the requirements of scientific-technical progress in agriculture.

This situation engenders the need to pay greater attention to this phenomenon and to search for differential forms and methods of transforming the dual occupational population into single occupational.

Conditions of the Transformation

The transformation of the dual occupational population into single occupational will be achieved in Poland under the influence of:

1) a rapid rate of economic growth in the country and the increase of new places of work in industry and services in the cities;

2) the planned development of co-operative and communal apartment construction in the cities and suburbs, making possible the transfer of migrants from the villages;

3) changes occurring in the consciousness of the rural population called forth by the rapid socio-economic and cultural development of the country.

The transformation of the dual occupational population into single occupational was treated in Poland as one of the policy elements for the rapid and planned conversion of the socio-economic structure of the country.

Previous Forms of Transformation

The transformation of the dual occupational population into single occupational, in regard to the place of residence, proceeded in the past in the following forms:

— permanent change of residence to the city, above all, to apartments in dense, high-rise construction;

— remaining in the former place of residence, in a rural settlement configuration, while still commuting to work exclusively outside agriculture;

— moving in an unorganized manner to a village or settlement close to the place of work in non-agricultural sectors of the economy.

The previous forms of transformation were not sufficiently adapted to the needs and preferences of the dual occupational population. They delayed the process of transformation itself and led to the existence of deformities in the settlement network. The progressive concentration of places of work in the cities was not accompanied by the concentration of the population in the selected settlement units. Instead, it favoured the strengthening of the group of people commuting to work.

Peasant-Worker Settlements

For the purpose of accelerating the process of transformation connected with the change of residence, construction of peasant-worker settlements is being planned. These settlements should:

1) facilitate the concentration of the dual occupational population in discrete settlement units conveniently located in relation to the place of non-agricultural work;

2) secure for this population in the settlements the intermediate conditions between village and city in order to reduce the adaptive difficulties in the new place of residence and;

3) ensure the possibilities of additional income from agricultural production on designated plots of land;

4) accelerate and strengthen the single occupational orientation of the dual occupational population.

So conceived, the settlements ought to fulfill two basic functions:

— the residential function

— the agricultural production function.

The agricultural production function ought to be gradually reduced as the single occupational non-agricultural orientation of the residents in these settlements is strengthened.

The peasant-worker settlements might be the answer to the need for reducing the social costs associated with the obtaining of manpower for non-agricultural sectors of the economy from distantly located areas. These settlements would reduce transportation costs and would, from an economic point of view, be a more rational pattern of settlement.

Methods of Transformation

Economic planning permits considerable freedom in regulating the course of transformation of the dual occupational people into single occupational. In addition, the following are taken into account:

1) the priorities of the general public;

2) the needs and possibilities of the national economy;

3) the preferences of the dual occupational population.

The influence of the state on the course of transformation occurs in an indirect manner through the creation of suitable external conditions, chiefly material, which stimulate this process. A planned economy permits control of this process while at the same time respecting the freedom of decision and the interests of the population concerned.

The transformation does not occur at the expense of agriculture and the dual occupational population. Its costs are borne by the entire society.

SUMMARY

The transformation of the dual occupational population into single occupational in the Polish situation is a matter beyond discussion. The only subject for discussion are the matters of the rate of transformation, its spatial and material scope, and selecting the forms and methods of the transformation.

The determinants of selecting a place of residence for the dual occupational population exert a basic influence on the course of the process transforming the dual occupational population into single occupational. Choosing a place of residence in the older, rural settlement configuration or in the new, urban or suburban configuration leads to certain social costs.

The higher profitability, from the viewpoint of social costs, of transformation by permanent rather than partial migration, that is, partial migration in which taking a job outside agriculture is not accompanied by a change of residence, depends on many factors.

The transformation is a process in which current expenditures can be treated in the long term as investments. The amount of these expenditures depends on both the level of economic development and the time period considered.

With a simplified input-output analysis of the social costs of transformation, one solely arrives at a determination of the border beyond which further commuting to work ceases to be socially profitable, and more suitable is the encouragement of permanent migration. This border is the magnitude of mobility, which depends on the degree of economic development of a given region and the entire economy.

Such a cost analysis is particularly useful in regions which are rapidly industrializing. It can be the basis for delimiting the foundations of a residential policy which should stimulate the selection of a residence location desirable from the social viewpoint and justifiable economically.

One of the forms guiding the decision of the dual occupational population in their choice of a residence location that is consistent with the above analysis of social costs and conforms to the preferences of this population can be, in Poland, the peasant-worker settlements. These settlements ought to facilitate the shift of the dual occupational population to a single occupation and to shape, in a planned manner, the process of this spatial transfer and the concentration of the population in urban centres of growth.

SOME REMARKS ON THE DEVELOPMENT OF CAPITALISM AND SPECIFIC FORMS OF PART-TIME FARMING IN EUROPE

Giordano Sivini

Part-time farming appears with different features in the various stages of capitalist development in which the agricultural activities have different economic, social and political functions. We shall consider this problem in order to stress the specific forms of part-time farming in the different stages of development and their possible survival in the present situation.

THE PHASE OF TRANSITION TO CAPITALISM

Medieval economy is a closed economy. The serfs, tied to the land, have the means of production directly at their disposal. They produce for their own subsistence and owe the lord a rent which historically takes different forms of dues in labour, in kind or in money. Produce covers almost the entire range of necessities. The fundamental object of production is food (cereals and breeding), and the producers are agricultural labourers who are also craftsmen. They live in enlarged family units, the exchanges between these units being limited.

From the 14th and 15th centuries begins a process of disintegration of the feudal structures which transforms the relations of serfdom. Though the serfs are still bound to the land, the prevalent form of dues becomes that of payment in kind, and later, in money. This changes the relation of subordination, since previously any increase in productivity did not have a positive effect on the producer, directly controlled by his lord who claimed the surplus. Now, as the dues become a part of the produce or, even more so, a sum of money, the increase of productivity, besides supplying the means for sustenance, leaves a surplus for sale so that the producer can begin to accumulate money. Since, in this period the duties of the serfs are only customary, the accumulation of the producer is increased through the loss of the real value of the rent in money. Besides, the rising need for money of the feudal nobility, to bear the costs of wars and luxury goods, makes it possible for the serfs to ransom their duties. Independent production on small plots of land begins to grow. At the same time the independent producers begin to divide in different strata according to their capacity for production and achievement. There are some family units which bring to market only agricultural produce and others which also supply "industrial" goods. The first forms of part-time appear with the division of labour within the peasant family unit, to the end of producing exchange values and not only use values for home consumption. The capitalist relations of production replace feudal relations in two ways. The merchant classes, which arose in the interstices of the feudal system of production, in agreement with the State and the nobility interested in regaining and exploiting the land, extend their control over the industrial production in its existent forms of domestic industry and manufacture arisen under the shadow of absolute monarchy. On the other hand, the wealthier part of the independent producers, provided with accumulated funds, increase industrial and agricultural production through home work and hired labour. They become true capitalist entrepreneurs, still on a small scale but interested in suppressing privileges and monopolies. Capitalism has its origin then, in Western Europe, essentially among the independent producers, and the bourgeois revolutions (English and French) aim at reinforcing these classes politically; but capitalist relations in agriculture develop differently, with different forms of exploitation which underline the different stages of the industrial revolution, that is, the passage from the capitalist exploitation of the producers holding the means of production, to that of the hired labour. We find the deepest transformation in England, where the dominance through the centuries of the land enclosure system brings about the formation of a rural proletariat which supplies both the industrial and the agricultural labour market. At the same time, it sustains the demand for consumer goods and precociously stimulates production. Conversely, in France, where the appropriation of the independent producers had eliminated the system of open fields in an age when, as Bloch says, there were more lands than men, there are no grounds for large scale exploitation of agriculture and for the early development of industrial production. In Eastern Europe, including Prussia, capitalism grows slowly through the initiative of the mercantile classes and the support of the absolute State which still holds agriculture in feudal chains.

The growth of agricultural productivity, beginning from the second half of the 17th century, seems to have had a strongly propulsive function in the industrialization of the various European countries, still so different in their phases of transition to capitalism. The increase in population brings about what Adam Smith described as a virtuous circle, which brings about a larger stock of fodder, hence more cattle, more manure and therefore still more cereals. In the long period, the wheat growers, after satisfying all the needs of home and foreign markets, helped by improved ways of communication, spread to distant lands obliging those that produced at higher prices to withdraw from the market. On the other hand, the latter had appeared on the market since the times of the rent in money. In the presence of competition it becomes necessary to increase the production of manufactured goods for the market: knitwear, straw, lace, nails, paper and others. So we get a concentration of rural industries based on home work in densely populated regions (with more "interesting" markets) not suited to cereal growing. This specialization is a premise for a regional division of labour and will later influence the development of industry. Part-time farming thus takes on the character of market production, providing the agricultural producer with a necessary income supplementary to the production for home consumption. That this is the purpose at the origin of the phenomenon is made clear by the fact that mercantile capital was invested in rural home industries, especially knitwear, at least a generation later than the production started by local population. On the trails of mercantile capital followed the capital accumulated in the wheat regions, where the scattered domestic industries had decayed. This capital had been previously invested locally in plants for the transformation of agricultural produce, such as mills and cellars, but these plants required much heavier capital investments.

275

Slowly, all European countries are involved, through the enlarging of the markets, in this process of regional division of labour. In the poorer regions of shepherds, as in the Alpine lands, rural domestic industry becomes an alternative choice to emigration, offering full employment to the youth of peasant families. The division of labour and the specialization within the productive domestic unit spreads, wherever agriculture regresses, favouring part-time employment and being an alternative to urbanization and to vagrancy. A similar alternative is not possible for the producers of wheat regions, interested since the 17th and 18th centuries in the development of techniques to increase productivity through higher investments of capital and reduction of labour.

From this general development of the regional division of labour some areas of Europe must be excluded, such as Southern Central France, where the relations of production in agriculture reduce the process of specialization, while the scattering of local rural domestic industry shows a general backwardness and narrowness of local markets. Other areas are also marginal, because the feudal structure is still intact and any home industry is organized by the lords mainly for long distance trade.

The Stage of Competitive Capitalism

In western Europe domestic rural industry is a phenomenon specific to the phase of transition to capitalism, characterized by the incomplete subordination of labour to capital. This phase lasts as long as it is possible to obtain the combination between the availability of land (owned or rented) and the ownership of the agricultural and industrial means of production. The expulsion from the land and the formation of a stronger proletariat increases the demand for consumer goods. Production needs to be widened in scale. The expropriated worker, even if he consumes less than when he produced for himself and for his household, must now purchase **all** that he needs. The home market becomes stronger and on this basis it is possible to build a greater export industry. The passage from water to steam power implies a much higher organic composition of capital. This fact determines the new dimensions of production, frees industry from the bonds of natural resources and cancels the former seasonal character of factory labour, breaking the last ties of the not yet urbanized labourer with the land. Fluctuations in production now depend on the market and supplies rather than on horse power; so it is still possible that besides the permanent group of factory workers, temporary labour may be needed and sought among the rural population.

In the stage of competitive capitalism, the relative autonomy of agriculture compared to industry may be deduced from the average levels of profit, from the balance of the terms of exchange between agricultural and industrial products and from the competition strength on the labour market. However, such a situation can be seen only in England and not only owing to the impetuous capitalist development of agriculture, but because after the repeal of the corn protectionism, in a system of free trade the productive forces in agriculture develop further with irrigation, greater use of fertilizers and mechanization. In most other European countries industrial expansion, favoured by State protection, produces an unfavourable home market for agricultural produce, even worsened by the increase of the organic composition of agrarian capital. The polarization between firms able to invest heavily and the mass of small and medium firms politically anti-capitalist which urge the State to pass redistributive measures, increases. In this situation home labour is determined by the competition of industrial capital, finding a limit in the level of development reached by the productive forces in agriculture and in industry. To Sombart it seems like a decentralized industry and to Marx, like an external branch of the factory, but it is essentially an expression of a weak capital forced by competition to decentralize production and to subcontract the production to increase the exploitation of labour, especially when it fostered the process of factory legislation. Unlike the rural domestic industry in the phase of transition to capitalism, which developed craftmanship and piece-work habits later utilized in manufacturing, the home work in this phase does not require particular qualifications and, where it is flourishing, it tends to involve all members of the peasant family without any particular specialization.

Though originally a transitory expression of the relations within capital in a certain stage, rural home work appears, in a situation of polarization of agriculture, also as a relative resistance to the expansion of the capitalist relations. In fact, it maintains in the farm labour force that otherwise would have to choose between hired work and unemployment. Other forms of resistance are found also in temporary jobs outside the farm, in unskilled daily work or piece-work. These activities are offered by small industrial plants with low technological level, seasonal character, searching for productive flexibility and, sometimes, for activities not standardized. Because of the limited means of communication of those times, we cannot speak of commuting as a specific form of activity.

The Stage of Monopoly Capitalism

The trend towards the formation of monopoly capitalism, which developed in England under a system of free trade through the elimination of secondary businesses and various forms of precarious work, materializes in Germany on a large scale, and to a comparatively lesser extent in other European countries, behind a complex screen of protective tariffs which allow weaker productive structures to survive. The centralization of capital is a limit to competition, but at the same time it favours the growth of a speculative financial capital from trade activities and land rent. The prices of industrial products fixed in an oligopoly or monopoly system makes the terms of trade "move against" the prices of agricultural products. Centralized and speculative capital yields higher rates of profits thanks to the diffusion of the share-capital principle and this further discourages investments in agriculture. The growth of national capital supports the development of colonialism and imperialism and consequently weakens the working classes; moreover, it becomes more "redistributive" at home through the exportation of industrial overproduction and the appropriation of the social produce by the weakest national formations.

The State intervention in agriculture has become ordinary business since the last twenty-five years of the 19th century after the crisis caused by the competition of American wheat and Australian wool. The agricultural policy put into effect by national governments has a double function:

a) a productive function which aims to support all farms indiscriminately and obliges the weakest producers to exploit their family labour, while it allows capitalist farmers to earn increasing extra profits;

b) a function of controlling the industrial labour market and, by changing the measures of support, allowing capital to hire labour under the best terms. Only within these limits do peasants continue to become proletarians, even though the process is reduced and the polarization in agriculture slows down. The processes peculair to this stage which take the place of the previous ones are, on the one hand, the improverishment of peasants, and on the other the split in the highest strata of the farmers, since some of the capital invested in agriculture merges with industrial and financial capital, also for reasons of control of the distributive sector.

The prices of the goods which producers put on the market are adjusted to the subsistence level of a peasant family, minus the share of the State intervention. The large farmer adjusts his prices to those costs and gets rates of profit comparable to those typical of monopoly capitalism; this becomes a stimulus to the interpenetration of capital in various sectors. The agrarian bourgeoisie that does not participate to the process takes possession, instead, of rents coming in, at various levels of rural social stratification, from tenancy and "métayage".

As the exploitation of peasants worsens, their standard of living declines and capitalists can take possession of increasing surplus labour on the market, instead of directly controlling the productive process. With reference to that, Jollivet points out the fact that the legal form of ownership which characterizes peasant production for the market in the capitalist mode of production, is equivalent to the contractual relation of hired labour and has the very same function of getting surplus-value and concealing this very function. The State often limits peasants geographical and occupational mobility and thus productive structure in agriculture becomes rigid and the countryside relatively isolated. Outside the farm grow activities which are not important for the market and are typical of poor and closed economies: agricultural labour, unskilled work, hunting, shooting, fishing and precarious forms of commerce and craftsmanship. The demographic pressure on the land decreases thanks to various colonization policies. These are the forms, hardly important at all, of part time farming which are peculiar to this stage of the development of capitalism and co-exist here and there with other forms typical of previous stages.

The Stage of International Capitalism

After the Second World War, the most advanced capital obliges national monopolies and oligopolies to compete on the free international market. National capital centralizes in order to face stronger foreign capital, which sends some of its own production abroad. Multinational companies are the expression of the most advanced and aggressive capital and of amalgamations, mergers, take-overs, and other forms of business combinations with national capital. Fifteen years after the end of the Second World War, thanks to the industrial development, there is a situation of full employment in Europe. The under-employed labour force moves from agriculture to industry.

People emigrate or leave the land while industrial production grows. The income of peasants is supplemented by the remittances made by emigrants. Peasants move from mountainous areas down to the valleys and, whenever they can, settle near industrialized zones in order to be able to commute, at lower costs, between the factory and their small holdings, without actually leaving them. For the same reasons, they try to get rid of some forms of primitive capitalism such as "métayage".

Productivity increases at a faster rate than real wages; non-productive consumption is encouraged in order to absorb all that is produced. Not only does the State guarantee the peasant family a minimum subsistence level but it now encourages the peasant to re-place working capital with fixed capital, men with machines, fertilizers, insecticides, etc. Proletarization and polarization characterize agriculture during this stage and this is a consequence of its increasing dependence on the market. The entrepreneurial attitude of the peasant changes. Up to that moment his production for the market had depended on the needs and food habits of his family. What he brought to the market was the overproduction, not of goods, but of "remains". Now he must specialize if he wants to get more favourable "terms of trade" for his products in relation to industrial goods; nor can the farm itself meet all the needs of the peasant family.

The Common Agricultural Policy has supported the prices of agricultural products since 1960 and has tried to meet a threefold need of capital:

a) continuing to extort surplus value from producers who are formally independent;

b) obliging them to resort to the market through the increase in the organic composition of capital and through the raising of the minimum subsistence level in agriculture;

c) guiding them towards the maximization of the production of commodities. The level of the support prices is such that it does not pay the farm business which produces at higher costs and thus it has to get out of the market. If the peasant wants to avoid that, he must increase his productivity. In fact, the productivity of labour in agriculture increased by 88% in the European Economic Community (EEC) between 1961 and 1971, whereas the productivity of labour in industry increased by 66%. That same threshold determines also the level of the extra profits of the capitalist farm and the amount of capital which can be obtained through an increase in production. The gap between the average income of large farms and the average income of small farms became wider between 1964 and 1974, and so did the gap between the average income of the most advanced agricultural regions and the average income of the most backward agricultural regions. Moreover, in this situation, long-term problems of overproduction have become inevitable.

Public expenditure to support the Common Agricultural Policy has gone beyond all possible financial forecasts and it will be difficult to sustain it. At EEC level, a new alternative is prevailing. It aims to favour the most efficient farms by relating the support prices —

which should be verified every year — to the productive efficiency of the most modern farms and by making farmers support the costs for overproduction. Furthermore, it tries to set up larger markets including all Mediterranean countries in order to establish a new regional division of labour based on a more specialized allocation of resources.

This new Common Agricultural Policy takes shape in the 1970's while capitalism is going through a major crisis. The fall of the average level of profits makes it necessary to stop encouraging nonproductive consumption in order to increase the level of profit itself. The modern organization of agricultural structures is not a minor objective of capital; but if the agricultural directives of the EEC were put into effect, they would push a great number of small farmers out of the market. Several Governments cannot impose this massive expulsion from agriculture even through indemnity, at a moment when industry cannot offer new jobs and itself begins to expulse labour.

CRISIS OF CAPITAL AND PRODUCTIVE DECENTRALIZATION

Capital gets involved not only in the fall of the rate of profit, but also in the reduction of the exploitation rate and of the level of production. The different interpretations of the crisis have in common the fact of stressing the increasing insubordination of labour, as a result of the process of standardization and concentration of the working class (resistance to rhythm increase, refusal of piece-work, absenteism, protest and strikes, higher wages, increased control on the conditions of production). Besides, it is generally agreed that this fact is a serious obstacle to the full employment of plants. The efforts to overcome the crisis aim at recovering nonproductive expenses in order to raise the level of profits: this is a problem which concerns the economic formation as a whole, but it also concerns the solution of problems peculiar to the capitalist mode of production, in so far as it is necessary to have control over the labour force again and eliminate the causes of the increase in the average costs of production because of unused capacity. The development of productive decentralization (together with the increasing centralization of capital) seems to answer these needs.

The decentralization of production from developed countries towards underdeveloped countries had already begun after the Second World War. At first it was mainly a movement of American capital, but later it became a common practice. The crisis of the 70's seems to encourage a systematic research for the best productive conditions, both at international level and within "economic communities" and single countries. Decentralization takes place in those areas where the working class is weak and concerns the least qualified productive activities, that in the central areas determine higher conflict. At the same time the levels of scale of some productions are modified in order to achieve greater flexibility. The old idea according to which the creation of new industrial "poles" will eliminate the "congestion" of the centre, is also discarded. The most recent models seem to favour new forms of vertical integration, that is, a new industrial organisation in which minor industries are completely dependent on a major company. This new system spread all over the countryside, thus creating a network of small and medium firms down to the home work. This makes it necessary to "redefine" the

280

whole territory without break between town and countryside. The debate about the subordination of small productive units to large companies has been very vague up to now. On the practical level, we can see two types of empirical relations. On one side, the direct system of subcontracts and secondary supplies; on the other, the use of mediation with the function of promoting, co-ordinating and controlling production. On this level we find examples of competition which might suggest the relative independence of small and medium-sized firms from the large companies. In this situation part time farming would only be, once again, a form of answer of weak capital to competition and crisis. We have already seen this particular form of part time farming, that we named "transient", during the stage of competitive capitalism.

If we consider the relation between international capital and national capital, locally supported by forms of State capitalism, we can advance the hypothesis that the new structure of production through vertical integration is a new way of maximizing the appropriation of surplus value. The competition existing between small and medium-sized firms does not eliminate their subordination to large companies. On the contrary, it allows the latter to be reorganised by entrusting small firms with a kind of external management of branches not easy to govern and whose efficiency is dependent on the market. This also applies to the various forms of commission and subcontract for supplies, in which large commercial companies and new industrial branches are also interested.

In this perspective, the setting up of industrial firms in the countryside develops a kind of part-time farming which cannot be considered "transient". Ephemeral manifestations of part-time farming might depend on the mobility of capital in relation to industrial restructuring and to competition. However, in this case the forms that part-time assumes are ephemeral, not part-time itself.

In this stage of development of capitalism, the specific forms of part-time farming are commuter activities and home work. However, we may advance the hypothesis that part-time farming is becoming a form of the capitalist mode of production specific of the present stage of capitalist development. If industries spread in the countryside and the peasant family becomes involved in some kind of industrial production, also marginal producers will remain on the land, once they can acquire additional income. This seems to contradict the general trend — supported at the European level — towards the modernization of farm structure through the elimination of marginal farms. Some governments are still hesitating about whether to push marginal producers out of agriculture, since there are no alternative jobs for them. However, if the EEC authorities should decide to relate the level of the support prices to the costs of the most efficient farm businesses, without previously restructuring agricultural assets, and if the European market were to be opened to the agricultural products coming from the other side of the Mediterranean, small producers would be pushed out of the market but would not leave the land and would surrender their labour force to the weakest branches of the decentralized industrial structures.

Final Remarks

I have tried to describe the specific forms of part-time farming during the various stages of development of capitalism, focussing mainly on their origins and characteristics. The problem has been considered in its fundamental elements of historical determination in order to underline that the specific forms of a phenomenon depend on its relation with the economic formation, and even on the fact of being one expression of the dominant economic process of the formation. Therefore it is essential to analyse the determination of productive forces both in agriculture and in industry.

I think that an empirical analysis risks dealing in the same fashion with phenomena which are defined with the same term, but are expressions of different systems and different structures. Capitalism does not develop synchronically everywhere. The economic formation is a combination of various modes of production; for the period considered, after the transition phase, the capitalist mode of production is dominant. At the same time an economic formation is also a combination of stages, one of which, after the transition phase, becomes dominant.

When one examines the social phenomena of a particular historical period, one encounters both the specific forms of that phase and of that stage of development and the survivals of forms belonging to previous phases and stages. The danger of confusion is obviously greater when one conducts a comparative analysis dealing with different situations and different historical periods. This paper is only a kind of introduction to further studies which will, in due course, take into account the specific internal relations of part-time farming (farm-family; production-consumption; etc.) and it should help with the interpretation of empirical data.

NOTES AND REFERENCES

It has been difficult to find historical studies on part-time farming; nor has it been easy to understand and overcome the disagreements shown by historical texts, in particular those dealing with the phase of transition to capitalism. I have mainly referred to **Studies in the Development of Capitalism,** by M. Dobb and particularly to the debate between P.M. Sweezy, R. Hilton, C. Hill and H.K. Takahashi published in **Science and Society** between 1950 and 1953. E.L. Jones has examined the regional division of labour in "Le origini agricole dell'industria", in **Agricolturea e sviluppo del capitalismo,** Roma, Editori Riuniti, 1970. On the other forms of part time farming F. Chessa, **L'industria a domicilio nella constituzione economica odierna,** Milano, Vallardi, 1918, has been very useful. I do not think it necessary to mention all the studies on part-time farming that were used. Very useful from the interpretive point of view were: M. Jollivet, "Sociétés rurales et capitalisme: principes et éléments d'une théorie des "sociétés rurales", in **Sociétés paysannes ou lutte de classe au village,** Paris, Colin, 1974; same author, **L'utilisation de la notion de "classe sociale" en sociologie rurale,** in "Bulletin d'épistemologie sociologique", 1966, n. 3; G. Mottura and E. Pugliese, **Agricoltura, mezzogiorno e mercato del lavoro,** Bologna, Il Mulino, 1975, C. Daneo, **Agricoltura e sviluppo capitalistico in Italia,** Torino, Einaudi, 1969. The information concerning the Common Agricultural

Policy is taken from **Bilan de la politique agricole commune. Communication de la commission au Parlement et au Conseil,** 26th February 1975. On productive decentralization in Italy in the present crisis, with reference to other countries, a vast debate has developed. See in particular, "Economia e politica industriale", 1974, nos. 6, 7-8, and **La piccola e la media industria nella crisi dell'economia italiana,** Roma, Editori Riuniti, 1975 (two volumes).

EPILOGUE

The question of whether part-time farming is a problem or a resource was not resolved at this meeting. It probably never will be, because, as the bulk of the papers and discussion confirmed, the phenomenon is a complex reality and an attendant part of almost all rural systems. As such, it defies simple definition and cannot be considered a universally positive or negative element; such judgements depending upon the context of time and place. The meeting, accepting the definition that all remunerated non-farm work done by farm operators constitutes part-time farming, established that with a given amount of information an objective typology can be formulated. Similarly, the concept of transition, commonly associated with part-time farming, was broadened to include a 'persistent' group which, in the current Ontario experience, appears to be predominent. In terms of identification, the 'motive' for part-time farming was explored as it was confirmed that part-time farmers theoretically choose to hold two jobs, although alternative theories of structural determinism were discussed. Classification based on objective assessment of characteristics and motives was the major outcome of the opening sessions.

A second feature of the meeting, which reflects the status of research into part-time farming, was the reporting on the phenomenon from different areas in North America and Europe. The pervasiveness of part-time farming in most rural systems was demonstrated, as was the wide variety of interpretations of the phenomenon and its role within the systems. Data sources were also debated and it was agreed that Canada, even without the Census cross-linkage material, has a wealth of information on this subject. Only in the instance of hobby farming and small scale part-time farming was there any controversy over the associated benefits or problems.

Little was resolved in terms of the relationship between government policy and part-time farming and this situation needs to be more fully explored. Despite the claim that part-time farming should be quietly ignored, the question remains in some areas as to its legitimisation within existing structures. There was general concensus at the meeting that part-time farming was an inherent part of most rural systems, and did not require special policies to protect or promote it. On the same level however, its role must be further understood to determine if punitive neglect is justified as a rural development strategy. It would seem that under a number of circumstances, mainly those associated with declining rural areas or underdeveloped economies, part-time farming could have a very positive developmental role and might well be institutionally encouraged. The symposium was not planned to give full attention to policy questions, but only to introduce them via the need to identify and understand the problems associated with part-time farming. A further meeting devoted to the questions of government policy and rural planning would be appropriate when further work on the implications of part-time farming has been done. The initial step of legitimisation has been achieved in most countries, even by farmers' unions, and the next research phase will be to address specific problems or strategies pertaining to part-time farming in rural development.

The symposium served as a useful catalyst to identify and bring together many of the leading researchers with interest in the question of part-time farming. The exchange of information and ideas proved to be an invaluable exercise and it is proposed to continue Guelph's role as an intermediary in this field by establishing an international register of research on part-time farming. In this task we gratefully acknowledge the support and co-operation of the F.A.O. It is anticipated that future research in Geography at Guelph will concern the impact of part-time farming, both in the historical and contemporary context, on land use, agricultural productivity, and social dislocation. In this way it is hoped to contribute to a better understanding of rural development.

Symposium Organizers
A.M. Fuller
J.A. Mage

LIST OF PARTICIPANTS
(*Symposium Contributor)

DR. D.M. ANDERSON,
Chairman,
Department of Geography,
Careleton University,
Ottawa, Ontario.

*PROFESSOR A.G. BALL,
Acting Dean,
Ontario Agricultural College,
University of Guelph,
Guelph, Ontario, N1G 2W1

KEN B. BEESLEY,
(Student/University of Waterloo)
310 Niska Road, Apt. 606,
Downsview, Ontario

R.E. BENOIT,
Rural Development Officer,
Alberta Agriculture,
Box 1540,
Barrhead, Alberta, T0G 0E0

*R. BENSON,
Community Planner,
Ontario Ministry of Housing,
Queen's Park,
Toronto, Ontario

RAY D. BOLLMAN,
(Graduate Student,
University of Toronto)
2 The Maples,
100 Bain Avenue,
Toronto, Ontario.

DR. DON BOSTWICK,
Department of Anthropology,
Colorado State University,
Fort Collins, Colorado

DR. PETER BRASHER,
Tiny Tay Peninsula Planning Board,
Box 186,
Midland, Ontario

DR. G. BRINKMAN,
School of Agricultural Economics
and Extension Education,
University of Guelph,
Guelph, Ontario, N1G 2W1

RON BROWN,
Regional Planning Branch,
T.E.I.G.A.
Queen's Park,
Toronto, Ontario

*DR. M. BUNCE,
Department of Geography,
Scarborough College,
University of Toronto,
West Hill, Ontario, M1C 1A4

RONALD G. BURNETT,
Assistant Town Planner,
36 Main Street South,
Halton Hills, Ontario

*DR. ADA CAVAZZANI,
Dipartimento di Sociologia e di
Scienza Politica,
Universita Degli Studi
Della Calabria,
Cosenza, Italy

DR. E. CEBOTAREV,
Department of Sociology,
University of Guelph,
Guelph, Ontario, N1G 2W1

PROFESSOR V. CHANASYK,
Director, School of Landscape
Architecture,
University of Guelph,
Guelph, Ontario, N1G 2W1

*DR. D. CHRISTODOULOU,
Agrarian Reform Policy Officer,
Human Resources, Institutions
and Agrarian Reform Division,
F.A.O.
Via Della Terme Di Caracalla
00100 — Rome, Italy

DR. E. WALTER COWARD JR.,
Department of Rural Sociology,
New York State College of
Agriculture and Life Sciences,
Cornell University,
438 Warren Hall,
Ithaca, New York 14850
U.S.A.

H. CROWN,
Director, Rural Development
Branch,
O.M.A.F.,
1200 Bay Street,
Toronto, Ontario

*DR. R. CROWN,
Director, Farm & Rural
Development Division,
Economics Branch,
Agriculture Canada,
Ottawa, Ontario K1Y 0N2

GARY DAVIDSON,
Director, Huron County
Planning Department,
Court House,
Goderich, Ontario

BASIL DORION
Counsellor,
Tiny Township,
Midland, Ontario

DR. R.J. EDWARDS,
Economic Research Service,
U.S.D.A. P.O. Box 352,
Tennessee State University,
Nashville, Tennessee, 37203

DR. W. FINLAY,
School of Agricultural Economics
and Extension Education,
University of Guelph,
Guelph, Ontario N1G 2W1

A. FORD,
B.C. Department of Agriculture,
Farm Business Management,
Room 303 Provincial Building,
Duncan, British Columbia

W. FREEMAN,
Rural Data Section,
Census Agriculture Division,
Statistics Canada,
Ottawa, Ontario

*PROFESSOR GLENN V. FUGUITT,
Department of Rural Sociology,
University of Wisconsin,
240 Agricultural Hall,
1450 Linden Drive,
Madison, Wisconsin, 53706.

*DR. A.M. FULLER,
Symposium Organiser,
Department of Geography,
University of Guelph,
Guelph, Ontario N1G 2W1

PROFESSOR DYZMA GALAJ,
Director, Institute of Rural
Development,
Polish Academy of Sciences,
Krakowskie Przedmiescie 30,
Warszawa, Poland

JOHN GARDINER,
Lecturer,
Kemptville College of Agricultural
Technology,
Kemptville, Ontario K0G 1J0

DR. M.J. GAUTHIER,
Universite du Quebec a Chicoutimi,
930 est, rue Jacques-Cartier,
Chicoutimi, Quebec G7H 2B

J. GELLNER,
(Student, University of Guelph),
54 University Avenue,
Guelph, Ontario.

*DR. J.L. GIRT,
Department of Geography,
University of Guelph,
Guelph, Ontario N1G 2W1

B. GUNN,
Ridgetown College of Agricultural
Technology,
Ridgetown, Ontario N0P 2C0

*PROFESSOR P.HACKMAN,
Department of Agricultural
Economics,
University of Helsinki,
007100 Helsinki 61,
Helsinki, Finland

P. HALE,
Ministry of Natural Resources,
Richmond Hill,
Ontario

PETER HANNAM,
Executive Member, Ontario
Federation of Agriculture,
R.R. 2, Guelph, Ontario

R.C.F. HILL,
52 Cartier Crescent,
Scarborough, Ontario

W.R. HOCKRIDGE,
British Columbia Department of
Agriculture,
Ste. 202, 1136 103 Avenue,
Dawson Creek, British Columbia

*PROFESSOR D. HOFFMAN,
Director, Centre for
Resources Development,
University of Guelph,
Guelph, Ontario N1G 2W1

JUDY HONE,
Regional Planner, T.E.I.G.A.,
Apt. 504, 650 Parliament Street,
Toronto, Ontario

M. HUQ
Graduate Student,
Department of Geography,
Carleton University,
Ottawa, Ontario

*PROFESSOR G. HUTCHISON,
Office of Continuing Education,
University of Guelph,
Guelph, Ontario N1G 2W1

*PROFESSOR R. IRVING,
Chairman,
Department of Geography,
University of Waterloo,
Waterloo, Ontario

L.N. JOHNSON,
Resources Manager,
Conservation Branch,
Ministry of Natural Resources,
1008 Colborne Street,
London, Ontario

*DR. GWYN JONES,
Agricultural Extension &
Rural Development Centre,
The University, London Road,
Reading RG1 5A0, England

DR. P.D. KEDDIE,
Department of Geography,
University of Guelph,
Guelph, Ontario N1G 2W1

J. KHAN,
Graduate Student,
Department of Geography,
Carelton University,
Ottawa, Ontario

STUART L. KRAMER,
Research Economist,
Planning and Research Secretariat,
Saskatchewan Department of
Agriculture,
Administration Building,
Regina, Saskatchewan

*DR. KENNETH KELLY,
Chairman,
Department of Geography,
University of Guelph,
Guelph, Ontario N1G 2W1

R.L. LAYTON,
Graduate Student,
Department of Geography,
University of Western Ontario,
London, Ontario

J. LEBLANC-COOKE,
Statistics Canada,
5 Temporary Building,
Ottawa, Ontario

DR. DEANE LEE,
Associate Professor,
Department of Food and
Resource Economics,
University of Massachusetts,
Amherst, Massachusetts 01002

*PROFESSOR A. LERNER,
School of Agricultural Economics
and Extension Education,
University of Guelph,
Guelph, Ontario N1G 2W1

MS. C.E. LONERO,
Regional Planner, T.E.I. G.A
5th Floor Frost North,
Queen's Park,
Toronto, Ontario

*DR. J.A. MAGE,
Symposium Organiser,
Department of Geography,
University of Guelph,
Guelph, Ontario N1G 2W1

D.M. MACKAY,
Farm Management Consultant,
Canada Department of Agriculture,
156 Nassau Street,
Charlottetown, P.E.I.

DR. K.J. McKENZIE,
Chief, Farm Management Service,
Agriculture Canada,
R.R. 3,
Arnprior, Ontario

P. McLEAY,
Faculty of Humanities,
The Polytechnic,
Wulfruna Street,
Wolverhampton, WV1 1LY
England

DR. JANET D. MOMSEN,
Research Associate,
Department of Geography,
University of Calgary,
Calgary, Alberta

*DR. MAREK MUSZYNSKI,
Institute of Rural & Agricultural
Development,
Polish Academy of Science,
Warszaw, Poland

HENRY F. NOBLE,
Senior Economist, Land Use Section
Economics Branch,
Ontario Ministry of Agriculture & Food,
Parliament Buildings,
Toronto, Ontario

BILL NORTHCOTT,
Tiny Tay Peninsula Planning Board,
Box 186,
Midland, Ontario

JOHN VAN NOSTRAND,
Rural Planner/Architect,
Ministry of Housing,
North Pickering Project,
950 Yonge Street,
Toronto, Ontario

HELEN E. PARSON,
P7 — 170 Erb Street West,
Waterloo, Ontario N2L 1V4

*DR. B.B. PERKINS,
Economic Policy & Planning,
Economics Branch,
Canada Department of Agriculture,
Ottawa, Ontario K1A 0C5

JEAN POIRIER,
Environment Canada,
Project Co-ordinator,
2-288 Cathcart Street,
Ottawa, Ontario.

DR. B. PROUD,
Chief, Farm Income and Prices Section,
Agriculture Division,
Statistics Canada,
5 Temporary Building,
Ottawa, Ontario

*PROFESSOR L. REEDS,
Department of Geography,
McMaster University,
Hamilton, Ontario.

*DR. J.C. RENNIE,
Executive Director of
Research and Education,
Ontario Ministry of
Agriculture and Food,
1200 Bay Street,
Toronto, Ontario

PROFESSOR L· RUSSWURM,
Department of Geography,
University of Waterloo,
Waterloo, Ontario

*DR. VIKAR SAFVESTAD,
(County Agriçultural Board),
Lantbruksnamden,
Box 610, 551 02,
1 Jonkopings Lan,
Sweden.

CARL F. SCHENK,
Senior Planner,
Niagara Escarpment Comission,
232 Guelph Street,
Georgetown, Ontario L7G 4B1

DR. JUAN F. SCOTT,
Lands Directorate,
Environment Canada,
Place Vincent Massey
Hull, P.Q.

DR. A.J. SHAWYER,
232 Bernard Avenue,
London, Ontario

PROFESSOR ROBERT SINCLAIR,
Department of Geography,
Wayne State University,
Detroit, Michigan 48202,
U.S.A.

ANDREW SIRKI,
Farm Management Consultant,
Manitoba Department of Agriculture,
Box 100,
St. Pierre, Manitoba

DR. G. SIVINI,
Dipartimento di Scienze Politica,
Universita degli Studi della
Calabria,
Cosenza, Italy

J.C. SLOT,
Agricultural Specialist,
Food and Land Development Branch,
O.M.A.F.,
1200 Bay St.,
Toronto, Ontario

BARRY SMIT,
Graduate Student,
Department of Geography,
McMaster University,
Hamilton, Ontario

EARL SORENSEN,
Graduate Student,
Department of Agricultural Economics,
University of Massachusetts,
Amherst, Massachusetts,
U.S.A.

*G. STOCK,
Rural Development Counsellor,
Small Farm Development Program,
Box 450,
Sangudo, Alberta, T0E 2A0

D.N.G. STONE,
Department of Geography,
University of Winnipeg,
Winnipeg, Manitoba

L. TOMPKINS,
Rural Development Branch,
O.M.A.F.,
1200 Bay St.
Toronto, Ontario

MICHAEL TRANT,
Graduate Student,
School of Agricultural Economics
and Extension Education,
University of Guelph,
Guelph, Ontario N1G 2W1

*DR. M. TROUGHTON,
Department of Geography,
University of Western Ontario,
London, Ontario

ANTHONY USHER,
Park Planning Branch,
Ministry of Natural Resources,
98 Dowling Avenue, #2,
Toronto, Ontario M6K 3A4

JAMES WALSH,
Graduate Student,
Department of Geography,
McMaster University,
Hamilton, Ontario

PROFESSOR INGOLF VOGELER,
Department of Geography,
Northwestern University,
Evanston, Illinois, 60207,
U.S.A.

*R. WIETFELDT,
Director of Research,
Ontario Federation of Agriculture,
387 Bloor St. E.,
Toronto M4W 1H9

DR. G. WALKER,
Department of Geography,
York University,
Downsview, Ontario

TOM WILLANS,
42 Liverpool Street,
Guelph, Ontario

PETER R. WALKER,
Director of Land Use Planning,
c/o Murray V. Jones & Associates Ltd.,
209 Adelaide Street East,
Toronto, Ontario

CONFERENCE STAFF — DEPARTMENT OF GEOGRAPHY

Delphine Abrahamse
Graduate Student

Doug Begg
Graduate Student

Gail Finlay
Student

Mario Finoro
Technician

Heather Fuller
Geographer at Large

John Galloway
Graduate Student

Bill Hodgson
Graduate Student

Michael Holland
Student

Rick Knutson
Graduate Student

Michelle Phillips
Graduate Student

Brian Reynolds
Chief Technician

Peter Stoddart
Graduate Student